TOUCHED

TOUCHED

A Painter's Insights into the Work of
LIANE COLLOT D'HERBOIS
A New Mystery School Teaching

·

MARIE-LAURE VALANDRO

LINDISFARNE BOOKS | 2012

2012
Lindisfarne Books
An imprint of Anthroposophic Press / SteinerBooks
610 Main St., Great Barrington, MA
www.steinerbooks.org

COVER & BOOK DESIGN: WILLIAM JENS JENSEN

COVER IMAGE: Relief of Akhenaten and Nefertiti
making an offering to Aten (the Sun), an aspect of Ra
(c.1300 BCE); Egyptian Museum, Cairo

LIBRARY OF CONGRESS CATALOGING-IN-PUBLICATION DATA
Valandro, Marie-Laure.
   Touched : a painter's insights into the work of Liane Collot
d'Herbois : a new mystery school teaching / Marie-Laure
Valandro.
      p. cm.
   Includes bibliographical references (p. 264).
   ISBN 978-1-58420-128-1 (pbk.)—
ISBN 978-1-58420-129-8 (ebook)
   1. Collot, d'Herbois, Liane, 1907–1999. Art therapy.
3. Imagery (Psychology)—Therapeutic use. I. Title.
   RC489.A7V35 2012
   616.89'1656—dc23
                                              2012018154

Contents

PART TWO: ON COLOR

Dedicated to Dorothea Sinker Pierce, Janny Magger, and all painters devoted to the work of Liane Collot d'Herbois. And, last but not least, to all lovers of art.

What is logic? Logic is the anatomy of thinking, and one studies anatomy by means of corpses. Logic is acquired through the study of the corpse of thinking. It is certainly justified to study anatomy by means of corpses. It is just as justified to study logic through the corpses of thinking. But one will never comprehend life by means of what has been observed on the corpse!

—RUDOLF STEINER[1]

Must every piece of writing be skillfully composed if it can be of service to us in some other way? Is a lack of formal design so fatal? Perhaps the wealth of wisdom in Goethe's Wilhelm Meister is fatal for those who know everything and have nothing more to learn.

—RUDOLF STEINER[2]

"You must paint as you do mathematics!"

—LIANE COLLOT D'HERBOIS[3]

Rudolf Steiner once spoke of a picture of the Earth as it can be seen by the dead (Berlin, Jan. 4, 1918): a globe floating in the space of the universe, its western hemisphere aglow with all the colors from red to yellow, its eastern hemisphere radiant with all the colors from blue to violet. In between is a band of green. In the middle of the blue-violet a living, golden, crystalline structure arises—the New Jeruzalem. To a spiritual consciousness, looking at the Earth from the circumference of the universe, the Mystery of Golgotha was like the birth of a radiant star in the blue and violet of the aura of the Earth. This color meditation is an imagination that can be nourishment for the dead.

—LIANE COLLOT D'HERBOIS[4]

1 *Materialism and the Task of Anthroposophy*, Dornach, April 29, 1921, p. 187.
2 *Metamorphoses of the Soul*, Nov. 25, 1909, p.115.
3 Written to author in 1996.
4 *Light, Darkness and Colour in Painting Therapy*, p. 250.

PART ONE

BLACK & WHITE

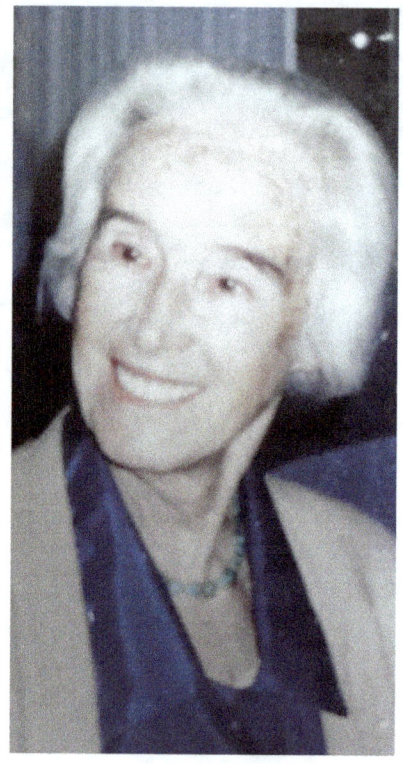

Liane Collot d'Herbois (1907–1999)

First Meeting

In my life, I have been on countless adventures and plan on many more, but apart from the joys and sufferings of marriage and motherhood, none has touched me as much or has been as mysterious and fulfilling as my adventures with colors. As a small child, I was already living very deeply with colors; I was the color of the *myosotis*, the light-blue forget-me-nots that abounded in the Burgundy countryside, or the red in the poppies of my grandfather's rocky farm fields. I remember sitting on a small terrace in a hotel in Rabat, Morocco, blinded by the African sun, and playing with colored pencils and attempting to draw what I saw: women dressed in black tents under the hot sun, surrounded by glaring white buildings. I was six and trying to understand how the Arabic language could be spoken by replacing my alphabet letters with the Arabic characters.

Now, many years later, with a zero appended to the six, I sit in a tiny house near Tintagel, England, where Liane Collot d'Herbois was born in 1907. My adventures in painting led me to meet this most unusual and gifted, larger-than-life human being in the 1990s. I met her work in 1988, when I was 40, through her book for therapists, *Light, Darkness and Colour in Painting Therapy*, given to me by a therapist friend.

Because I had been too practical and too poor to consider the life of an artist, I became a linguist and language teacher. Only at the end of a teaching day, I would attend classes in still-life and nude and portrait drawing, playing with oils, acrylic, and charcoal. I did impressionist-style paintings, copied Monet and Van Gogh, and made pure-color paintings. I used to love black, white, and red. I continued my training in art through most of my life, wherever I lived. In Paris, no one seemed to mind when I dropped in at the life-drawing lessons at the Beaux Arts to draw their nude models.

In 1990, my father died suddenly. He had been a self-taught Sunday-only artist, a former police officer, construction worker, inventor, born

3

architect, oil painter, lover of landscapes, and, when we were very young, an illustrator of fairy tales for us. After his death, I started painting more and felt closer to him as I did. I had no teacher, so I respectfully asked the flowers in my garden to be my teachers. I was an avid gardener, and there were plenty of flowers to paint. With the flowers, I learned about painting with watercolors, blending and trying to achieve just the right kind of red or blue or whatever was in front of me, especially the nasturtiums.

After having my two children, I quit teaching and started painting full-time, now in watercolors, in addition to my work as a translator, documentary film maker, and gardener, among other things. My children attended a Waldorf school as developed by Rudolf Steiner, and there I played with colors under the direction of several teachers, who introduced me to different techniques. I came upon the book published by the Magenta Group and written by Liane Collot d'Herbois, as mentioned earlier. The book revolutionized my work with colors. That was twenty-three years ago. I cannot overemphasize the excitement that this work has brought to me. Her book evoked everything I was looking for in the world of painting and color. I illustrated everything in her book in large black and white-paged notebooks and lived deeply with what she had given us, along with my studies of Rudolf Steiner's lecture cycles. I worked alone.

In the early 1990s I met Dorothea Sunier Pierce, and under her experienced loving guidance undertook further studies in esotericism and the work of Collot d'Herbois. Dorothea had studied in Europe in the seventies, beginning with the Hauschka method. She later studied with Liane, and they became friends. Dorothea, a Californian, is an accomplished artist, painter, serious anthroposophist, and esotericist. She organized several trips for Liane, and they continued a loving correspondence throughout the rest of Liane's life. It is thanks to Dorothea that we have Liane's book *Colour*. Dorothea was visiting Liane in 1976 and specifically asked her:

> "Please, Liane, put your artistic research into book form." Liane, Francine, and Dorothea went out, bought a tape recorder and the book began that very evening...with much amusement over how to operate this unfamiliar recording device. From then on, Francine was responsible

for all the typing, correcting, and note taking, while Liane held forth at meetings and conferences and responded to questions and so on.[1]

It is also through Dorothea that I became aware that Liane Collot d'Herbois was still living, and it was Dorothea who kept the flame alive for this important work in the United States. This has been no small task. With Dorothea's blessing and encouragement, I arranged for childcare for my two children and booked a flight to Driebergen, Holland, to meet Liane for several interviews to which she had agreed.

After my long transatlantic flight, as I stood at her door at the appointed time, I realized that she was not going to open the door. She was partially deaf and needed a hearing aid. I felt sad, having gone on such a long trip without being able to see her. I had written and thought she knew of my coming. So I left to stay with friends of friends. Finally she tracked me down—how I do not know—and another appointment was made. I nervously walked into the town of Driebergen, climbed the set of stairs, and once more rang the bell. This time she answered the door and looked me straight in the eye. "What do you want?" she said very coldly. I froze from her look! After this surprising welcome, I could do nothing but simply say why I had made this trip: "I just wanted to thank you for writing this incredible book and that is all!" Then I was ready to leave and go back to the United States having done what I wanted—simply to say "thank you." At that, Liane Collot d'Herbois's face changed instantly and she gave me a big smile and asked me in for tea and cookies. Of course, I had prepared a whole set of questions. She answered all of them and asked me to come again, which I did several times with more questions. I stared at the painting "Going over the Threshold," which she had been working on at the time. I wanted badly to tell her that I wished to paint like that, but she could read my soul, so that was not necessary.

That was the beginning of a new, unexpected adventure for me. I had asked her if there was any way we could have this kind of schooling, training

---

1   Told to the author by Dorothea Sunier Pierce in May 2011 at her home in Great Barrington, Massachusetts.

in painting, in the U.S. I felt there was no reason for students to come so far, when what was being done here could also be done there. It would be cost-effective at least. Liane Collot d'Herbois told me to come back in a week to meet Yanny Mager, who was to work with me *if* (Liane emphasized) we got along and worked well together. Then we could begin training in the U.S., because Yanny was her most gifted teacher and understood what she was doing. So this is what we did for several years until 2005, when it ended owing to the lack of students. Although I quit the schooling in a formal sense, Yanny and I still worked together on painting, sharing our findings and deepening the experience. In this way I continued painting and developed techniques for this demanding method, which might help future painters while still doing therapeutic work. My previous work in meditation has allowed me to plunge deeply into this art, thereby gaining profound insights that might also be helpful for others. Here Steiner points out the problem:

> Our present-day relationship to art arose; a relationship that is not merely cool but actually cold. Think of people in a modern city today, going through a picture gallery or exhibition. In actual fact, they do not meet with anything that stirs their feelings and with which they are intimately connected, but, to put it radically, they meet a pack of riddles which they can only solve if they go into the particular relationship the artist has to nature or to anything else.
>
> We are faced with one individual riddle or problem after another. And the significant thing is that while we think we are solving artistic problems they are in fact highly inartistic problems because they are psychological problems; problems as to how the artist regards nature, or world conceptual problems and things of that sort, which play no part at all when we consider the great epochs of art. What mattered in those epochs were real questions of art, real aesthetic questions, and these applied to the viewer as well, because the concern of the artists was *how* it should be done, not *what* he should do, because the *what* was merely the substance they were steeped in. You could say that our artists are no longer artists but people who observe the world from a particular point of view, and what they put into form is what their own special temperament leads them to notice. So these are psychological problems...and so on, but the essential aspect of *how* the work of art

is done has almost been lost in our time. People frequently do not have the heart to study how it is done.[2]

This book is the result of this adventure in painting. The work of Liane Collot d'Herbois is nothing but *how*. That is why she wrote to me, "You must paint as you do Mathematics." In other words, one must be a selfless painter, get rid of ideas about being great and put away all psychological problems; they have no place on the canvas. One must be selfless and truly surrender to the Color Beings, giving total dedication and devotion to them. A painting will reflect who a person is. There is no boundary in this work between who we are and what emerges. If we are steeped in personal problems, the colors will not shine; dirty colors emerge from our soul life. We need intense work on ourselves to paint colors in a selfless way. We cannot just apply red wherever we like because we feel like it. No, that has to be given up. The reds need to be painted where they belong, not where we *feel* they belong. Paint as you would do mathematics. This does not mean in an intellectual way; it means in an orderly way. Colors go where they belong. That is the reason this work is so difficult.

This amazing journey into the work of Liane Collot d'Herbois will include the work of Rudolf Steiner who was the inspiration behind her work and the total inspiration for my own work, and Ita Wegman who led Liane to become the great master painter that she was. It was under Ita Wegman's tutelage that Liane developed her incredible work, a work that is yet to be discovered. This book is a small attempt toward understanding the background of this new way of painting, which ultimately includes Anthroposophy or "wisdom of the human being," and Golgotha, the ultimate healing. It could also be called "painting: one path to the Christ" or "a path to Christ through watercolor painting."

---

2 Steiner, *Color*, Dornach, July 26, 1915, p. 62 (trans. revised).

Return to Tintagel

So that is why today I am walking through the streets of Tintagel in Cornwall, England. Liane lived here until she was twelve, interspersed with trips to Australia. I will be here for six weeks, trying to breathe the air, to experience the elements and the magic that Liane Collot d'Herbois breathed, trying to glimpse this wild Cornwall that she often described to us. Her life was full of wild stories, which shocked me when I heard them. Now, however, after walking on the cliffs around King Arthur's old castle, windblown, watching dark clouds over the ocean and this formidable coastline, I am not surprised that she picked this as her birthplace. She definitely was a child of the wild elements. I can see her as a small girl going over the hills to fetch some butter from the local farm or walking windswept paths amidst the small, cold, granite farm houses speckled throughout the rounded hills, a wild child who often fought with her fists. She was kept away from other children by her eccentric father. She would run and jump atop a horse and let the horse run until she was caught and punished for stealing the horse. She must have looked at the wild ocean and perhaps knew of this amazing destiny that would shape her into the great painter that she was. She often told us that Cornwall was one of the only places in England where one could still encounter people who had "the sight," or old clairvoyance.

Today I had a talk with a man working at Arthur's house—an amazing granite structure built in 1885—who told me that he knew of a woman at a farm nearby who was clairvoyant, and that she did not like it because she could see people's future, and she was afraid of this sight. Ita Wegman mentioned that people often drank much in order to avoid being bothered by this second sight.

Here we can see how much Liane was a child of the elements, living freely:

When I was little I had no one, no human being that I could look up to. Where we lived people were barbaric. As a child I have seen the most awful things: brutal fights, people bashing each other about, eyes being ripped out, awful. It was a wild place and the people were wild and the elements were wild. It was not so long before that, that by means of lights, they wrecked ships on the coast.

Some of the local people, nearly all of them, had a bit of control over the elements. One third of the people were clairvoyant. There was an old woman who nursed me, who was clairvoyant. She used to tell me the most frightening stories.

I remember a ship was wrecked on the coast one stormy night. The coast was very rocky there and it was continually breaking down. Whole cliffs fell over just like that. (In one place there used to be a house on the cliff, that one day had gone down completely.) In the place of the shipwreck the rock contained a special kind of gneiss, a very hard rock, and people had to blow it up in order to get down to the ship. They did not want to miss anything that might be down there. I wanted to go down there, too, but I had not got any shoes on. I could not go down, because the rocks were covered with sharp crystals. I had to go home and get my shoes to be able to go down over those crystals to the beach.

In those days it was a wild, wicked world, but I liked it. I knew the people too well; I saw them too well to be frightened by them or dislike them. And I was a ferocious child myself. I used to get involved in fierce fights. Nothing could stop me. I pushed people into the river sometimes. The girl who brought round telegrams was stupid and I did not like stupid people, so I pushed her into the river and I walked away. She survived, and came out all right.

Another time I was given a lamb and I was very fond of it. I kept it in the garden that ran down to the river. On one side, they used to hang up the washing in lines held up with poles underneath. A man who was working in the garden said he was going to drown my lamb. He was going to do all sorts of nasty things to it. I was so upset that I got one of those long sticks and I swung it round and hit him right in the face. Blood all over! It was terrible. I was of course sent to my room and I was not allowed to see anybody, for more than a day. Finally somebody came and asked me why I had done that, what had happened, and I could tell that he had threatened to throw my lamb into the water. And then I was forgiven and allowed to come downstairs again.[1]

Liane Collot d'Herbois left Cornwall to attend a boarding school and then went on to study at the art school in Birmingham. She had been a lonely child with amazing gifts. Her father kept her away from all religious training, and she was kept in a room by herself when religious instructions were given so as not to be disturbed by them.

Here we see her early connection to Anthroposophy. She was nineteen. From then on she was within the anthroposophic circles. She worked for several years in a Camphill home where her training as an art teacher was developed further.

This adventure in the work of Liane Collot d'Herbois brought me to visit St. Petersburg and Moscow for the icons, to London to marvel at Turner's paintings, to Holland to be awed by Rembrandts, to Florence to meditate on Fra Angelico and his murals in the St. Marcos Cells, and to Madrid, Toledo, and Barcelona to be spellbound by El Greco's paintings and by Picasso's enthusiasm. It also has led me to build a gallery in the middle of a farm in Wisconsin, because this kind of art needs to be hung in a suitable home.

The insights that I have gained from painting in the style as developed by Liane Collot d'Herbois have given me a greater understanding of many master painters, which I will share with the reader. I have chosen to discuss some of these painters and their masterpieces to show how these works reflect humanity's changing consciousness. Later on in the book, I will also share some of my observations on the use of colors as I experienced them in my world travels. Liane Collot d'Herbois's incredible discoveries and insights not only add a new understanding to the world of artistic creation, but she adds another dimension that derives from her

---

1   From author's notes on conversations with Liane Collot d'Herbois.

work with Anthroposophy and Rudolf Steiner's large legacy: that is the healing medical aspect of her work which, in the words of Ita Wegman, is the future of medicine.

But before I can share these thoughts I must establish the fact that Collot d'Herbois's work is that of the modern mystery school. The anthroposophic, or spiritual scientific path or, to put it another way, the "Rosicrucian path renewed" by Rudolf Steiner, will be mentioned many times in this book, as this path of painting is a true modern spiritual scientific approach, or Modern Rosicrucian Path, and that in itself is a significant challenge. The result will be far from complete, or even understandable—I know that even before I begin—but I must try with my limited faculties to bring some of my insights and understanding into this work.

Collot d'Herbois was a genius in the sense that she brought something new, totally new, into painting.

> It is only cosmos working when, for instance, in Germany, Goethe, Schiller, Lessing, Herder, and Schelling have written their works and then a schoolmaster comes along and recites the magnificent works and ideas of Goethe, Schiller and the others. The schoolmaster would not be able to recite anything that was not already there beforehand. Alternatively, let us consider people in another field. They base their work completely on what has developed over time. This is not the case with genius. Genius works out of the chaos. It is unique, in that a new spark comes into the human soul. Fresh concepts arise and take effect. In genius we find the marriage of the cosmos with chaos.
>
> No progress could come about if there were only outer causes, if these causes did not merge again into the chaos. By all earlier laws of effect being thrown back into chaos, genius arises. And through the effect of genius, something comes out of other worlds—something that was not taken from the past but is brand new. In every moment the world must again become chaos. The marriage of the past with the present is a union of the cosmos with the chaos.... New elements can come into being only out of the chaos, which must really unite with us, if we want to make a contribution to the progress of humanity.[2]

---

2   Steiner, *Rosicrucianism Renewed*, Berlin, October 1907, p. 104.

Collot d'Herbois's work bridges the gap between art and science. She was deeply spiritual, deeply Christian, and her paintings all dealt with deeply Christian themes, but she was very private about it. When we had our conversations, I told her that I was studying everything Steiner said about the Christ in the etheric and very sternly she said to me, "Keep that private!"

Her paintings were healing because of the way they were painted. Again I repeat this very important aspect of painting: "You should paint as you do mathematics."

She also told us that painting using the laws of light and darkness will heal the place or the person looking at the work, even though the painting might not be a masterpiece. These paintings are healing because they are painted according to cosmic laws, the laws of light and darkness. The work as painted is what heals (the "how" that Steiner mentioned in the last quote above), meaning taking into consideration the laws of light and dark. How the colors come into being when light and darkness meet. This has nothing to do with Newton's theory, to say the least, but Goethe's color theory put into practice and developed further by Liane Collot d'Herbois. However, the world being the way it is, her work has not received any attention and probably won't for another fifty years. She often said, "Darling, (she called us darling because she could not remember all the names) it is alright if this work dies out, it will come back when the time is right, perhaps in thirty or fifty years."

Great painters, men and women of genius, and teachers are always ignored because first of all not many can follow them, but also so that they can work in peace. She always told a few of us who took painting seriously that we ought to be "incognito," or as she calls it, "low level." We should not call attention ourselves, but just keep working and painting—study, paint, study. This is what I have done and still do. If we paint, study and meditate, the work will speak for itself. Suffer the loneliness of this work, but keep working with love and thankfulness and devotion. "Keep on, keep on" she always told us. And so a few of us do, in our very quiet places at the four corners of the Earth.

I have often quoted the following from Rudolf Steiner because it speaks so much to me when I feel totally alone in my work.

Art is eternal yet its forms change. And if you realize that art always has a relation to the spirit you will understand that both in creating it and appreciating it, art is something through which one enters the spiritual world. If one is a real artist, one can paint a picture in seclusion. Real artists do not mind who sees the picture, or whether anyone sees it at all, for they have done their creation in different company, in the company of divine spirit beings. Gods were looking over their shoulders. They created their pictures in the company of gods. What does it matter to a genuine artist whether anyone admires the picture or not. This is the reason why one can be an artist in total solitude. Yet one cannot be an artist without giving one's own creation an objective existence, so that it lives in the world, which one is also considering from a spiritual point of view. The creation to which one gives objective life must be alive in the spiritual atmosphere of the world. If one forgets this spiritual relationship, art goes through a transformation and changes more or less into non-art.[3]

Some of the topics which I will try to approach of course deal with images since painting involves an image. What is it that Liane brought to us through her painting technique? Light and dark, why? What is different? Where will it lead? What was she trying to accomplish? Steiner had asked a painter to paint in veils.[4] Liane developed a new way of painting in veils. What are we trying to accomplish when we paint this way? Why not just use colors? To answer these questions I will have to dwell deeply into such realms as first, second, third, fourth, fifth dimensions, negative space, threshold, imagination, inspiration, hierarchies, healing—all of these subjects will be touched in one way or another. Ultimately, however, the subject of the "Old Mysteries" will arise as well as the "New Mysteries" as they live in Anthroposophy.

---

3 Steiner, *Colour*, Dornach, June 9, 1923, p. 150 (trans. revised).

4 The technique of veil painting involves thinning the paints for transparency and then layering the paint, wet over dried colors.

It was a long journey into a world that I did not know, but which fascinated me the more I studied it. And the more I studied, the more complex it became and the more I loved painting in this manner, applying one layer over the other in a methodical, quiet, planned manner. This was nothing like the modern painters' way of splashing every which way or applying blobs of color to the canvas. Instead, this is a very slow way of painting, like playing chess. One has to think about the layers, before applying them, thinking all the time about where the colors need to go in reference to the light and the darkness. One studies the sunrises and sunsets hundreds of times and observes how the colors die in the sunset and awaken in the sunrise, different in summer, fall, winter and spring, different when it is dry or wet. All these observations are necessary in order to paint the colors as they arise, as the color phenomena live in nature and we try to duplicate the coming into birth and dying of colors on our canvas. That is the way Liane Collot d'Herbois painted. She was an extremely keen observer of nature and its phenomena, which led to her discoveries in painting and in healing. She saw the colors outside and the colors inside, which is the soul and thereby the healing aspect of this work—from the outer, to the inner—the way of Mystery knowledge. Moreover, there was no better teacher for Liane Collot d'Herbois than Ita Wegman, a close associate of Rudolf Steiner, a physician and a woman far ahead of her time, never mind who she was in her other incarnations!

Liane used to read catalogues when she was very young and memorize them in their entirety. This demonstrates her amazing memory and powerful sense of observation. That she did not miss anything is obvious when one reads her two books on colors. She was a true Goethean scientist, an anthroposophist.

All those years [during art school] I had very little to do with nature. I had never had anything to do with religion, but I had a feeling, I knew from my youth that there is more than what we see around us. I borrowed books from the library, read them one after the other and so I came to Buddhism. Buddhism I liked, but I thought "That is only for me alone. I cannot do anything with it in the outer world." I liked it, it has such noble striving, but only in one direction....

Anthroposophy (I mean by that Rudolf Steiner's books) I met when I was nineteen, I got the books from the public library in Birmingham. I had seen that there had come a school where they put children in a pram and played harps to them. I thought that terribly funny and I wanted to know what that was, so I got books about them from the library. The first thing was Goethe's "New Aesthetism," which I did not like. I thought it was silly. Then I got a little book about the Goetheanum. I did not like any of that, except the staircase and the organ. This was not what I was looking for and then I took "Knowledge of the Higher Worlds" and that was it. And so I came to Rudolf Steiner. I was still interested in Buddhism, but there came a point when Buddhism was no longer satisfying, because I could not do anything with it. And I thought that if something is spiritually true, one must be able to use it on Earth.[5]

Liane Collot d'Herbois always saw herself as a working woman rather than as an artist, because she had to provide for herself from an early age. She never married because she did not want to "iron a man's shirts" as she put it. She had another destiny.

---

5   From the author's notes on conversations with Liane Collot d'Herbois.

Approaching Darkness and Light

As I walk again from one of the nearby villages on the coastline, I marvel at the beautiful landscape of this fairytale-like area. Large soft hills still full of cows and sheep graze on immense green fields overlooking cliffs that plunge into the ocean. These hillsides fill the horizon, as do large farms still working as they did hundreds of years ago. Liane enjoyed this freedom of space where her larger-than-life spirit could run freely, undisturbed by the world's demands. She talked about reading Plato on top of one of the low roofs while her friends were in school, until one day she fell off. She was truly a Platonist with a mission—the mission to re-enliven painting and bring something entirely new into it. She wanted to bring mystery teaching once again into the field of painting and for that she needed to be born in a very unusual body.

When I was young and studied painting I heard many different things about how one was supposed to paint. I often found that very confusing and I thought that there ought to be something that people could have in common.

The fact that the colors exist is an objective truth. But people paint them in many different, subjective ways. When I worked as a therapist the longing to find a common denominator that could be accepted by everybody became even stronger. Over the years I gradually worked out the method of painting and its application in painting-therapy that are the content of this book. The basis of all that I have to say consists of two things: the cosmic threefoldness of light, color and darkness and the human being as the microcosmic threefoldness of spirit, soul and body, of thinking, feeling and will.[1]

We find ourselves here, right at the center of Rudolf Steiner's work, and right at the center of controversy: the scientific approach does not recognize

---

1   Collot d'Herbois, *Light, Darkness and Colour in Painting Therapy*, p. 15.

even to this day that we not only consist of the physical body, but we have a soul and a spirit. Scientists are still searching for the mysteries of life in brain chemistry. They say it is all in the brain, and perhaps we will discover a pill made out of some new substance derived from the brain, and all our problems will be solved. Steiner even mentions far worse for the future if this type of materialistic science continues. People in the future who have their own ideas or feelings different from the state's edicts—people with a soul—will be given a shot of a substance. This may prove true unless we begin to acknowledge the spiritual world. Liane Collot d'Herbois's instructions for a new way to paint represent a fight against the death of the soul and the spirit when only the body will be recognized.

Her whole work is a testimony to this simple statement of body, soul and spirit, or thinking (light), feeling (color), and will (darkness). To implement it, however, she told me herself, is another story, and it is a long, long apprenticeship and battle and there is no guarantee that one will be successful, meaning that one must always strive and never take anything for granted.

> If we really wish to grasp what art is, we must never forget that its fundamental concern must always and forever be to depict the battle between beauty and ugliness. Reality is achieved only by seeking a state of balance between them, and not when we accept the one sided reality intended for by Lucifer, and Ahriman....
>
> We cannot afford the luxury of cultivating beauty alone. To do so would be to escape from reality. Human beings today must boldly and confidently face the real battle between beauty and ugliness. We must be able to experience and share the battle between dissonance and consonance in the world.
>
> Experiencing this struggle means strengthening human evolution.[2]

In practicing Liane's book *Light, Darkness and Colour in Painting Therapy*, we experience nothing but this dissonance, consonance and the struggle to bring in harmony. As one can imagine, this work is transformative, life changing, and confrontational. And to lead a whole schooling in

2 Steiner, *The Archangel Michael*, Dornach, Nov. 23, 1919, pp. 137–138.

this work demands enormous forces; that is why it is taught by two people who can help each other and give each other support to face the challenges brought about by the students' struggle.

There is a story that Ita Wegman, not long before she died, was depressed by all the problems involved with her work and because she could see where the world was headed and felt cut off from the spiritual world. A new painting by Liane was brought to her and suddenly, full of enthusiasm, she stood up and said, "The spiritual world is here! The connection with the spiritual world is restored!" In Liane's words:

> I first met Ita Wegman during an international conference in England, before the war [World War II]. There were many people there from different countries, among them Elizabeth Vreede. Ita Wegman had various intentions and had made various plans for the future with all these people. She wanted to see me about something and we went into a room where we could talk. It was a very large and rather darkish room. On the walls were three pictures that I had painted. We went in and talked a bit, and after a while she turned around; then her eye fell on a picture of St. John the Baptist. She walked toward it, looked at it in silence for quite some time, then said, *"Ich bin frappiert; ich bin frappiert"* [I am struck; I am struck]. She must have had an inner experience when looking at the picture, because after that she changed all her intentions. All the decisions she had made were swept away and she did just the reverse of what she had intended beforehand. It took quite a lot of courage to tell all people that she had changed her mind, not being able to say why exactly, but it turned out to be a very good decision. She was so convinced and so certain that what she had experienced in front of that picture was something that changed all her decisions. And she stayed by it; nobody could make her change her mind again. Such was the influence a picture could have on her.[3]

In this story, Liane Collot d'Herbois of course does not mention herself as the one who painted the picture, because she is far too humble, but someone else's picture would not have had such a powerful influence on Ita Wegman. Her paintings have a power within them which touched Ita

---

3   From the author's notes on conversations with Liane Collot d'Herbois.

Wegman and caused her to experience something not of this world, but from the spiritual one.

This connection with the spiritual world is really what this book is about, what this kind of painting is all about, and what Liane tried all her life to share with us. I am going to do my best to dwell deeply into what that means from all kinds of approaches. It will sound complicated and chaotic, and so it is! Again, this is mystery school work.

Here is the center of Liane Collot d'Herbois's work. Her paintings brought something not of this world to the Earth. Many years ago, as I looked at a picture of one of her paintings, I immediately told myself, "This is the way I want to paint." What attracted me, I could not describe, but I knew that the quality present in that painting was what I wanted to achieve, and I worked nonstop to school myself in this marvelous way of painting. Most of the time I did this alone because that is the way this work is done. Liane brought the other world into this earthly world, and her whole schooling and training consisted of bringing this unearthly quality. This is the world of light and darkness, and their meeting is the world of color.

As one reads these words they seem abstract, but if one meditates on them and realizes for a second what it is we are doing as we try to paint in this manner, one could frighten oneself at the sheer audacity of it, and one might shy away: "What? I am working with primordial creators! No thank you! This is too much for me." As Liane says, one has to stay low-level and totally humble about what one is trying to accomplish, because it is a monumental task. The best way is to "keep working, darling."

In the macrocosmic sense, light and darkness are the Primordial Creators. They form the great cosmic polarity from which at the beginning of time all creation originated. Darkness is the first. It is the all-enveloping, all-pervading, all-carrying mother of substance. Darkness is the expression of cosmic sympathy, continually pouring out, enveloping, and carrying. It is the carrier of warmth, of love and of gravity—that force of attraction that is an expression of sympathy. Darkness fills, it gives substance, but in itself it is formless and it has no possibility of giving form, as it can make neither a center nor a circumference.

Darkness was before light was, it is the very first principle of creation and it is also the mightiest....

Light is an altogether different element. It is an expression of cosmic antipathy. It radiates from a center to a circumference. It carries the impulse for form. It is clear, cold, finished. Near its source it is stronger, further away it gradually becomes weaker and weaker, until it altogether dies out.

As soon as the cosmic light shines out into the cosmic darkness a great movement occurs. Out of its sympathy the darkness moves toward the light, trying to absorb it into its own being. By its force of antipathy the light pushes the darkness away, sweeps it aside, cuts through it, making a path for itself along which it can pursue its course. Cosmic antipathy meets with cosmic sympathy and the result of their interaction is movement in space. The light creates space as it pushes the darkness away. The darkness moves: away from the light, toward the light, in waves, in spirals. The darkness makes many movements. It does not move out of itself, it carries the impulse for movement and that is awakened into actual movement as soon as the light shines forth.[4]

This is a new language that Collot d'Herbois uses, one she had never encountered in her art studies. It is a common language for painters that allows them to make some sense of colors, how the colors want to be painted, how they literally come into being. Being stands behind the colors, which is what Liane wanted us to experience. Training her students meant that they had to experience the cosmic powers of light and darkness and the coming into being of the colors. As students, we experience these processes with charcoals applied with our hands on charcoal paper; we experience the meeting of light and darkness. This is a far cry from conventional artistic training these days. The meeting of light and dark is sometimes a tender one. Sometimes it is a high drama; sometimes both, but it is an experiential meeting of cosmic forces. The result of this experiential meeting is healing, a balancing of our selves. Some have more darkness, meaning they live more in the realm of willing with not much thinking. They act, so working with the antipathy of light brings some radical changes and

---

4   Collot d'Herbois, *Light, Darkness and Colour...*, pp. 15–16.

difficulties. They have to start thinking, "Where does the light go? How does it go? How does it move? That person then experiences something that is not really present in their constitution, something more will-like, acting without thought. This working with charcoal then balances out their lack of thinking. Other kinds of people who are thinking all the time—we might say people who have much light in their constitution—lack the will aspect. They think too much and never act. They do not enter the will-sphere of action. Working with darkness is a great challenge for these people because they want only forms. Light brings form and control, while entering the sphere of darkness means creativity and giving up control. Entering the will sphere and starting to act brings fear. All this comes into the picture when such a person works with light and darkness.

Part of the genius of this work brought to us by Liane Collot d'Herbois is the experiential element. As we work with the charcoal on the paper, it looks like a very simple deed, applying it lightly with our hands, entering into the process, living with the cosmic forces of light and darkness, actually experiencing their powers deeply within ourselves. Liane gave us twelve such exercises for charcoal, and each of them has a specific effect on the soul/spirit, and as students, we are called upon to experience all twelve of these exercises several times in the training in order to feel the difference of the light and the darkness and their meeting, whether the light is close or far away.

> There are twelve fundamental light and darkness exercises for charcoal and each of them has its own specific effect on the soul. In these exercises one can have varying standpoints over against the source of the light: it can be near or far away or at a medium distance. When it is far away the drawing will have a moonlight atmosphere, as it comes closer it will assume a more Sun-like quality. When the light is very close there will be a strong radiating effect....
>
> Let us begin with light that is at a medium distance, neither too far away nor very close.... This exercise has an enlightening effect, and it will help logical thinking. When the darkness is drawn in front of the medium light, one gets a stronger connection with one's will, one incarnates a little deeper into one's will....

Imagine now that the source of the light is very far away. That means that the picture will only be dimly lit and that the light diminishes quickly.

The light in these pictures is soft, slightly hesitant, misty. It reminds one of moonlight. It has a dreamy quality and as such it has to do with a slight excarnation. The darkness of the metabolic system rises in a very vague manner, creating a protective, warm shelter that carries a person.

In therapy one sometimes wishes that, because it can calm people and help their nervous system. It releases them from the world of necessity. People want that release sometimes, because the world of necessity hurts them....

When the source is quite near, the light will radiate strongly and therefore fan out....

When one draws the movements in the space behind this light one gets an exercise that will help to control the impulse of the blood when this impulse is too strong... Drawing the darkness in front of this light that is so close brings about a cleansing of the will.

When we draw the charcoal light and darkness exercises that are described above, we work with variations on the theme "threefold human being." These are all different pictures of man when we look at him from the point of view of light and darkness. The drawings in which the light comes shining in from above more or less depict man in his present stage of development. The exercises with the light in the center of the paper represent a stage of development that we are rapidly growing in to: One as it were sees oneself in the darkness and there is no light on one's path—except for the light that one carries within oneself.[5]

Only after describing this work in this manner do we really penetrate the coming into being of colors, which is a meeting of the light and darkness. Liane Collot d'Herbois is the only one who has developed such a method of working. Herein is her genius. The power that resides in working in this manner cannot be ignored. But it requires a long apprenticeship, which modern human beings are reluctant to pursue. We live in

---

5   Collot d'Herbois, *Light, Darkness and Colour...*, pp. 33–36, 38.

a fast world and expect to acquire something in weekend training and call ourselves experts. That is not possible in this field. Rudolf Steiner mentioned that it would take him thirty years to develop a skill, such as becoming an accomplished painter. Liane herself repeatedly mentioned the difficulty of this path and that the explanations are easy but putting them into practice is another story! The beauty of it is that what comes through our hands does not lie; it tells all, whether it comes from the healer or the one to be healed.

As we work this way, it is nothing but an enormous struggle because we are constantly faced with our selves, and most of the time what shows up is not pretty at all. We actually see it, and transforming what emerges is part of this powerful work and thereby the healing element. I can assure you that working in a room full of people actively engaged in light and dark charcoal work is an incredible experience if it is conducted in a serious manner. The person who conducts must have a high moral standard and have abandoned all feeling of power and selfishness. If that is not the case, this work is dangerous, because it calls up negative forces. One can literally feel the power. We are, after all, working with forces—cosmic forces—and are actually experiencing light and darkness. This work is not to be taken lightly. Sometimes students have to leave the room; they cannot cope with such work. In it we go beyond making pretty pictures and for some it is too much. One can always come back later when one is ready, or take up another kind of schooling.

> If as human beings we were to devote ourselves solely to beauty, we would be cultivating forces that would lead us into Luciferic channels. In the real world, beauty exists no more one-sidedly than evolution, which is always accompanied by devolution. The merely beautiful, used by Lucifer to fetter and blind humanity, seeks to free us from earthly evolution and make us independent of it. Beauty in that sense would sever our connection with the Earth. In reality what we are actually confronted with in the world is an interplay between beauty and ugliness—indeed, a fierce battle of the beautiful against the ugly.[6]

6   Steiner, *The Archangel Michael*, Dornach, Nov. 23, 1919. p. 137.

In this work, we learn to see each other on a different level, a level where words are not really necessary. This is the work of the therapist, to see who is in front of us, and how we can help that person to balance out what is missing. We actually learn how to see that on the paper, and the students, by seeing what others are doing, are learning even more. That is the actual training of the therapist. There is absolutely no judgment. One student can handle the light; another can handle the darkness, but each has to learn how to handle both, which is the beauty and power of this work. Liane Collot d'Herbois was a true genius, and Ita Wegman saw to it that she stopped working with children in the Camphill homes and started developing this technique so that we as painters can bring something new into the world of artistic creation and of healing.

It was Ita Wegman who invited me to Paris. In fact I went to Paris because of St. John the Baptist. I had an exhibition at a conference in Penmaenmawr and she came to see it. We had met before and so we already knew each other. One of the pictures in the show there was about John the Baptist and she especially liked it. She did not have much time to talk, but later she asked me to come and live with her in her house in Paris...

In those days, I could always stay at the clinic in Arlesheim. And when I was not well, Ita Wegman would take care of me. One time she made me come from Paris, because I was not well. I had a room on the ground floor. Elizabeth Vreede came to see me and she asked me if I would come and stay with her when I was better. I knew her well, and had stayed with her before, so I accepted the invitation gladly. Three or four days passed and then a nurse came in and told me that I had to go because the room was wanted. So I packed. I could not find Ita Wegman to tell her where I was going, but as I was coming back to the clinic for lunch, I decided to leave till then and I went over to Elisabeth Vreede's.

In the meantime, Ita Wegman came to my room to see me and found out that I was not there. When she found out what had happened she was furious and told the nurse she had endangered her karma with Ita Wegman, and Ita Wegman's karma with me by putting me out like that. A fearful row. For about a year that nurse would not come near me or speak to me because of it. She had never known that Ita Wegman could be so angry.[7]

From the beginning, I was enthusiastic about starting a school in this work of light, darkness and color. Being with the students was more than exhilarating, even though it was extremely difficult personally and more than demanding. I had a responsibility toward the students who came to me to be taught and I never forgot that.

These words of Rudolf Steiner can help in understanding light and darkness.

Aversion enables us to comprehend, and affinity enables us to love. Since our bodies have centers where affinity and aversion meet, this affects our social interaction as expressed in the process of teaching.[8]

---

7 From the author's notes on conversations with Liane Collot d'Herbois.

8 Steiner, *Practical Advice to Teachers*, Stuttgart, Aug. 22, 1919, p. 30.

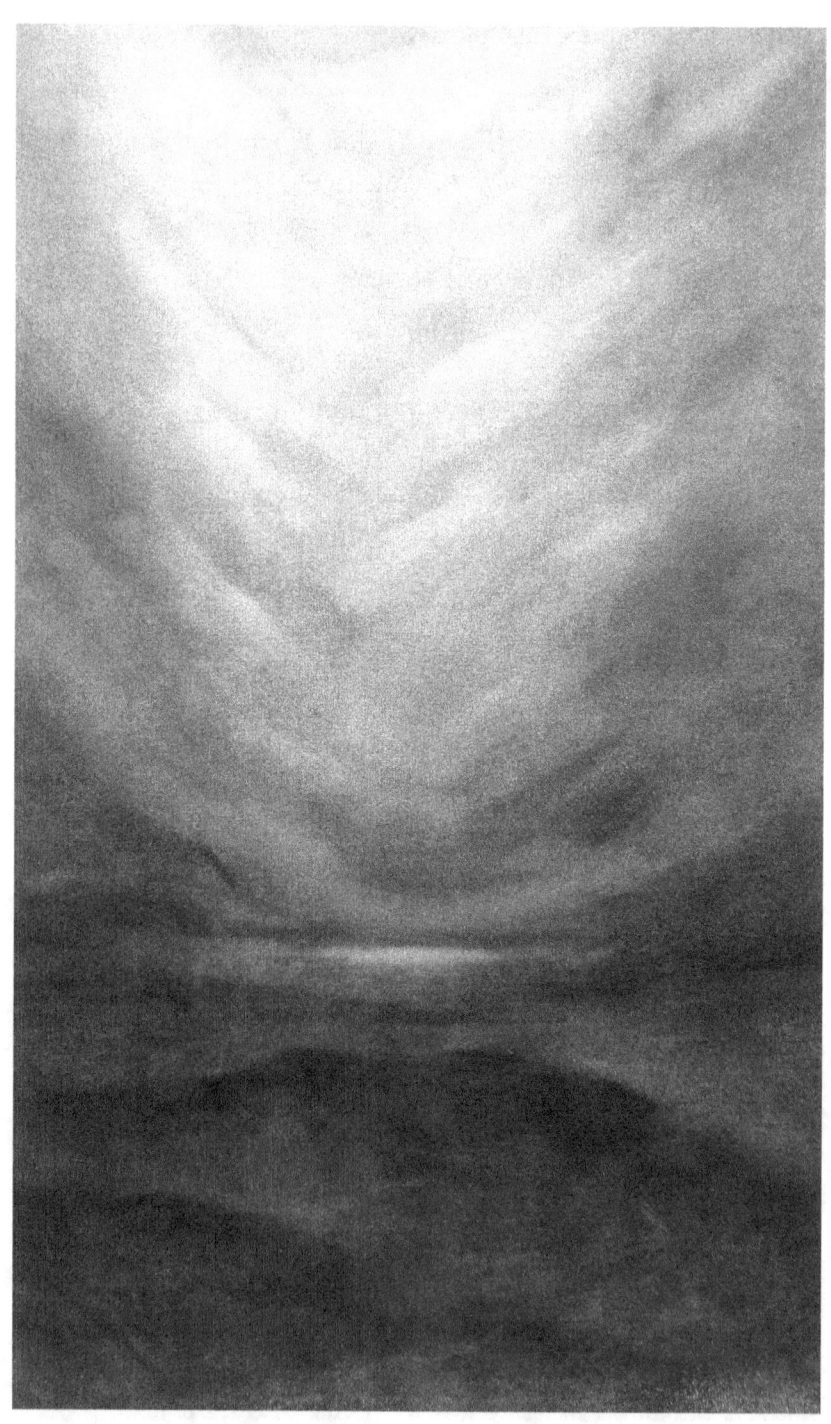

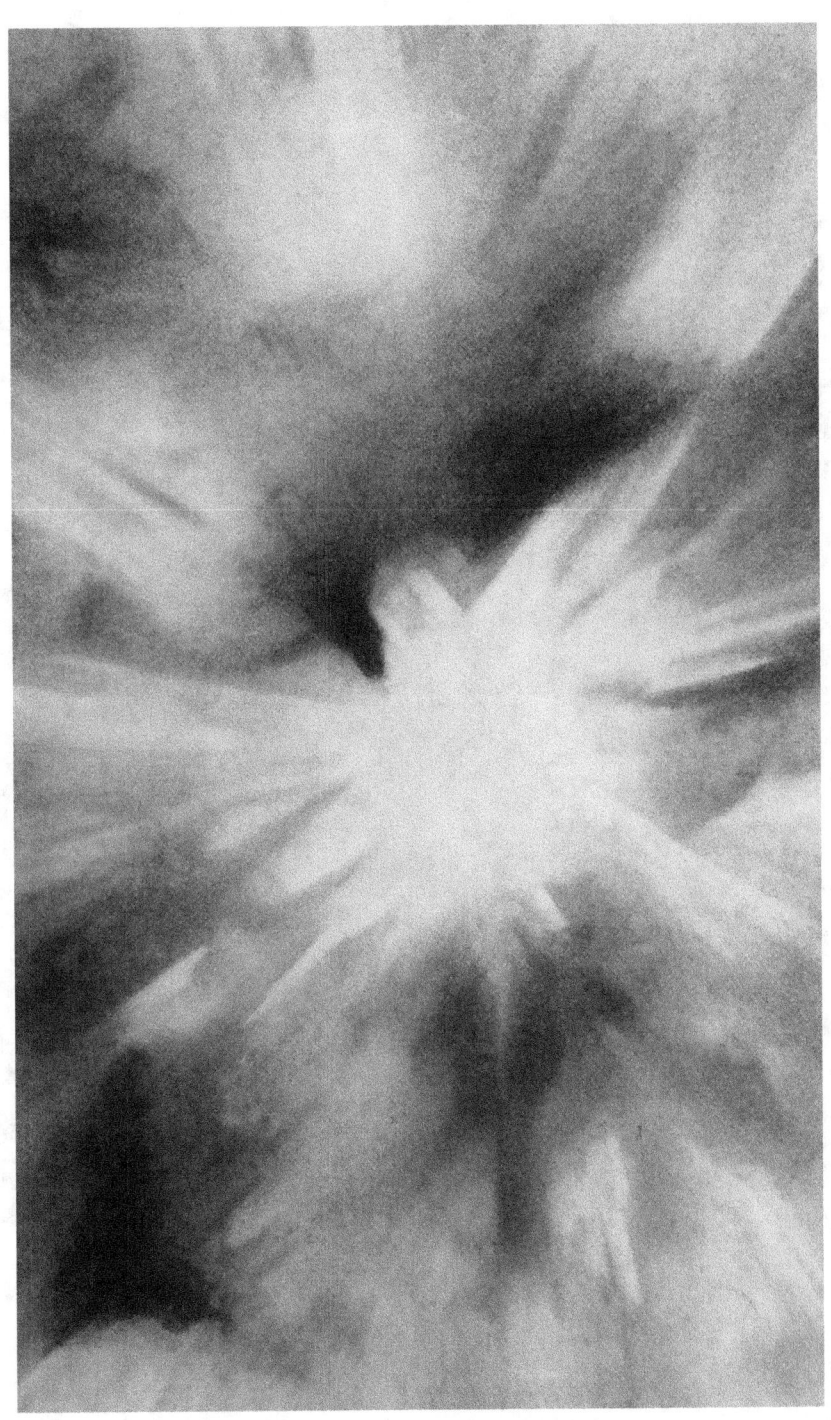

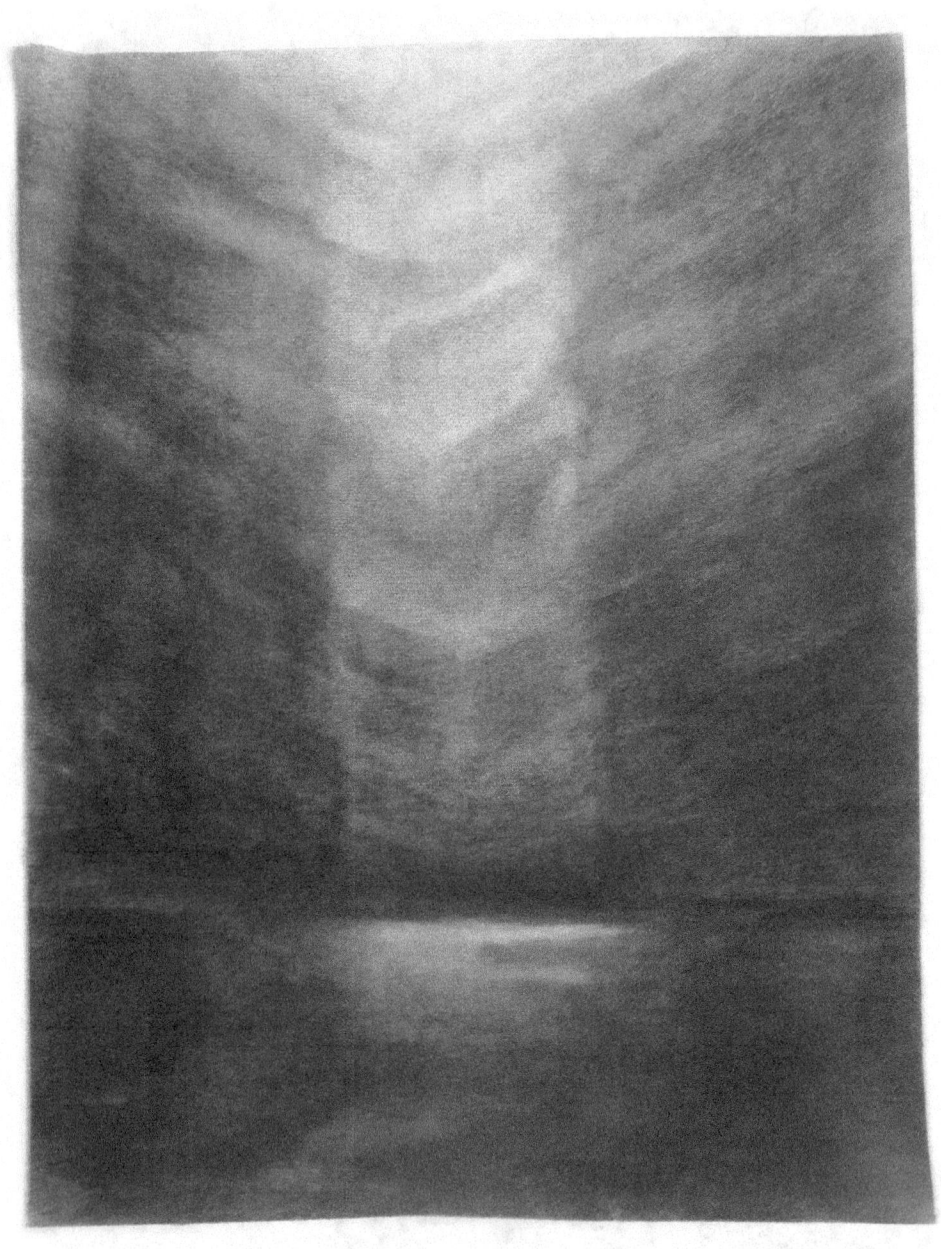

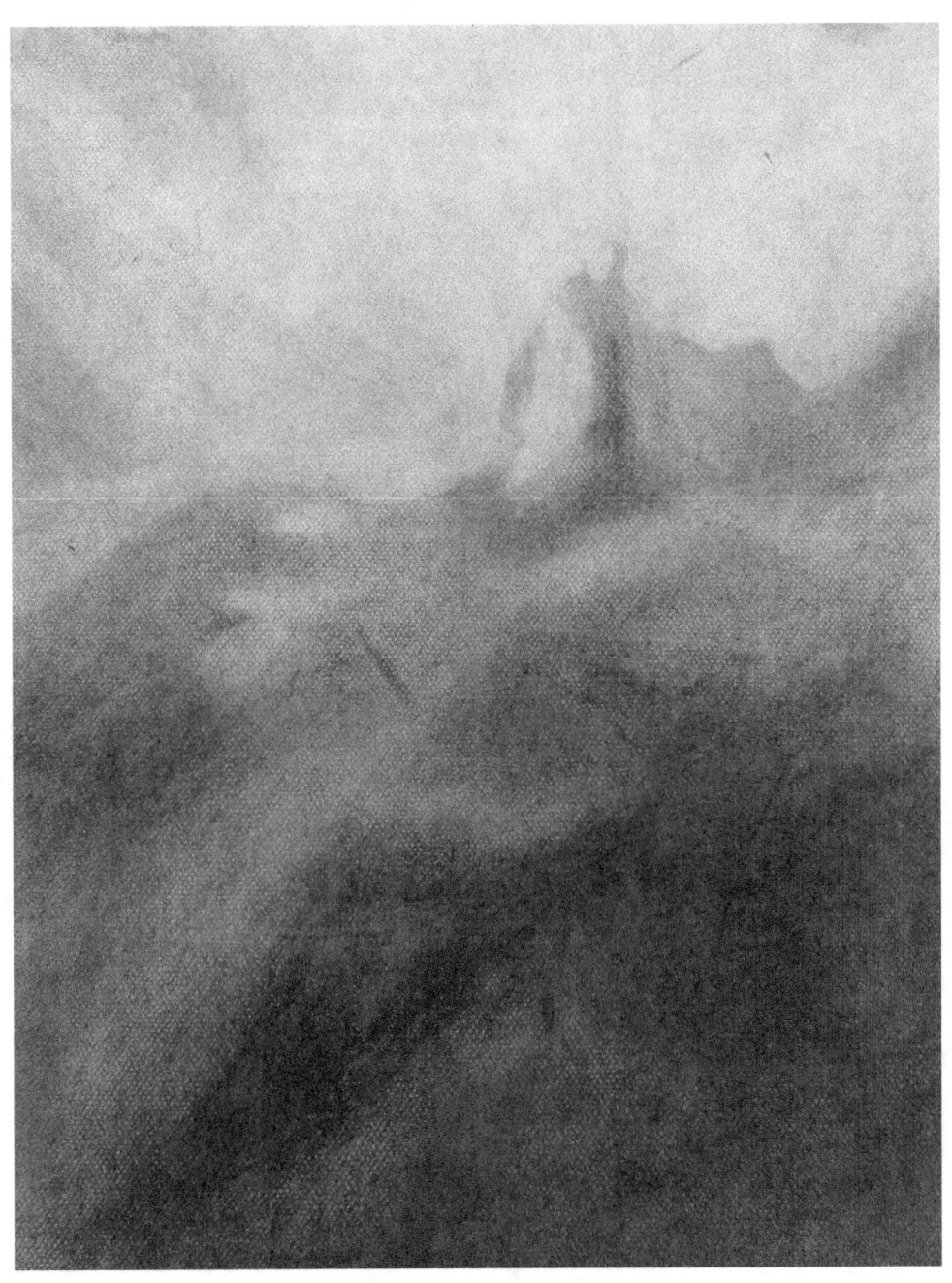

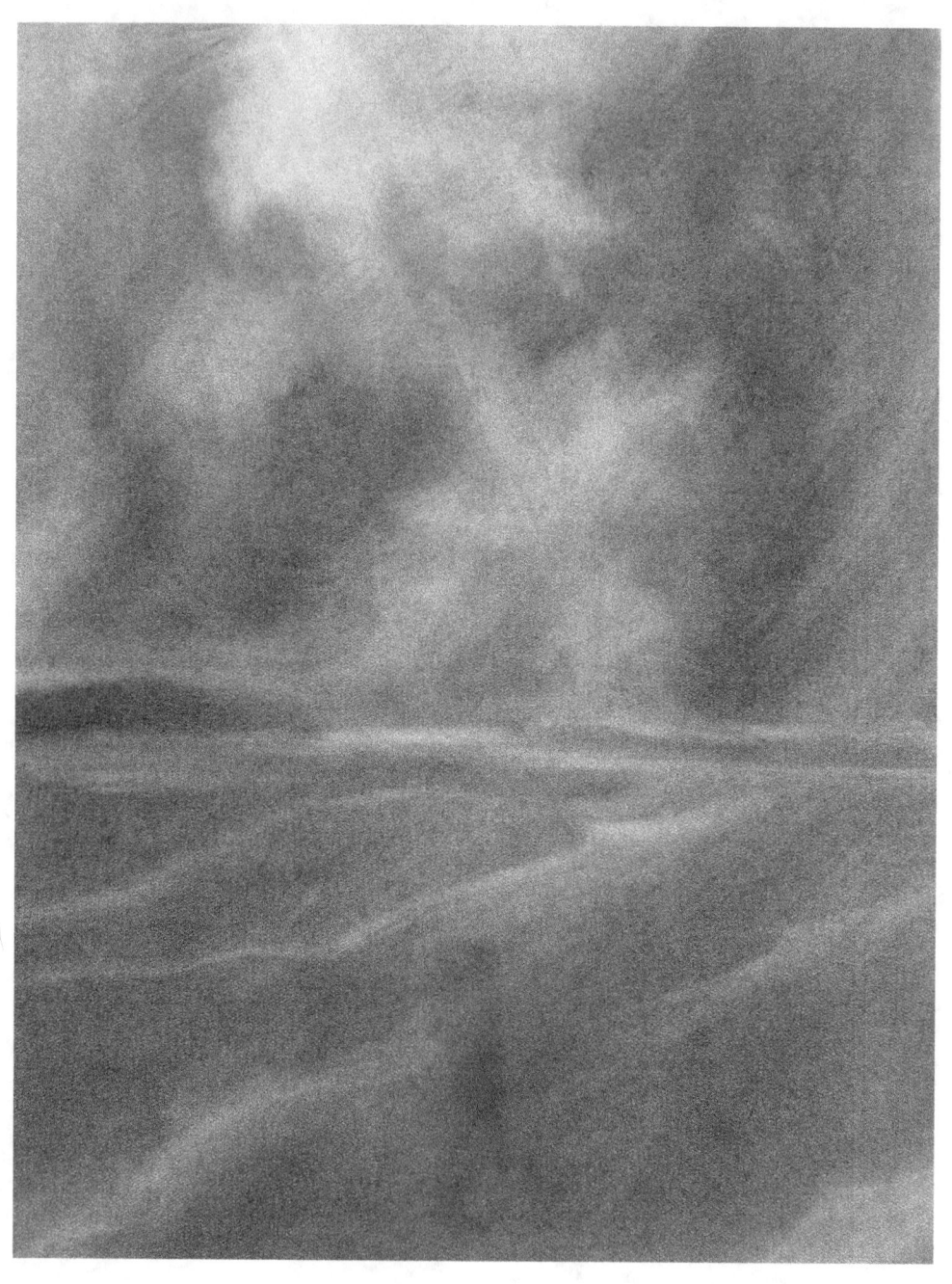

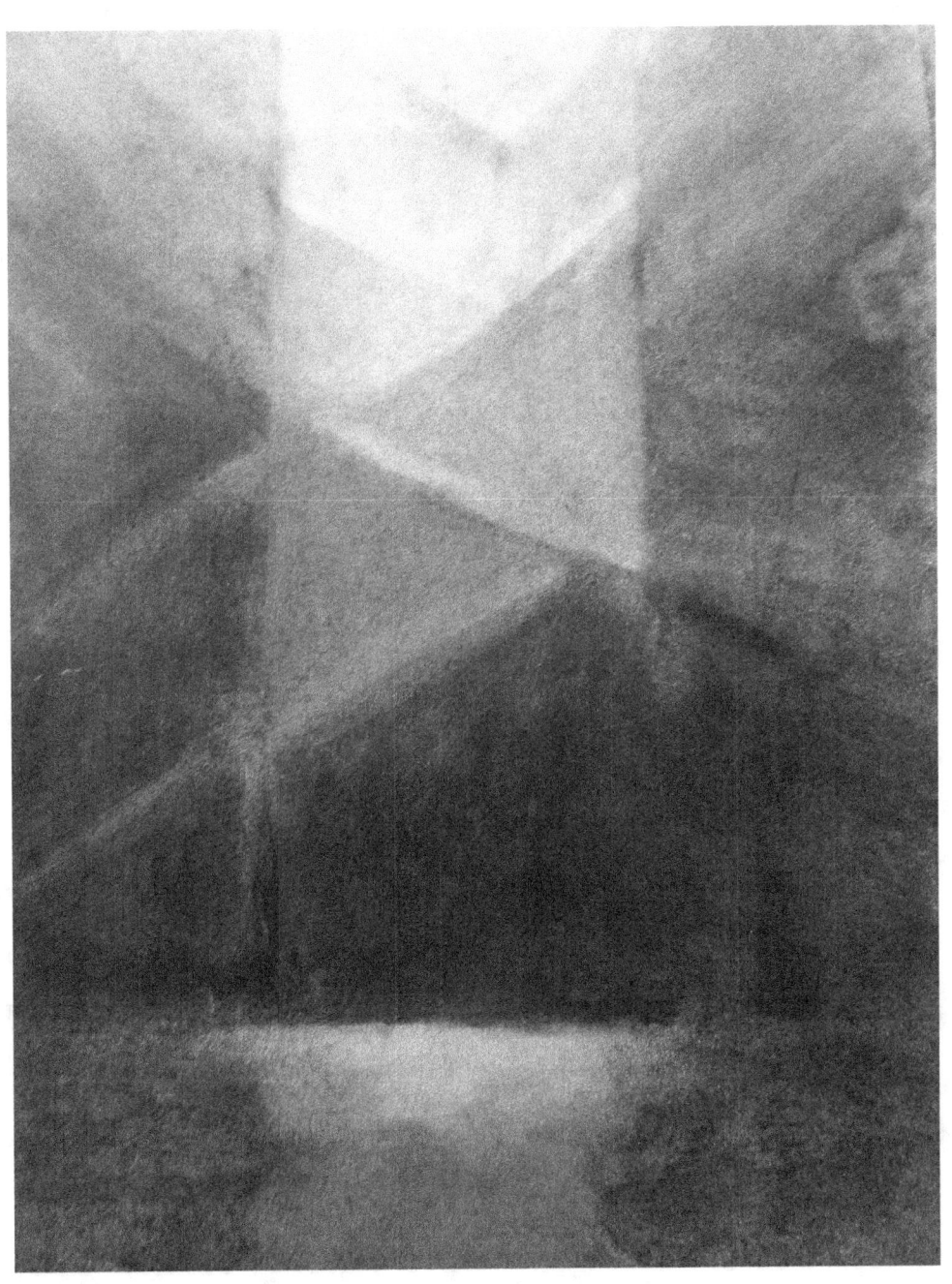

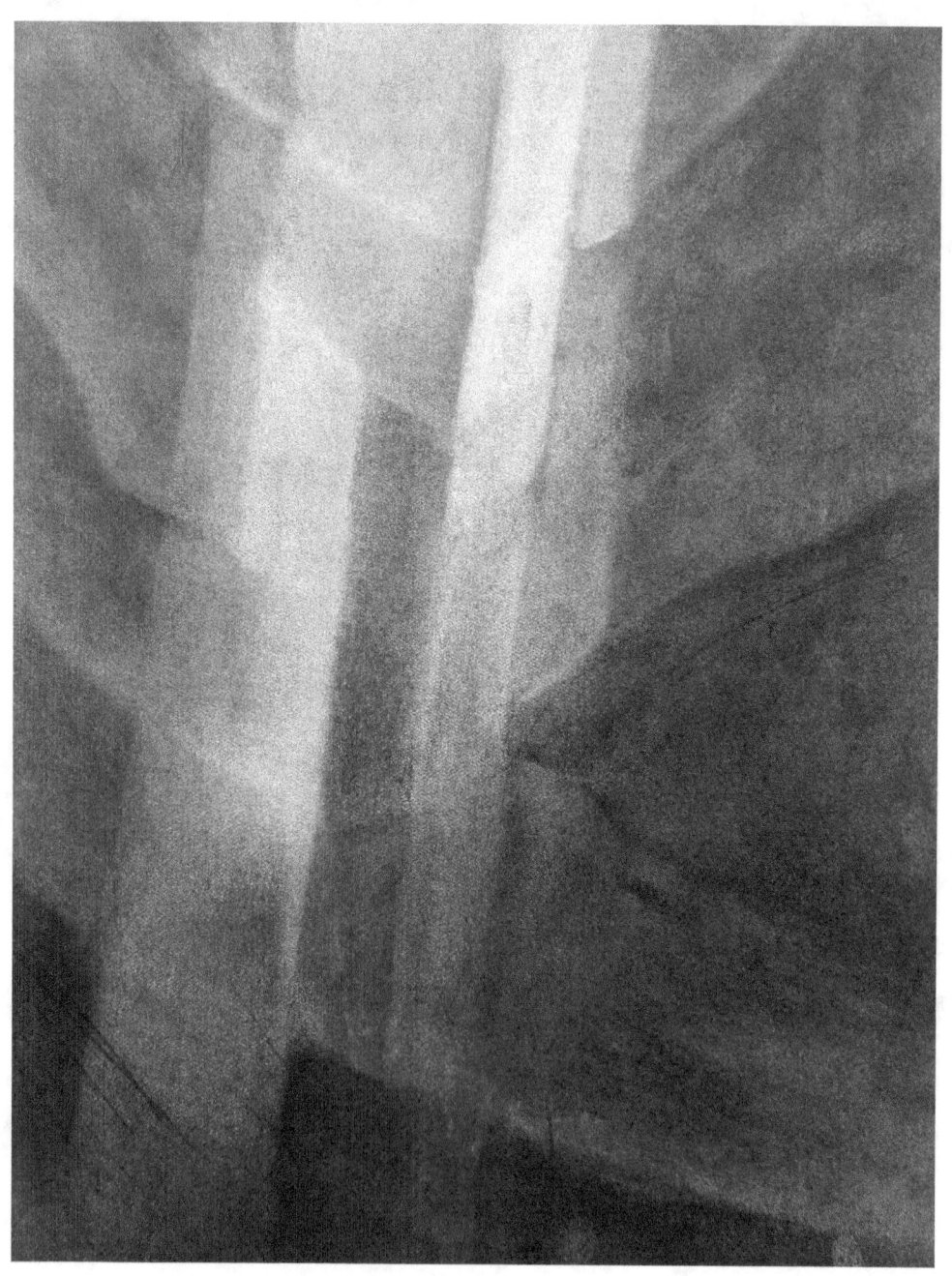

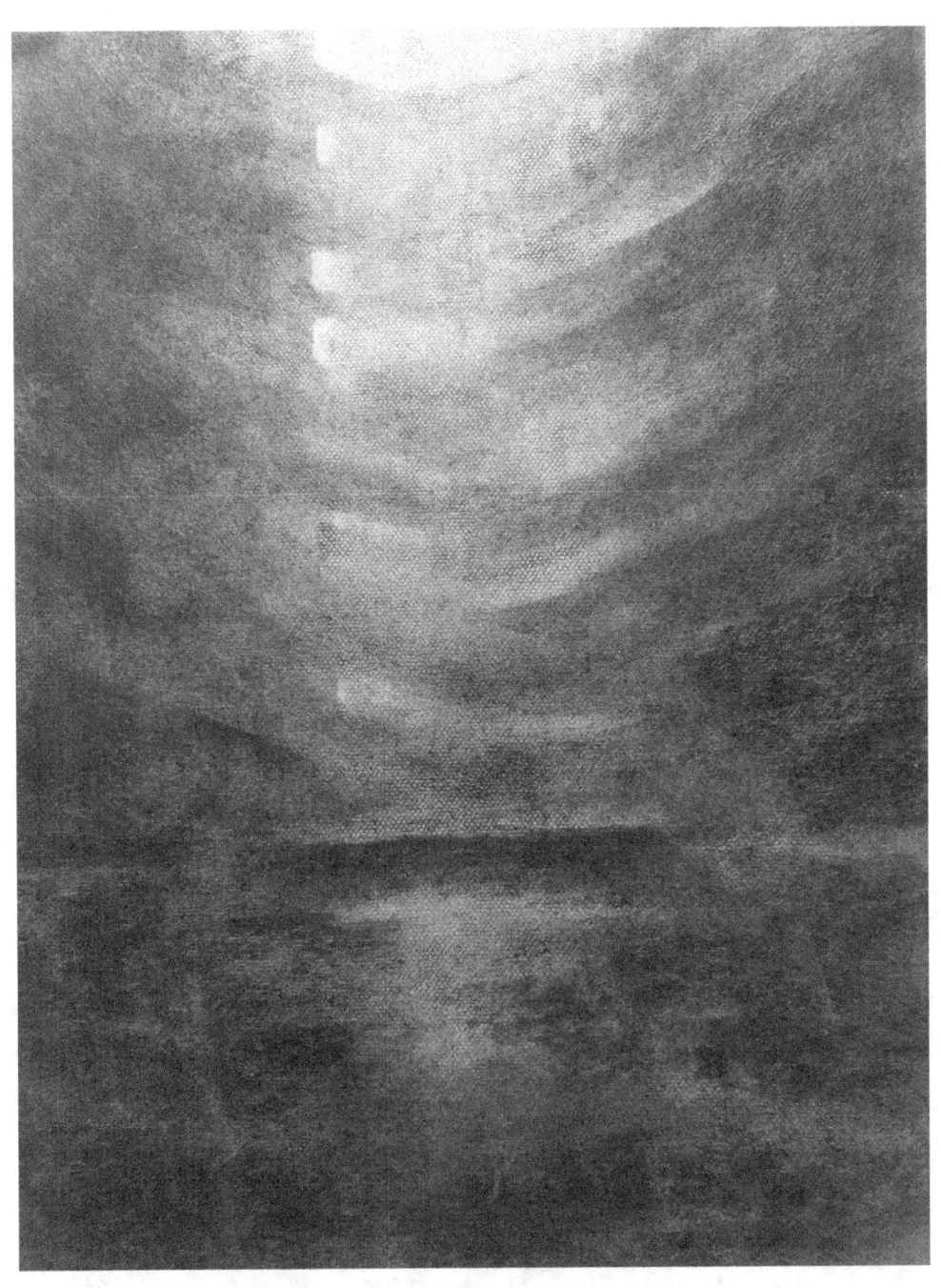

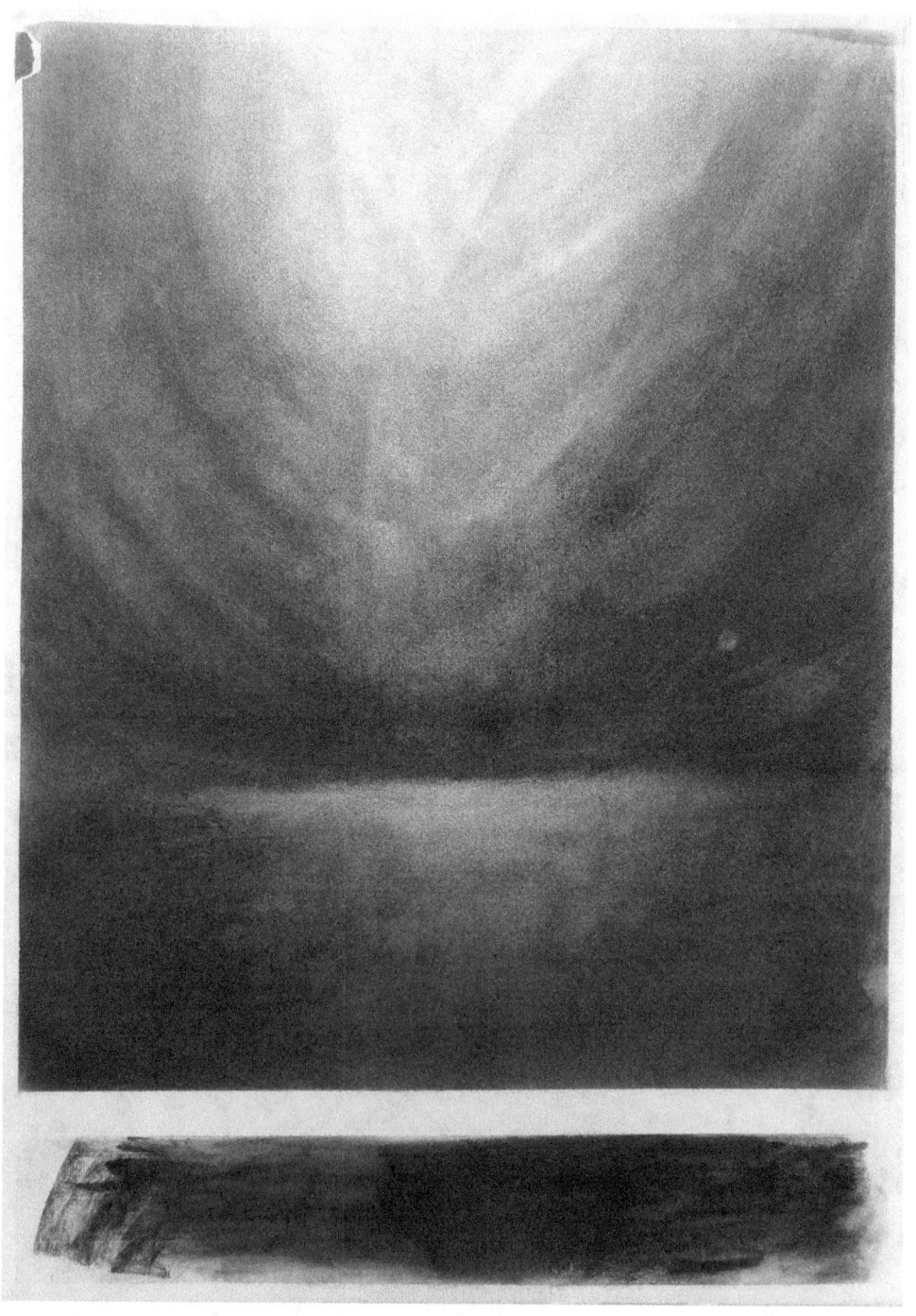

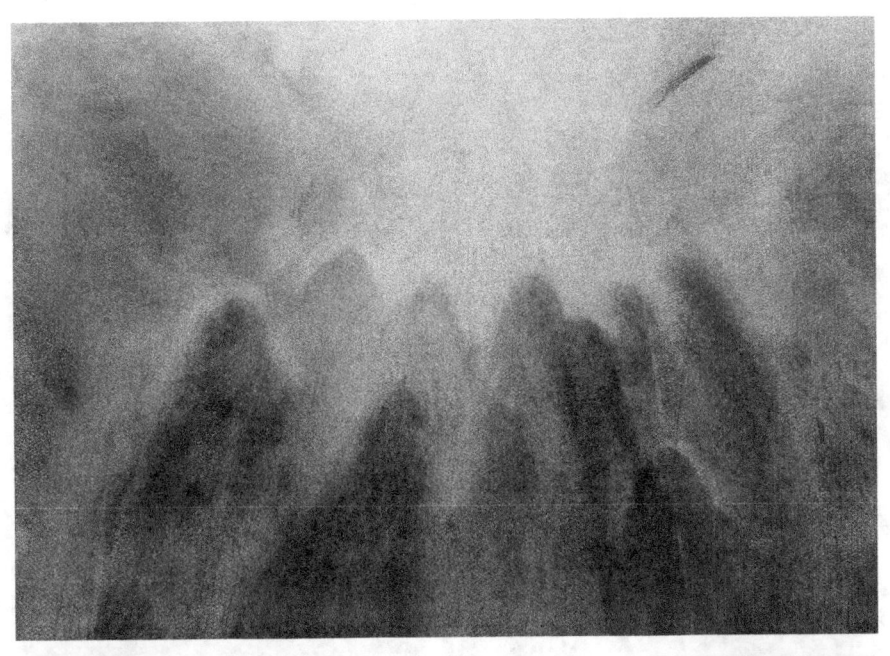

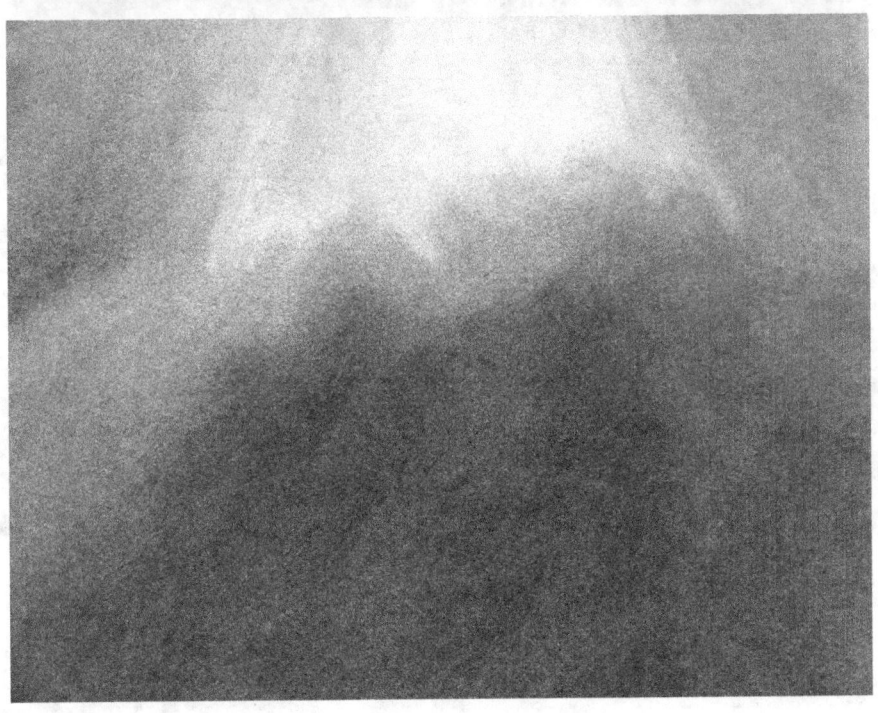

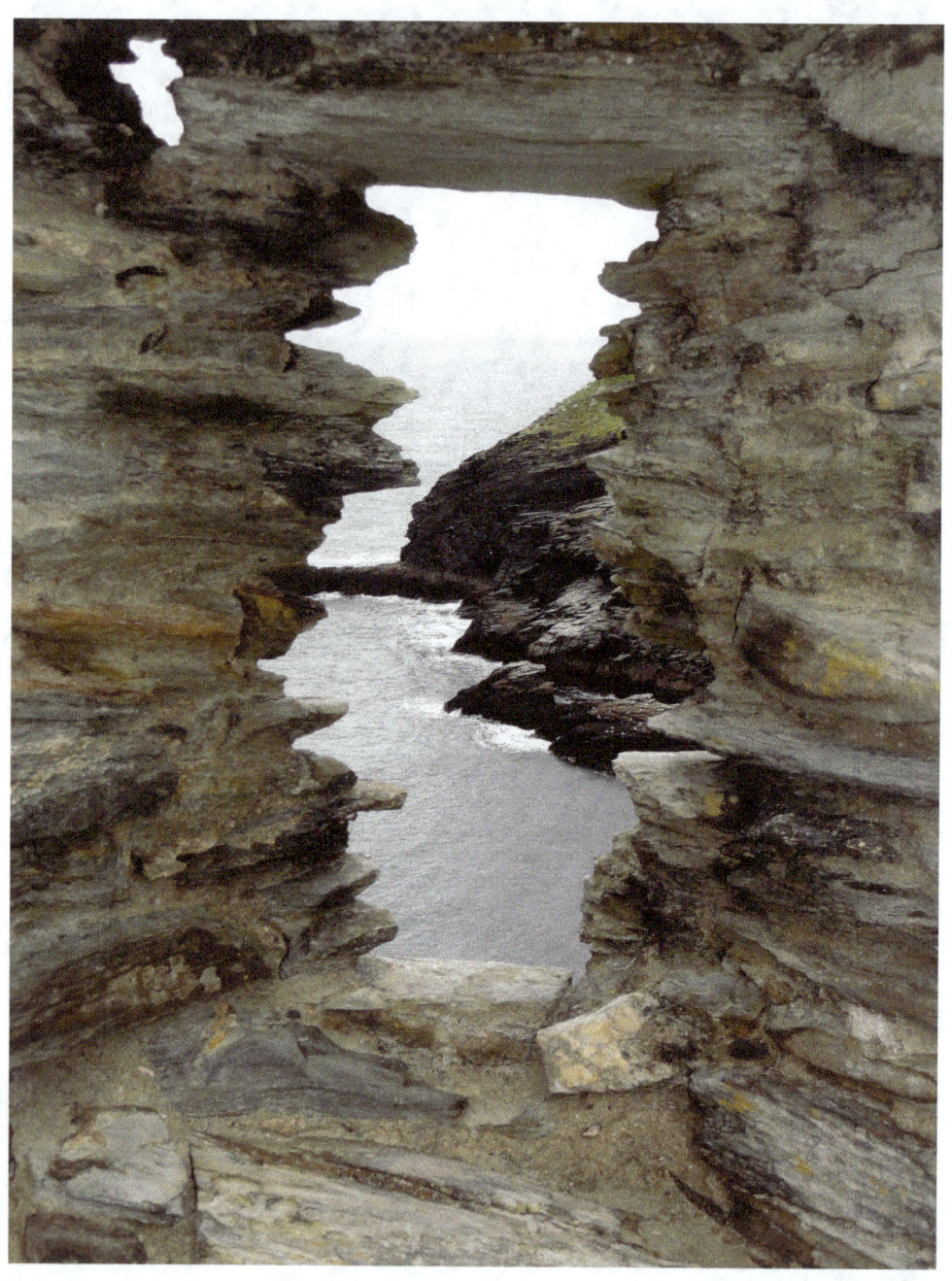

Observations in Cornwall

I cannot write this book without mentioning the logistics of living every-day life in this lovely town. Every afternoon I go for a walk, as I am today, I mingle with the English on holiday and folks walking with their children and their dogs. The coast walk is spectacular. I walk to the old church dom-inating the cliffs' landscape and see Tintagel Castle, what is left of it, in the distance. The list of vicars is written on the wall, an incredibly long line of them doing their job for 800 years. I stop to have one of Cornwall's famous cream teas: scones with jam and cream, the cream delivered fresh every day to local restaurants from the farm down the road. I am pleased to see that in England the good simple life has not been lost, and one can purchase fresh cream from local cows that are happy in the field. I hope it never changes. My tea tastes delicious, and I need the fat since on my trip to India last year I got amoebic dysentery and lost all of the little fat I had. Now I am happily making up for it. Traveling has its up sides and down sides.

Walking, I feel very thankful to be here in this unspoiled part of the Earth, looking at the setting sun over the quiet Atlantic Ocean from high cliffs that have seen so much history. Walking always helps me get my thoughts together and activates my inspiration for another session at the computer. Since I am here alone, I deliberately see or talk to few people all day, except for a few phone calls that keep me in touch with friends and family. Otherwise I am totally absorbed in my subject. It is just me, the books and the subject. I never know how my writing will turn out; it is a complete mystery. I am not the type to write a book with chapters 1, 2, and 3, and so on, all planned ahead. It is not the way I do things. I know what needs to be said, but it can't be in a format that is really dead. I leave that to others. I have to write and keep things alive, since the topic is how Liane Collot d'Herbois re-enlivened painting. With that as my subject, how can I write any other way? It simply can't be done. I hope the reader won't mind my unusual method; my intention is to match the text with my theme, keeping it alive and full of movement like the colors.

> In the world of living things, everything develops from within.... Things that grow and wane develop from within, and so it is also in the case of living thinking. [1]

Some won't like this writing style at all because the result will be highly imperfect. I accept my imperfections, but the book needs to be written anyway. Here is a passage from Rudolf Steiner's lecture of April 24, 1917, in Berlin, in which he explains his work with Goethe. I find it relevant to my work with Liane Collot d'Herbois, with Rudolf Steiner himself, and with so many others to whom I owe everything. One aspect of it—the fact that it is still alive—is so alive within me that I feel obligated to put it down on paper.

> Perhaps I may be permitted to speak from personal experience in this area, since these matters relate to the personal. Since my nineteenth year, I have been occupied continually with the study of Goethe, but I have never been tempted to write a factual history of his life or even portray him academically, simply because from the very first I felt the most important thing was that Goethe remained a living force. The physical man Goethe, who was born in 1749 and died in 1832, is unimportant. The important thing is that after his death his spirit still lives among us, not only in Goethean literature but also in the very air we breathe.
>
> This spiritual atmosphere that surrounds us today did not yet exist in ancient peoples. The ether body, as you know, is separated from the soul after death as a kind of second corpse, but through the Christ Impulse that informs us since the Mystery of Golgotha the ether body is now somewhat preserved; it has not completely dissolved. If we believe (*believe* in the sense I defined earlier) that Goethe has "risen" in an ether body, and if we begin to meditate on him, then his concepts and ideas come to life in us, and we describe him not as he was but as he is today. The idea of the resurrection thus becomes a living reality and we

---

1 Steiner, *Materialism and the Task of Anthroposophy*, Dornach, Apr. 29, 1921, p. 187.

believe in the resurrection. We can then say that we believe not just in ideas that belong to the past, but the living continuity of ideas, as well.

This is connected with a profound mystery of modern times. No matter what we may think, so long as we are imprisoned in the physical body, our thoughts cannot manifest properly. (This does not apply to our feelings and will, but only to our thoughts and representations.) As great as Goethe was, his ideas were greater than he was. The fact that his ideas were unable to rise to greater heights is because of the limitations of his physical body. The moment his ideas were liberated from bodily limitations and in a position to be developed by someone with sympathy and understanding for them, they could be transformed and acquire new life. I am referring here to the thoughts that persisted to some degree in his etheric body and not to his feelings and will. Recall that the form in which ideas first arise in us is not their final form.

Believe, therefore, in the resurrection of ideas. Believe this so firmly that you willingly seek union with your ancestors—not those ancestors to whom you are linked by blood, but with your spiritual ancestors. Believe that you will ultimately find them. They need not be those of Goethe; they might just as well be anyone else. Try to fulfill the injunction of Christ not to cling to blood ties, but to seek rather a spiritual relationship [Luke 14:26]. Then the thought of the resurrection becomes a living reality in your life and you will believe in resurrection. It is not a matter of incessantly invoking the name of the Lord; what matters is that we grasp the living spirit of Christianity and that we hold fast to the vitally important idea of resurrection as a living force. Moreover, those who draw support in this way for their inner life from the past learn that the past lives on in us; we experience the continuity of the past in ourselves. Then—it is only a matter of time—the moment arrives when we are aware of the presence of the Christ. Everything depends on our firm faith in the risen Christ and in the idea of resurrection, so that we can now say that we are surrounded by a world of spirit, and the resurrection has become a reality within us.

You may argue, however, that this is pure hypothesis. So be it. Once you have had the experience of being in touch with the thoughts of someone who has died, one whose physical body has been committed to the Earth and whose thoughts live on in you, then a time comes when you can say the thoughts that have newly arisen you owe to Christ; they could never have become so vitally alive without the incarnation of Christ.[2]

That is why I am here far from everyone I know. It is lonely but easier to be and live with these masters.

Strolling through this town, one gets a feeling for the English folks. Rudolf Steiner says they are the people of the "consciousness soul." I really never knew the English except through history. I find them totally lovely and charming. Of course, I see the other kind of folks here, too, covered in tattoos, drinking fellows and women. A lot of drinking goes on here. Nonetheless, there is a sense of lightness to many of them; as the old ladies stroll through town one notices that they do not like confrontation. They are extremely polite and drink lots of tea, and that aspect makes them diplomats, unlike the coffee drinkers of Italy and France, who love confrontation. I love confrontation myself, but it is wonderful to walk around in this light atmosphere in which things are accomplished in a polite way. It is a light atmosphere also because of the mica in the ground that reflects light, and that must also contribute to this light temperament. Perhaps they are all sanguine! I could learn something from that. This reminds me of how Liane Collot d'Herbois hated to confront people with unpleasant things. She left that job, like telling people off, to others. Someone else did it for her! How very English!

The other day, I went into the impressive hotel by Arthur's Castle to have a coffee, and there I saw the paintings of a local painter who is supposedly famous. He lives there, has his studio there, and his paintings—small, large, and very large—are hung everywhere throughout the four-story hotel. They show a lot of will and energy, but it is the same old stuff: colors thrown on the canvas with butterflies stuck on it or whatever suited his fancy, and the price for one painting was $30,000. All sorts of his colorful canvases were everywhere, sometimes in dirty colors. He had his name in all the newspapers and the whole world came to see his

---

2 Steiner, *Building Stones for an Understanding of the Mystery of Golgotha*, April 24, 1917 (trans. revised) pp. 176–177.

paintings including other artists, actors and other famous people. I spoke with him for a minute and asked him in my naïve way if he was interested in a serious conversation with me since I am also a painter. He, politely, did not answer my request and asked me if I had questions. I said I did not have questions, but just wanted to talk about art. Again he ignored my request. Then I mentioned that I have my own work and that I am also very busy working and do not need inspiration. It is true; I am deeply inspired. Again the conversation went nowhere. I presume he had nothing to say since he is such an important artist. This is a strange place. I left the almost abandoned establishment—the tourists did not go there for some reason. They preferred the town with its little tea restaurants full of life. This castle hotel was dead and full of the past (and ugly paintings that are not real art), a place for some rich folks to feel richer.

The scenery, however, is exciting and full of life. Walking on these lovely paths, I feel full of gratitude and thanks for the wind, the sea, the earth, the richness of the minerals and stones around me. In life nothing is lost, especially not our thankful mood for everything around us.

Entering the Work of Liane Collot d'Herbois

As we slowly enter the work of Liane Collot d'Herbois, we have to immerse ourselves into the meaning of the words *light* and *darkness*. This is a new language. Rudolf Steiner was tireless in bringing these cosmic imaginations for us to live with so that we could penetrate that world. Liane brought them to us as well. She worked with and became steeped in these imaginations. This led her to develop her very special approach to painting and therapy. Therefore, we must take the plunge ourselves into this world to understand this new approach to painting. Logic will not help us here; we must go beyond logic. We have to live with our feelings with the words and then perhaps get a touch of what it is that Liane Collot d'Herbois wanted us to experience and put into practice. For some, this approach will be tiresome and even boring, and they will leave these pages unread as too demanding. However, it is the *effort* that difficult passages demand that creates real understanding for that work. There is no avoiding it. My work would be a lot easier if we could ignore the effort that is required for merely understanding it. In a way, this is what protects such work. It is all out in the open, but the effort required to understand it keeps the unprepared away. Making it easier would not be in the spirit of this work, or the spirit of Rudolf Steiner's legacy.

In Rudolf Steiner's beautiful words:

I pointed out that first we perceive the world of light phenomena. In other words, in outer nature we see all that is made visible to us by what we call light. I said that we must view this light as dying thoughts of the cosmos—that is, cosmic thoughts that were, in the remote past, thought worlds of particular beings, worlds of thought through which cosmic beings perceived their cosmic secrets. What was thought in those remote ages shines down on us today as a kind of cosmic corpse, dying cosmic thought. This is what shines down on us as light....

During the Saturn evolution, for instance, all that existed of humanity was a kind of automaton. You know, too, that the cosmos was inhabited then just as it is now. However, other beings at that time were at the level humanity occupies today. We know that the spirits called archai, or "primal beginnings," were at the stage of today's human beings during ancient Saturn. They were not human beings such as we are today, but they were at a human level. Although they had an entirely different constitution, they were at the human stage. Archangels were at the human stage during ancient Sun, and so on.

Thus, when we look back into remote ages, we realize that during those previous Earth evolutions, those other beings lived in the world as thinking beings with human characteristics, just as we live in the world as thinking beings today. What lived in them then, however, has become external cosmic thought. Nevertheless, what lived in them as thought and would have been externally visible only as their light aura is now seen in surrounding space as the acts of light. We must see dying worlds of thought in these deeds of light. Darkness, of course, also plays into these acts of light and, in contrast to light, darkness reveals what can be called will on a soul-spiritual level, or *love* in Eastern terms.

Thus, when we look out into the world, on the one hand we see the illumined world, but this illuminated world would be transparent to our senses and we would not see it if darkness did not become perceptible within it. In addition, on the first level of the soul we have to regard this darkness interlacing the world as something that lives in us as will. Just as the outer world can be seen as a harmony of darkness and light, our inner world, insofar as it enters space, can also be seen as light and darkness. However, light is thought, or mental image, to our own consciousness, and the darkness within us is will that becomes virtue, love, and so on....

We reach a worldview that sees outer nature as the result of earlier moral processes and light as dying thought worlds. This makes us realize that the thoughts within us, while they live in us as thought forms, owe their origin and motivation to a very remote past....

What is in us now in its first stages of development will then shine out as external phenomena. Certain beings will then look into the world just as we do now on our Earth, and those beings will say, "A world of nature gleams around us. Why does it gleam as it does? It is because of the kind of actions human beings carried out on Earth. What we see around us now is the result of what earthly humans bore within them as new beginnings."

We are here now, beholding outer nature. We can look at it as dry, abstract intellectuals, and we can analyze light and its phenomena as physicists do in their laboratories. This would be to analyze them with inner coldness. This may well produce some splendid, ingenious results, but we would not be meeting nature with our full humanity. The only way to meet nature with our whole being is to feel our way into the color phenomena of sunshine, the blue of the sky, and the green of the plant, and be sensitive to what we hear in the rippling waves—for I am using the word light here in relation to all the sensory impressions and not just the light perceptible to the eye.

What do we actually see through our sensory impressions? We see a world that can certainly lift our souls and appears in a certain sense as the kind of world we need for meaningful contact with a meaningful world. If we merely analyze the world intellectually as physicists do, we are not applying our full humanity. To apply our full humanity we have to realize that what gleams and sounds around us is the last glimmer of what other beings developed within themselves in the remote past, and we should be thankful to them. Then we will not survey the world as dry physicists but become filled with gratitude to those beings who for millions of years during the ancient Saturn epoch lived as we do today, as human beings who thought and felt in such a way that we have this glorious world around us now. It is indeed a realistic worldview when, instead of making us dry intellectuals, it fills us with gratitude to those beings whose thoughts and actions in the remote past brought this impressive world into existence.

Just think of this picture for a moment with the necessary intensity and fill yourselves with a feeling of indebtedness to our remote ancestors for creating our surroundings. Let us fill ourselves with this thought and then come to realize that we will have to base our thoughts and feelings on the kind of moral ideal that will make those beings who come after us feel equally grateful to us for their surrounding world, just as we can do toward our ancient ancestors, who, through the effects of their work, literally surround us as shining spirits. Millions of years ago, the shining world we see today was a moral world. Millions of years hence the moral world we now bear within us will become a shining world....

Eventually, gratitude toward the remote past when beings actively worked to form our natural surroundings as they are, and a feeling for the tremendous responsibility that falls to us through the fact that our moral impulses will become shining worlds.... Our thoughts will become shining light. The moral world order will come to revelation. The moral world order of one time becomes the physical world order of another, and the physical world order of one period was at another time the moral world order. Everything of a moral nature is destined to become physical.[1]

If the painter up the road had an inkling of what is said here, I think he might start painting in a different way, but he did not want to have a conversation. What a shame!

As this passage demonstrates with such powerful words, we are responsible for making our future, for the future of humankind, and Liane Collot d'Herbois was fully conscious of her task as a painter. What she brought us was a way to paint that would add some morality to the world of artistic creation—first, by making us aware of the powers of light and darkness, and then the birth of colors. Rudolf Steiner gives lecture after lecture on the evolution of humanity, with which we must live to work as Liane described. One cannot exist without the other. Her work was born from the work of Rudolf Steiner; it grew out of Anthroposophy, and by that she meant Rudolf Steiner's books.

As students, we can put it this way: The more we steep ourselves in the work of Rudolf Steiner, live with it, meditate on it, and love it, the more we will be able to paint as Liane Collot d'Herbois has suggested. We have to lift the words light and darkness out of their tomb and have them reborn within us through our hands, by practicing light and darkness in charcoal work.

She wanted us to create paintings out of this moral world of colors that Goethe touched upon and she developed fully. However, that was only a

---

1 Steiner, *Colour*, Dornach, Dec. 10, 1920, pp. 96–99 (trans. revised).

beginning, with much more for us as her students to develop and take even further. She said, "Now you have to work in the darkness." Her meaning is very difficult to understand, but I have gained a glimpse of it after so many years of intense painting and meditating. She meant that we have to start being conscious in our will, which is the future. It is a task with which many masters have dealt and was the sacred work of the mystery schools of the past, and now Anthroposophy, as explained in *How to Know Higher Worlds* and *Intuitive Thinking as a Spiritual Path: A Philosophy of Freedom:* willing is thinking, and thinking is willing. In other words, the work that Collot d'Herbois brought to us is the work of a mystery school in which we use colors and charcoal to break through to the spiritual world. We can see now the kind of task she had come into the world to give, and the forces she had that could bring this to birth. She was an initiate; there is no question about that. The choice to be born in that village in West Cornwall was no event left to chance. This story from her youth reveals her destiny as an initiate.

> I became very ill [she was nine]. I remember the disease was quite pain-ful. I experienced so-called death for a time. My mother had specialists come in from London. The one said it was blood poison, the other said it was rheumatic fever, another said my back, my vertebrae had to be punctured, and then I would be a cripple for the rest of my life. My mother said that it would then be best to let me die. And so they sat down and waited for me to die. And I did "die." Telegrams saying that I was dead were sent out all over. I was covered with a white sheet. I became less and less and less. I was away, in a place where it was very light. The extraordinary thing I remember about it was the extreme objectivity. I did not see the Earth anymore. Everything was so objec-tive, and one was also objective oneself. One did not have the ordinary everyday feelings. Time passed, obviously. In the end I had to go back to Earth, but I did not want to go down again. I tried to resist, but I was pushed and it became darker and darker. At last I was back on Earth again. It was very painful to come back into my body. I had been away quite a while, about a day and a half. I remember it quite well.[2]

---

2   From the author's notes on conversations with Liane Collot d'Herbois.

A friend mentioned that the age of nine years marks half a moon node of 18 years and an initiation. It is quite extraordinary for a child to be so conscious at such an early age. Here is Liane Collot d'Herbois's recollection of realizing herself as being "I."

I did not say "I" of myself before I was five years old. Until then I had a rather dreamy consciousness. I lived with my grandmother in Cornwall. I walked for hours, miles all over the countryside. To me the whole landscape was alive, living. I had a friend, a big elemental being who lived on a hill over the moors. I read later that he'd had a big fight with Michael. Michael [the Archangel] had to fight him, because this elemental being made so much noise. The people living nearby could not stand it any longer, and they asked Michael to come and fight this big elemental being. Anyway, he was quiet when I knew him, and I was very fond of him.

I did not feel myself as really separate from things. I suppose I did not realize I was on Earth. One day my grandmother sent me to a farmhouse far away over the moors to get butter. I trotted off happily and came to the farmhouse. I was given the package of butter that was in a bag, and I went back home with it.

The land there is all silica, all decomposed granite. I was walking on a white, shiny path; the Sun was in front of me. I enjoyed the lovely sunny day and walking down that beautiful white path. I was daydreaming. Suddenly, from nowhere, out of the blue sky, there was such a tremendous clap of thunder that I dropped the butter. I had such a shock! And for the first time in my life I said "I."

I cannot explain what it was like. Suddenly I was something I did not want to be. It was an awful shock for me, suddenly to see the world like that. I felt that all and everything had left me and that I was alone. I remember saying to myself: "Is that more than I, more than me, or am I more than that?" That was my great question. I picked up the butter from where it had fallen onto the crystals of the road. I did not notice anything or mind anything about the butter at all. I was so preoccupied and unhappy and, in a way, frightened—that I was an "I." It was a most awful experience. I did not like it at all. All had been so nice before.[3]

---

3 Ibid.

Training in Light, Darkness, and Color

Now it is time for me to go for a walk on the rainy cliffs. It seems to me the tourists might stay home today. I will enjoy the misty atmosphere, the clouds, the wet path, and be thankful for the person who walked these paths as a child and kept her fierce temper intact, so that later as an adult she could give us this wonderful gift of painting with her elemental strength. The hills here might have something to do with her vitality, courage, and fierce temperament. I might imbibe some of it for this important task of writing I have set out for myself.

I start out from the village, decide to have a cappuccino with the locals, then go north on the cliff walk toward Boscastle. The ocean is engulfed in a gray mist adding to the magic of the place, a few locals are walking dogs and children, then as I go on it becomes deserted. The cliffs are high, dominating the soft gray ocean with a few foamy waves. The seagulls fly to their nests hidden in the tall cliffs, and on the meadows coming straight to the cliff walk the gentle grazing cows, and the ponies eat what is left of the grass. The air is soft, not cold, and here and there one can see the beautiful white rocks incrusted with all sorts of minerals. They used to mine tin here in these beautiful rock formations, and the Romans came all the way here to trade. The ground is really very alive with these gems/minerals and one can feel their powers, if one has an "ear/nose" for them. It is most wonderful, again, to be here and I can see why I came here to write. I am overwhelmed with thankfulness for what I am able to experience in this very special place on Mother Earth. I breathe very deeply the air, the ocean, the rocks, the cow and pony smells, the mud, the blackberries eaten by the handful, and feel that I cannot be more full than now, and if more is coming I will explode from delight. I always liked walking in wild places and here I must say I have my fill. I cannot ask for more than this.

Again, it is no mere chance that Liane grew up here. This is a powerful place and it preserved Liane's wild nature. Here she was allowed to live freely, to roam freely among the elemental forces coming from the Earth, the ocean and the fast-moving air that is always changing with rain, clouds, storms, winds. Nowadays it would be difficult to provide a child with such a wonderful place to live. I tried myself to give that to my children so as to preserve their inner wildness, their courage. Children growing up in the city become little intellects much too soon, and their wonderful wild natures are killed. That lack of experiencing wilderness creates untold harm to their young souls. This destroys their willpower for the future even before they are grown up. Many of them do not have a chance; they end up in the therapist's hands. Liane often told about the lack of movement in the soul, apathy, and this comes from this kind of dry childhood.

Walking on these special grounds reminds me of all that. If Liane had not grown up in this very powerful spot, she would not have achieved what she did. I am looking over my own childhood and I must say that I was very lucky myself to have grown up a bit in this kind of wilderness: at the Italian/French compound there were no books except a few fairy tales, no television, no radio, no music except instrumental music, gardens full of vegetables, strawberries, small alleys to roam through, rabbits and chickens to play with, an orchard where we climbed up cherry trees, large shade trees, making pasta from scratch, and jams. Then at my grandfather's farm, which was very poor, there were work horses, cows milked by hand, fresh churned butter, garden planting, walking on small paths through the woods to the village to buy huge breads, hanging out at the very large kitchen table, sleeping in the attic with all my aunts and uncles, listening to music played by my uncles and aunts at night in the candlelight—there were so many of them we had our own band—eating Camembert with my grandfather, playing with lambs, German shepherds and more. No one ever told us what not to do. We were simply free to run around, and to that I owe my love of nature, of freedom, of the Earth, and of the wilderness in nature and in myself. I am always troubled when I see the poor cooped-up children living in the city. I feel the harm done to their souls; their little souls take on a grayish color.

Children need to run and experience freedom of movement without elders constantly telling them what to do. We make them invalid by all our constant orders—don't do this, don't do that. This does not mean we should not discipline them, but that is another story.

≈

Imagine that you are floating in an endless space. All around you is a nebulous atmosphere that is dark and warm. At first you don't see anything but darkness, but you feel that you are being carried by this warmth that is there and that it carries you along with it in very slow movements.

After a while you begin to realize that you must be moving toward light, because in front of you and all around you the darkness dimly begins to glow with a beautiful purple, the color we call magenta. The magenta envelops you and still you feel that you are being carried, but now by this color and by its warmth. Gently it moves you on and the darkness gradually becomes a little lighter. The magenta seems to glide away to the sides and in front of you the color changes to a deep carmine. You are beginning to vaguely discern the movements that the dark atmosphere makes, pulsating, rolling, coming together and dispersing again, but all still hardly perceptible. The movements carry you with them. They become quicker and stronger and you find yourself traveling through a world of vermilion. To your left and to your right the atmosphere is a little denser and there the carmine still lingers. The movements gain more speed, taking a more upward course and now you come to a world of orange, the vermilion receding on either side of you. In front of you the orange suddenly opens itself, moving aside, and you feel that you are being pulled toward the yellow that you see there radiating in front of you. Here the movements are almost linear, pulling you along forward and upward to the point where they are split up by the light into small fluttering patches of yellow-green that accompany you till you stand in front of the splendor of the light itself. You feel drawn toward it, toward that pure unveiled light that has the color of a clear emerald. It takes you into itself and you can look through it, gazing out into ever deepening depths of blue. You step out of the light, leaving it behind you and you find yourself in the geometrical movements of the turquoise. On either side they soften to a cobalt blue. Here the atmosphere is no longer warm and nebulous; it is clear, crisp, and crystalline. As long as you had the light in front of you the darkness carried you toward the light, with movements that were gradually ascending. Now, with the light behind you, you are being borne away from it by retreating movements that go gently downward. Here the darkness allows itself to be pushed away by the light. You come to a cobalt blue that envelops you, carrying you down to the uncertain movements of the Indigo. The light grows weaker, reflecting softly on the hesitant movements of the darkness. Then you come to the mysterious violet, where the movements are still slower and almost horizontal. You realize that if you would still go further you would come to the great boundary where the light finally dies out.

Although we speak of many colors and give them different names you must think of color as of one substance, one great cosmic substance that is incessantly in movement and its movements are due to the infinite variety of interactions between light and darkness....

All we have said about the cosmic aspect of the subject also holds good for the human being. In us the light of consciousness and the darkness of substance meet and interact in many ways and between these two poles there is the many-colored world of the soul. The activity of destruction that is in the light makes a path that is necessary for the incarnation of the "I." The creative activity of the darkness builds up and maintains the organism that is the vessel for this incarnation. The color in its arising has more affinity to darkness than to light, because it is carried by darkness and movement. Color *is* movement. The manifestation of our soul lies very much in the sphere of movement. Therefore you can look upon the soul, as something that has a much more intense connection with the world of movement and darkness, which in the human being is will, than with the world of light, which in the human being is thinking....

There is a great difference between the darkness that is meant here and evil. I do not mean here a soul-darkness, but the darkness of will that carries us....

It takes a long time to study light and darkness properly, but we will have to accept that.[1]

The whole of the training of the painter lies in this passage. Every sentence here is experienced by the painter in dozens of very specific exercises developed by Liane Collot d'Herbois. Each exercise is a crystal-clear detail on how to paint the color, with specific movement to show the movement of the colors toward the light (the reds) or away from the light (the blues). Each painter has to learn how to paint the colors. Specific colors are used, and they often have to be bought from different companies, for example Winsor & Newton or Schmincke, to have the exact color that is needed. A long apprenticeship is necessary for those who have not previously played with colors. The color from little jars filled with very light colors and water is applied in a quiet manner in a veil, working from left to right with a large brush of at least one inch width. One never applies another veil unless the preceding veil has dried totally. This is an exercise in itself. To control one's temper can be difficult but not impossible. I am a case in point since my temperament is choleric; but that temper has its positive side—energy! Of course, I always enjoy a good lively argument.

Living in colors this way, painting them in this manner, is healing. We worked on all these exercises, some of them designed specifically for students on the American continent. Liane had the Americans in mind when she gave us certain exercises. Some of the colors she gave us were astonishing to work with. They brought me some amazing visions of my past lives just by the color she told us to use. There are some forty of these exercises, each rich with cognitive feelings. Each addresses certain areas of the soul life, with specific healing aspects to all of them, which the students experience and assimilate. This becomes their "book." Students, again, do not need any books, as they have worked it through and have become their own book. Then they can teach out of that well-earned knowledge. However, these color exercises have to be experienced; they are not to be given out as recipes because giving the colors themselves will not make one bit of

---

1   Collot d'Herbois, *Light, Darkness and Colour...*, pp. 17–19.

difference. One must go through the very rigorous schooling in charcoal work and experience those fully, then start with the veiling exercises, spending at least three days on one specific exercise. Moreover, if I use carmine with indigo and some emerald, for example, this means nothing to someone who does not go through this rigorous schooling/training. One has to live deeply into the colors with love, with devotion, and selflessness and then the colors cooperate and help us.

Here Steiner discusses the task:

Art will never arise from scientific concepts or from abstract theo-sophical concepts, at least nothing but empty allegory and formal symbolism. The thoughts of the modern world about the world are in themselves inartistic and actually aspire to be so. Consider the colors and what our scientific view has made of them. Vibrations of the most abstract part of matter, the ether, etheric vibrations of so many wave-lengths, and so on. Imagine how far removed the waves of vibrating ether envisaged by present-day science are from the living quality of color. How could it be otherwise than that we forget altogether to pay any attention to the life and essential quality of color? At the end of our last gathering, we pointed out that the element of color is funda-mentally flowing and alive, and that our soul life lives in it. I said, too, that a time will come when we will again recognize the living connec-tion between the flowing world of color and the colored objects and creatures around us.

People find this difficult because, having to develop their "I" dur-ing Earth evolution, human beings have ascended, so to speak, out of this flowing sea of color to the level of clear self-awareness. With their "I" people lift themselves out of the flowing ocean of color in which the animal world is still fully immersed. If an animal has green, brown, red, black, or white feathers or fur, it is because of its whole relationship to the flowing sea of color. Just as we look at objects with our "I," an ani-mal looks at them with their astral body, and the forces of the animals' group soul flow into their astral bodies....

Owing to the kind of relationship that exists between an animal's astral body and the group soul, sensitivity to the living creativity of color flows into an animal. Moreover, just as our hand reaches out to grasp an object we long for, the animal's whole organism is affected by the living creativity of color that flows straight in and colors its feathers or fur....

This living participation in color has been submerged in people, to the extent that human beings have begun to develop their "I." We would never have been able to develop our "I" if we had remained united with the living sea of color to the degree that, on seeing a red color or rosy dawn, for example, we would have been aroused to transfer the dawn colors in a creative, imaginative way to areas of our skin.... In constitution, human beings had to become neutral toward this flowing sea of colors. The color of our skin in temperate zones is essentially the expression of our "I" and shows absolute neutrality toward the waves of flowing color outside us, and we have it as a result of our ascent out of that color sea....

Our physical, body, and astral bodies evolved during the Saturn, Sun, and Moon periods of evolution, and our "I" during the Earth evolution. Human beings must find a way to spiritualize the astral body again and permeate it with "I" activity. Doing so, for the sake of developing our "I" we must rediscover the moving waves of color from which we emerged while looking at us and taking stock of our surroundings as a swimmer would do when stepping ashore. We are, in fact, living in a time when we must begin to immerse ourselves in the spiritual activity at work in natural forces—that is, immerse ourselves in the spiritual forces behind nature—if we are not to lose all contact with the world. We must rediscover the way to live with colors, to experience their inner life, and not just look at them and paint with them externally. It will not help, from the perspective of painting, to study the play of colors by merely staring at them. The only way is to enter, with our whole souls, the way red or blue moves and to feel the living quality of the colors. We must bring to life what is in the color, not by practicing color symbolism, which is the worst possible thing, but by actually discovering what is in color, in the same way as the power of laughter is in someone who laughs.[2]

This is what Liane Collot d'Herbois developed with genius, thanks to her very keen scientific mind, her love of color and painting, and her work as a spiritual scientist under the guidance of her master, Ita Wegman.

---

2 Steiner, *Colour*, Dornach, July 26, 1914, pp. 62–65 (trans. revised).

This aspect of the schooling is the preparatory step toward an under-standing of light and darkness and colors. It is to train ourselves and live with the cosmic forces of light and darkness and the beings of colors. A student needs at least four years of this technical schooling in painting and charcoal work, and that is only if the person is talented enough to under-stand its anthroposophic background and does the necessary studying of that. No wonder there are not enough students; the task is almost impos-sible. Then, however, the students will grow into it and they will feel what the Color Beings are through such intensive work. We do not need a book in this schooling. After a while, the work lives within us; we carry it with us. That allows us to teach or paint, or work with patients. The process has become part of us if we have penetrated it deeply enough, and there is no end to the depths we can achieve. Unlike doctors who constantly look up information in their very thick books, we become the book. Besides, there really is no book to follow.

However, as Liane says, the school might die down for a while, but new talented students will come. I met some of those students; they were very young, and many of them happen to live in Russia or are from Russia where I was visiting prior to coming to Tintagel.

Working in this manner, you can begin to see how great the task is. It is not only to paint. We have to train ourselves in meditation, serious medita-tion, as we paint. We have to enter what is the realm of the etheric, the flow-ing world of forces in which all living beings live. When one looks at a red object, for example, and closes one's eyes, then one sees green, a faint green color. That color does not exist physically; we see it with our ether body. This is connected with what is called *thinking with the heart* forces, rather than the intellect. Embarking on this meditative journey is another serious part of the schooling of the painter that must be included; otherwise the painter gets lost in subjectivity and cannot even consider painting in veils.

As painters we need to transform ourselves totally, to surrender to the colors and let them speak, and that can only be done if we do the exercises in Steiner's *Knowledge of the Higher Worlds and its Attainment* or other such spiritual practice. Without this training, paintings are just something to play with, and not what Liane Collot d'Herbois envisaged bringing to us, or what Rudolf Steiner describes in his lectures on color.

In *World of the Senses and World of the Spirit* Steiner spells it out even more strongly. We are enmeshed in the world of Lucifer and Ahriman. We do not have the right relationship to these forces, and therefore we have a more selfish, self-centered influence.

> The only way to learn the right and true relation is to reestablish it. In human beings as they exist in the world today, subject as they are to luciferic influence, the relation between "I" and astral body is not in order.... A correct and proper relationship will come about when human beings undertake wise, energetic, and patient self-discipline and acquire the qualities we describe with such terms as *wonder, reverence, feeling in harmony,* and *surrender*. The relationship between "I" and the astral body is such that an unbiased observer will have the impression that the relationship is now a true one, that the "I" has now cancelled and undone what came in through the luciferic influence (selfishness). The original relationship can be corrected again only by developing these four qualities of the soul in the very highest degree.[3]

The canvas becomes a place where beings incarnate via the colors we paint with respect and devotion, forgetting ourselves in the process. The other world touches our earthly world via our paintbrush. We have gone through the threshold and work with the higher beings. That is the true meaning of being a Collot d'Herbois painter, and this with true humility. Otherwise, we deal with grandiose maniacs or queens of schools, like the artist up the road with his paintings on all four floors of the hotel, thinking he knows it all.

Here Rudolf Steiner talks about this in different words:

> We come to know the inner nature of color and...we can foresee a time when an artist's preparation will mean a moral experience in color of this kind, when the experience preparatory to artistic creation will be much more inward and intuitive than it ever was in past ages.... They

---

3   Steiner, *World of the Senses and World of the Spirit*, Hanover, Dec. 29, 1911, p. 41 (trans. revised).

will take hold of people's souls and enliven them with a tremendous sense for artistic creativity, whereas the materialistic culture that has entered our modern age has dried up the soul and made it passive. Souls must be stimulated again by a power from within; they must be taken hold of by the inner forces of things....

You will gradually reach the point of becoming so perceptive for living links, that you will recognize the moments when the spirit approaches individual human beings. In the future, the world will no longer be explained as unequivocally as it is now—based on physical causation; instead, matter will be relegated to its proper place and people will realize that there is more than material phenomena, as spirit shines through it.

We have seen that colors and sounds are windows through which we can ascend spiritually into the spirit world, and life brings to us openings through which the spiritual world can enter our physical world.... If we interpret this phenomenon correctly, we have to say that spiritual life flows down to us through this window. It is clear to us that such forces flowing into us cannot be explained on a strictly material level. So there are windows in the tones through which we ascend from the physically material world into the spiritual world; and there are windows through which, if we remain in the physically material world, the spirit can descend to us.

If we do not perceive the fact that the spirit descends to us through such windows, it is like someone who cannot read opening a beautiful book.[4]

Here, in a conversation with Margarita Woloshin, Steiner talks about this very subject:

To work out of a dreamlike, visionary state of subdued consciousness is not the way to the new painting, but rather an awakening in feeling and willing. "If you were able to bring your heart to rest, then you would see what is within you," Dr. Steiner said to a painter. The heart of human beings who no longer feel pain and happiness on their own account, but for whom feelings are harbingers of spiritual facts, becomes an organ for the new art of painting. When the light of daytime consciousness

---

4 Steiner, *Colour*, Dornach, January 1, 1915, pp. 77, 82–83 (trans. revised).

penetrates the darkness of the world of will, human beings experience by means of color, now imbued with being in their own soul, the color in nature as imbued with being, as well....

"Art is related to death," Dr. Steiner once told us. "Like death, it takes away maya and reveals true 'being.'" Released from the weight of matter, from what has become, into the realm of the living-becoming, color works to redeem the dead world through the art of painting. In transferring things from their existence in three-dimensional space onto the surface, it grants them a new existence in a new space. In this space, the "inner" of the human being manifests as the "outer." The external world, however, becomes ensouled, becomes inner experience. Time becomes space. The spiritual light of Lucifer and the heavy darkness of Ahriman become color in Christ.[5]

---

5 Stebbing (ed.), *Conversations about Painting with Rudolf Steiner*, pp. 150–51.

Love and Knowledge

This time I go to another little village on the tiny, narrow winding road to the coast. I leave the car by a beautiful stone farm and follow the coastal path, crossing the cow fields and the fields full of sheep up into the hills and stop to look down the cliff by the ocean. What a surprise, a beach cove with a tiny village lies below with a pleasant hotel, restaurants, cafés, and swimmers and surfers in wetsuits by the water's edge. I have discovered where the sporty crowd hangs out. I find a way down the cliff into the village. It is very busy, with dogs out on the beach, children in wetsuits, happy families swimming in this frigid water. What a pleasant sight. I noticed that in the dollhouse where I am staying there were some wetsuits, and some surfboards, so tomorrow I will go myself, because I love the water and it is agony for me to watch the ocean and not get into it. I breathe in the warm air of the late afternoon and watch as the Sun goes down. The surfers come out, full of life, ready for the evening and probably very hungry. The wet rocks on the beach are encrusted with mussels, just as I used to find on the coast of Brittany, France, where we vacationed when I was in my early teens.

I sit on a terrace with other happy bathers, drink coffee, and then climb back up the cliff and proceed in a different direction back to the car through more meadows. In one of the meadows I come face to face with a beautiful brown bull. I slowly move away so as not to disturb him. I am truly beginning to love this place. There are many coves and little villages to discover in my afternoon "getting lost" walks and they are all within a mile or so of each other. I am sure that Liane ran through all these places in the region where she lived as a child.

When I was little the landscape in Cornwall was beautiful. Our family had a house by the sea. Opposite there was another house on the cliff and that was all. The water used to come up to the doorstep. In addition, there was always color, flashing and shining in water and storm. It was wonderful. The elements really were more my home on Earth than anything else. I used to roll over the rocks in ecstasy when there was much foam.

In Cornwall they use to have their churches far outside the village, in the country. We always had to walk a long way for funerals and baptisms. In spring and early summer the woods would be full of bluebells and on the way, sometimes, under the trees, one could see no green at all, only the beautiful cobalt blue carpet of the bluebells as far as the eye could see. Another time I would lie down and roll amongst the primroses. I used to eat them. I ate beech leaves and primroses. I used to dig up earth-nuts, whatever plant that was I do not know. I used to like the taste of fish eyes, don't ask me why.[1]

I have to say, I am ecstatic myself as I walk in these paths, and nothing makes me happier. I am probably living with the elements myself, as is everyone who comes here. What is it that is enormously satisfying when one treads on these paths up and down the cliffs? There is a primal feeling of power, of being alive, of joining the elemental beings who live in these wild places and are happy that we connect with them, especially with so many cows grazing here. The earth seems very happy and that is also part of the magic of this place. The animals still live here: ponies, sheep, horses, and cows. The clouds yesterday dropped their load on the scenery, so the paths are very muddy, but never mind.

It might seem that I am going a bit off track with the subject that follows, but without it nothing would come into being. It is important and part of this work, part of working with Spiritual Science. Nothing would get done if this was not present. This is the discussion of love—love that we feel when in love, when we feel that kind of love for everything in nature and everything in general. It is a way of knowledge, a way to acquire knowledge. I once asked Sergei Prokofieff, a prolific author, how he could write such enormous books with so much in them, especially with the many footnotes. He said simply, "love." I never forgot that. When I write, it is the

---

1   From the author's notes on conversations with Liane Collot d'Herbois.

same—love for the subject, ultimate total love for what I am writing. The same thing holds true for what I paint, complete love. Nevertheless, one must also acquire discipline and schooling. On the other hand, you can love all you like, but when also approached as a path of knowledge, writing is extremely powerful. Besides, there is no other way, but unfortunately this does not guarantee a book.

One of my favorite writers, Walter J. Stein, was a disciple of Steiner. He wrote his thesis on the subject in the 1900s:

> Again and again in later times, I thought about this question, entering into it more and more deeply in the successive periods of my life, and as I did so I realized increasingly that the way into the inner life of nature is only possible by entering the secrets of the human soul. It is not science about nature, but the perfection of our own human faculty of love, which leads us by and by to pierce through the veil of nature. It was Rudolf Steiner who encouraged me to work out such thoughts more fully and to develop them at length into a theory of knowledge for spiritual cognition, showing that it is not the intellect but love that penetrates into the cosmic secrets.
>
> In my doctoral dissertation I went into the subject thoroughly, also in its historical foundations. A few remarks must here suffice. Whenever we are thinking we forget ourselves, the thinker, altogether. We live in utterly selfless devotion to the object of which we are thinking at the given moment. This devotion does not rise into our consciousness, but it is there. All that comes into our consciousness is the result of thinking, namely the resulting act of knowledge. But we can render conscious in the way R. Steiner has shown—in his *Philosophy of Spiritual Activity* [*Intuitive Thinking as a Spiritual Path*]—this otherwise unconscious element in thought. We can bring into the field of consciousness the love and devotion that live as a rule unnoticed in the act of knowledge. When we do so, we discover that all knowledge really rests on love and moreover, that all truly selfless love is knowledge.[2]

I mention this topic, because without this love I cannot write. I am writing because I have such love for the subject, painting, anthroposophy, for

---

2   Stein, *The Death of Merlin*, p. 40.

everything actually. Whatever I do is based on this. I did study philosophy, love of wisdom, when I was young, and now I am just implementing this love of wisdom. It has become alive through Anthroposophy, the wisdom of humankind.

Here Rudolf Steiner talks about forgetting as a stage in spiritual development. Forgetting is extremely important. As Walter Stein mentions, in the act of thinking we forget about thinking; it is a selfless act of which we are not aware. Without forgetting about thinking, no thought would come, and hence the selfless devotion of the act of thinking.

> One can gain help in enhancing the power of forgetting if we further develop, through self-discipline, a quality that appears in ordinary life as the ability to love. Naturally, it can be said that love is not a cognitive power; it does not concern knowledge. This may be true today because of the way cognition is understood. Nevertheless, here it is not a matter of keeping the power of love only as it appears in ordinary life. Here the power of love needs to be developed further through working on oneself. We can achieve this by keeping the following in mind....
>
> If we want to be honest about what is really happening, we would have to say that we are merely swimming along in life's current. However, those who wish to become spiritual scientists must take their development into their own hands through a particular discipline. For example, one could use a habit (small habits can be of tremendous importance), and within a certain time transform it through conscious work. In this way, we can transform ourselves in the course of our life. We are transformed by being in the current of life, as well as through the work we do on ourselves with full awareness. Thus, when we observe our life panorama, we can see what has changed in our life as a result of such self-discipline.
>
> This works back in a remarkable way on our soul life. It does not have the effect of enhancing our egoism; rather, it enhances our power to love. We become increasingly able to embrace the outer world with love, to enter the outer world more deeply. Only those who have made efforts in such self-discipline can judge what this signifies.... We enter whatever our thoughts penetrate with much stronger personal

involvement. We even enter the physical mineral world with a certain power of love—the world that, when approached merely quantitatively, leaves us indifferent. We clearly feel the difference between penetrating the world with only our weak power of mental imaging and penetrating it with the developed power of love.

You may be offended by what I am saying about the developed power of love. You may want to insist that the power of love has no place in one's quest for knowledge of the outer world—that accurate objective knowledge comes only from what we obtain by logical intellectual activity. Certainly we need a faculty that can penetrate the phenomena of the outer world by means of the bare sober intellect alone, excluding all other powers of the soul. However, the outer world will not give us everything it has when we try to get it in this way. The world will give us everything only when we approach it through the power of love that strengthens one's mental activity. After all, it is not a matter of demanding and expecting nature to unveil herself to us through some theory of knowledge. What is truly important is to ask how nature will reveal herself to us. How will she yield her secrets to us? Nature will reveal herself only when we penetrate our mental powers with the forces of love.[3]

The other aspect of this love is discussed here by Steiner as he explains the different stages of modern Rosicrucian initiation:

Once we have understood the relationship between microcosm and macrocosm, we can move on to the sixth stage—becoming one with the macrocosm. We then become friends with everything in nature...to some extent, similar to the love that remains between husband and wife. A sunflower, a violet, the lion, a tiger, or some other form in nature all appear differently. As differentiated as the love between husband and wife, likewise the whole cosmos appears differentiated. What is within us flows outward and is connected with a metamorphosis of the heart. The etheric and astral bodies transform the heart to become a voluntary muscle. Here, esoteric teaching will have the effect of spreading light as it perfects itself even more.[4]

---

3   Steiner, *Anthroposophy and Science*, pp. 70–71 (trans. revised).
4   Steiner, *Rosicrucian Renewed*, Munich, May 19, 1907, p. 53 (trans. revised).

It is superfluous to mention, especially with this work, that if there is no love for painting, for colors, or for light and darkness, we simply do not have a work of art. As mentioned earlier, in this schooling we must give up the notion that we will make our mark in the world as a painter. We must give up painting for recognition, for money, for self-satisfaction, even for beauty. That is what Steiner refers to when he mentions the love and the selflessness that occurs in the act of thinking, without which we would be incapable of a single thought. Here is the same process: there will be no painting in the Collot d'Herbois method if there is no love and selflessness. We are there as servants of the Color Beings, who want to be painted as they should be as they come into being. Then, what wants to come in through the windows of our hands and onto the white canvas can incarnate. Thanks to selflessness, the selfless act of painting, we objectively develop the heart as an organ of cognition. That is the work of a mystery school.

Alchemy and the Fourth Dimension

Liane mentioned that she had wanted to work in an apothecary. She loved chemistry, and later, with Ita Wegman, she developed her own plant colors.

> It was Ita Wegman who showed me the direction in which I could develop myself as a professional painter. She told me that I had to paint for people: "You should paint pictures that bring healing. The important thing is that they mean something to an individual or institution. Let them remind people of the spiritual world." That is what she wanted me to do and that is what I have always tried to do.... Ita Wegman made me see that the most important thing the artist can do is not express oneself; the artist should create for other people. So my main interest is not in art, but in the fact that one can give another person something.[1]

I can safely say that, because of her unusual upbringing, Liane Collot d'Herbois was most definitely involved in mystery school work in the past, especially in her association with Ita Wegman. The elemental forces that she brought into this incarnation have their roots in mystery school work. What she brought to us, her students, was the work of the mystery schools, but transformed for our modern consciousness. It is all about alchemy. She was a great alchemist. The alchemist shines through her love of stones, chemistry, her involvement with making colors, her paintings, and her books. The radiance of her paintings is the alchemist at work, and her insights into the colors, as well as into illnesses, is also alchemy.

What else could she give us, her students, but this work with charcoal, carbon, in order to transform ourselves into the philosopher's stone, the diamond? But we had to get our hands dirty with carbon and apply it to the

---

1   From the author's notes on conversations with Liane Collot d'Herbois.

white paper, and sometimes we would have charcoal on our faces, on our noses, we were so immersed in it.

How did she ever arrive at this genius idea of applying carbon charcoal to a piece of paper with bare hands, of getting our hands totally black with it and working on the surface of the paper for hours? Using this method—thinking (the upper part of the paper), feeling (the middle), and willing (the lower part)—how did she manage to read the human being from existing knowledge of the threefold human being? She did this by struggling to bring light into the darkened charcoal paper, to bring in the light from the top of the paper. It sounds extremely simple, but it is far from that.

We never work with a subject, but simply with darkness, letting the light shine in. We work with the cosmic forces of light and dark. What comes through our hands simply is. We work with what is. This is alchemical work at its simplest. Liane Collot d'Herbois was not born in Tintagel, Cornwall, for nothing. It is the seat of the Arthurian legends of knights sitting at the Round Table. One can even visit Merlin's cave. I cannot resist bringing up the illustrious knights who roamed this area hundreds of years ago and left their imprint. Many writers have come here over the past centuries, searching, and they still do.

Liane Collot d'Herbois was surrounded by these powerful streams. She grew up with them and ignored them. She told Ita Wegman that she could not stand Parcival, but grew to like him later and painted the Parcival theme several times. Making these analogies may sound a bit trivial, but walking in these special places, I cannot ignore the history and myths that really shaped the continent. The knights were sent throughout Europe to help fight the people's wild untamed forces. Liane follows the tradition of the Mysteries by giving us a method by which we can fight our own lower forces and show through our paintings, our work, that the spirit can shine through the transparency of the colors. The point is to become transparent in our soul with nothing to hide. In the charcoal work, it is all there and nothing is hidden; all is transparent for everyone to see. Carbon is black, but the diamond, transformed carbon, is transparent.

Here is Walter Stein on alchemy and the Knights of the Round Table:

At this point, I must bring in some alchemical concepts. All organic substance consists of carbon. But neither plants nor animals, nor human beings are black. Therefore it must be possible for carbon to undergo a process in which it acquires all colors. The carbohydrates, for example, are also carbon in the language of alchemy. But what is the supreme achievement of Creation? It is the color of the human skin. It can be black, it can be red, and yellow, but it can also turn a hue of green in envy, red in anger, yellow in jealousy, white and red in noble frame of mind. So what is the human skin in alchemical terms? It is the canvas on which the soul paints....

Why is it specifically Sir Tristam who receives enlightenment about the secret of the color of carbon?

Because Tristam, Lancelot du Lake, Lamorak de Gales, and Beaumains knew the secret of the Philosopher's stone, that is, the constitution of the healthy body, the faithful soul, and the victorious spirit. For those are the substances that constitute the philosopher's stone. The philosopher's stone is the human being.... Love is the greatest artist. It uses every color to paint the soul on to the body so that it shimmers through. We should not forget the soul! But not despise the body either. Chemically it is nothing but black carbon. But the alchemist, the soul, makes this black carbon shimmer with every color. Let the genuine spirit, the noble soul, shimmer in the healthy body....

Alchemy, which played such an important role in antiquity and in the Middle Ages, is a science almost completely forgotten today. It is thought of as the precursor of chemistry. We smile about the strange ways of times past and reassure ourselves that in chemistry we possess the real and true knowledge that the Middle Ages were seeking. That is certainly correct to a large degree; a whole series of discoveries were made in chemistry by the development of alchemical ideas. But that shows no appreciation of real alchemy, originally a teaching of the mysteries. The fundamental truths of alchemy are not primarily related to substances, although it does make all kinds of preparations particularly for medicinal remedies, but to the nature of the human being itself.[2]

The schooling of the student is nothing but working on the body, the soul, and the spirit. Liane always reminded me during our conversations:

---

2 Stein, *The Death of Merlin*, pp. 133, 135.

"Darling you must be on the Earth. You must have your feet on the ground. Then you can heal." She said that most people are not on Earth, not properly incarnated on Earth. In other words, they are not present here in their body, but are elsewhere. We cannot ignore our body and the Earth.

As Walter Stein put it so well, "The constitution of the healthy body, the faithful soul, the victorious spirit that is the substance of the philosopher's stone" is the human being. Furthermore, we cannot ignore the other aspect of the production of the philosopher's stone, which has far-reaching importance for the future:

> The fourth stage of initiation is the production of the philosopher's stone. Modern scholarship has made a fairy tale out of it. In a certain respect, the scholars are right, because if it were really as science imagines it, it would be nonsense. However, producing the philosopher's stone is the highest stage of development toward which the human being strives.... We need do nothing other than to examine the process that cosmically preserves the human being in the present epoch: the breathing process. We breathe in and out. We breathe in the oxygen of the air and give back to the surrounding world carbon dioxide, a poisonous gas in which we could not live. The plant takes in the carbon dioxide constantly, keeps the carbon for itself, and builds up its own body out of it. It gives the oxygen back to animals and human beings. Thus, the plant, animal, and human being form a whole, in the context of the breathing process.
>
> The human being needs the plant today. The corpse of the plant, which takes the form of black coal dug out of the Earth or of transparent diamond, is something that we ourselves have within us, but we cannot use it. We have to hand it over as breath of life to the plants. The plant builds its own body out of carbon dioxide. It can do what human beings cannot yet do but will be able to do later. Imagine this process: The taking in of carbon dioxide by the plant; the sending out of oxygen, which is transferred into the interior of the human being.... thus the flowing together with the plant world, which is taken into human nature; then we build up for ourselves a pure, chaste body, just as the plant does today.
>
> Human are on the way to becoming beings able to carry out this process consciously; in this way, we will be able to develop the chalice

of the Holy Grail within ourselves. The breathing process has not reached completion; it is being perfected and is poised to perform a task within the human being that today takes place outside the human being and to transform the human substance that is pervaded with *kama* [the subtle body of desires] into pure, chaste substance. That is true Alchemy. We will become capable of performing the alchemy through which we will also learn to transform the cosmos. The symbol for this process is the Holy Grail. We cannot dismiss this high ideal simply because it is millions of years away; rather, it must be attained according to the maxim "Continual dripping hollows the stone." Those who make the breathing process rhythmical attain their goal gradually. The philosopher's stone is the carbon, the substance for the building of the human body in the future. This process of transformation is alchemy in the Rosicrucian sense.[3]

Now we enter even more deeply into this work. This will require the reader to exercise the capacity of thinking! Here Liane Collot d'Herbois discusses the tragedy of the light:

The physical daylight is the distorted reversal of the light of the first dimension. It is the luciferic messenger, bringing illusion.

This daylight that we live in does not in the first place come from the Sun, it comes from the Earth. The Earth's atmosphere is lit up, daylight is part of the atmosphere of the Earth. Our day consciousness is dependent on that outer light. Seen from another point of view our consciousness and light are the same. Light has a destructive influence, even as our consciousness has a destructive influence on our organism. And the light itself is dying.

Part of the spiritual world is retreating from the Earth and some of its tasks of creative activity now fall on the human race. The daylight is no longer ensouled and filled with life-forces as it still was in the times of the Greek civilization. Human beings now have to perform that task and the ensouling of the light depends very much on our morality and on the quality of our thinking. And with the prevailing materialism of today we constantly look at the tragedy, at the dying of the light. We have to ensoul the light.

---

3 Steiner, *Rosicrucian Renewed,* Munich, May 19, 1907, pp. 51–52.

Color can give life to our thinking and one way to ensoul the light is to think color as vividly as one can. That is a kind of meditation and meditation is the one truly free, moral deed man can do on this Earth. All the rest of our life is mainly necessity.

In this connection there is one more aspect of the light that we ought to consider and that is that in the human being as well as in the cosmos one can distinguish an ascending light and a descending light. At work in both are angelic beings that are different from one another. Nonetheless, they are not antagonistic but work together.

The ascending light is an all-diffused light that has no center. It is a luminosity that has no space, it brings a certain spacelessness. As such it belongs to the second dimension, which in the human being can be transformed into the fourth dimension. Because in the human being this ascending light is the light of life that wells from the heart. It works in the purification of the astral body. And the more we grow from the consciousness of the head toward the consciousness of the heart, the more we grow toward the fourth dimension. In the world of color this light of life is represented by the "peach blossom," a color that hovers between magenta and cobalt violet.

The descending light has an altogether different quality. It radiates from a center and it carries destruction. But through the destruction it brings space and consciousness and in that way it serves Creation. In the world of color it is represented by viridian green. In the human being the descending light is related to thinking, the thinking that can be transformed into pure thinking when it comes into the right connection with feeling and will. Then it meets with the ascending light that wells from the heart and is carried by it.

I hope that the above will mean more to the reader of this book than just a few adjectives to the functions of the green and the magenta. It means a lot that one can think color and be conscious of its inner being. That one can paint and have a connection with color that is based on an understanding of its origin in light and darkness. Because in dealing with color one is dealing with the world of angels and in that world the thinking of color is an actual deed, a reality that will go on into the future where later, very much later, one will be able to perceive it in the outer world.[4]

---

4 Collot d'Herbois. *Light, Darkness and Colour...*, pp. 25–26.

Rudolf Steiner offers helpful comments on the fourth dimension, which help us understand what Collot d'Herbois wants to say.

Is it possible to use colors to suggest something that can replace the three dimensions? Once we have an overview of the element of color, we can arrange colors in a specific way that creates an image of three-dimensionality in two dimensions. Anyone can see that all blues tend to recede, while reds and yellow advance. Thus simply by supplying color, we express three dimensions. By using the intensive aspect of color to express the extensive aspect of three-dimensionality, we can compress the three-dimensionality into two dimensions....

When yogis (students of esotericism) want to ascend to knowledge of the higher worlds, they must gradually replace reflections with realities. For example, when they consider the plant they must learn to replace the lower dimensions with the higher ones. Learning to disregard one of a plant's spatial dimensions and substitute the corresponding dimension—namely time—enables them to understand a two dimensional being that is moving. What must the students of esotericism do to make the being correspond to reality rather than remaining a mere image? If they were simply to disregard the third and add the fourth, the result would be something imaginary. The following thought will help us move toward an answer. By filming a living being, even though we subtract the third dimension from events that were originally three-dimensional, the succession of images adds the dimension of time. When we then add sensory ability to this animated image, we perform an operation similar to the one I described as curving a three-dimensional figure into the fourth. The result of this operation is a four-dimensional figure whose dimensions include two of our spatial dimensions and two higher ones, namely time and sensory ability. Such beings do indeed exist....

Imagine two spatial dimensions—that is, a plane—and suppose that this plane is endowed with movement. Picture it curving to become a sensate being pushing a two-dimensional surface in front of it. Such a being is very dissimilar to and acts very differently from a three-dimensional being in our space. The surface being that we have constructed is completely open in one direction. It looks two-dimensional, it comes toward you, and you cannot get around it. This being is a radiant being; it is nothing other than openness in a particular direction. Through such a being, initiates then become familiar with other beings they describe as divine messengers approaching them in flames of fire. The description of Moses receiving the Ten Commandments on Mount Sinai shows simply that he was approached by such a being and could perceive its dimensions. This being, which resembled a human being minus the third dimension, was active in sensation and time....

Any being that lives in time frees itself from the three dimensional space, from the three ordinary dimensions. Time is the fourth dimension. It remains invisible within the three dimensions of ordinary space and can be perceived only with clairvoyant powers. A moving point creates a line, a moving line creates a plane, and a moving plane creates a three-dimensional figure. When the three-dimensional space moves, the result is growth, and development. There we have a four-dimensional space or time, projected into the three-dimensional space as movement, growth and development....

I would like to make you aware of the so-called *alchemical mystery,* because a true view of four-dimensional space is related to what the alchemists called *transformation.*[5]

Now we can go back to the task of the painter and the world of the second dimension versus the world of the third dimension.

It is through color perspective that a painting gains a relationship to the spiritual. It is strange that painters today mainly ask themselves whether they can transcend space by giving space more depth. They then try to depict a fourth dimension in a materialistic way. However, the fourth dimension can exist only through annihilation of the third, somewhat the way debts annihilate wealth. We do not enter a fourth-dimensional space upon leaving three-dimensional space—or, better, we enter fourth-dimensional space that is two-dimensional, because the fourth dimension annihilates the third; only two remain as reality.

If we rise from matter's three dimensions into the etheric element, we find everything oriented two-dimensionally, and we cannot understand the etheric unless we conceive of it thus. Now you may take exception by saying, "Yes, but in the etheric I move from here to there,

---

5   Steiner, *The Fourth Dimension,* pp. 116–117, 64–65, 74, 39.

which is to say three-dimensionally." Very well, but the third dimension has no significance for the etheric, only the other two dimensions. The third dimension expresses itself through red, yellow, blue, violet, as explained. In the etheric it is not the third dimension that changes, but color. Regardless of where the plane is placed, the colors change accordingly. Only then can we live with and within color; live two-dimensionally; rise from the spatial arts to those that, like painting, are two-dimensional. We overcome the merely spatial. Our feelings have no relation to the three-space dimensions, but only our will. By their very nature, feelings are bound in the two dimensions. This is why they are best represented by two-dimensional painting.

You see, we have to struggle free of three-dimensional matter.... Painting is an art that people can experience within. Whether they create as painters or just live in and enjoy a painting, it is an event of the soul. People experience inner through outer; experience color perspective.... In painting, it makes no sense to speak of anything as inside or outside the soul as "inside" or "outside." The soul is within the spiritual when experiencing color. In fact, what is experienced in painting—despite the imperfections of pigments—is the soul freely moving in the cosmos.

It is different in the case of music. Here we do not merge inner with outer, but enter directly what the soul experiences as the spiritual, or psychospiritual, leaving space entirely. Music is line-like, one-dimensional, experienced one-dimensionally in the line of time.[6]

The words quoted by Collot d'Herbois and Steiner are not simple. They contain immense wisdom and much power stands behind them. This is the work of a mystery school, one path among many through painting.

We are not talking about simple paintings here, or one wanting to paint just to paint. The work that Liane Collot d'Herbois brought to us goes far beyond the task of the painter. We are talking in fact about changing the world with our paintbrush while transforming ourselves in the process. However, this does not come to pass without sweat and tears. We are talking about healing human beings through colors, and this does not

---

6 Steiner, *The Arts and Their Mission*, Dornach, June 2, 1923, pp. 35–36 (trans. revised).

come about without suffering. As one very good, serious student who had finished the eighteen days of the course said to me at the end, "I have never done anything so difficult in my life!" She had to quit, because she needed to raise her two children, but she nevertheless had a taste of what real knowledge is; she had experienced it. It is not for the faint-hearted.

Entering the world of the fourth dimension is part of the work of the painter as Liane tries to explain to us. For alchemists, fourth dimensional space is related to transformation; a picture of carbon becoming a diamond is the task, as mentioned in the previous pages.

Spiritual Beings and Perception

I am spending the afternoon investigating the next coastal town due north on a tiny, more sinuous and narrow road by the coast. This town is much larger and full of tourists climbing the cliff paths. The river comes down from the highland, and snake-like, flanked by tall cliffs, falls into the sea. It is a lovely town hidden in a tiny valley. I find more local food and good walking. The tourist bureau contains pictures of illustrious visitors who have come here over the years, including Thomas Hardy and Alfred Lord Tennyson.

It is quite windy on the cliff tops. I gaze at the horizon and look for seals sitting on the rocks. The wind adds more life here; the waves crash onto the cliffs, and the rising sea engulfs the river as it flows from the valley. I find a hidden cove on the way that is full of surfers out for the last sunny days of the season. Next week I will walk here from Tintagel. It is only about five miles, which will be a wonderful walk some afternoon, sure to bring forth some inspiration.

It is really unusually alive here! I have visited many sacred places on this great Earth, and I must say this area has some amazing features. The quality of the stones, quartz and granite and everything we walk on, has lightness within it. There is also a primal power where the ocean crashes against these very old cliffs, which have been born out of the Earth through gigantic upheavals in the past.

Here is a long passage from Rudolf Steiner's *Rosicrucian and Modern Initiation*, from a lecture given in Dornach on January 4, 1924:

> Today, I would like to give you a picture of how scholars of that time [the Middle Ages] would speak to their students....
>
> The Seraphim would have been characterized as beings for whom there is no subject and object, for whom subject and object are the same thing. These beings who would not say that they are surrounded by

various objects, but that the world *is*—that I am the world, and that the world is I. Such beings know only *themselves*, and for them knowledge of themselves is an inner experience, which human beings might experience only weakly when filled, let me say, with *burning enthusiasm*. It is, as you know, often difficult to make a person today understand what "burning enthusiasm" means. At the beginning of the nineteenth century, people still knew this better than people do today. In those days, it could still happen that some poem was being read aloud, and people would become so filled with enthusiasm (forgive me, but it really was so) that people today would say they had all gone out of their minds. They were so moved, so warmed. Today, people freeze up just when you expect them to be "enthused."

By becoming conscious of this element of enthusiasm—rapture of the soul that used to come naturally to people of Central and Eastern Europe—by lifting this experience into consciousness and making it the complete content of consciousness, people had to form an idea of the inner life of the Seraphim. As a bright, clear element in consciousness, filled with light, so that *thought immediately becomes light,* illuminating everything—such was the idea that people formed about the element of consciousness of the Cherubim. In addition, the element of consciousness of the Thrones was conceived as *sustaining, bearing the worlds, in grace....*

One would then have gone on to say that the choir of Seraphim, Cherubim and Thrones works together so that the Thrones found and established a kind of seed, or kernel; the Cherubim let their own light-filled being flow out from this center; and the Seraphim wrap the whole in a mantle of warmth and enthusiasm that radiates far out into cosmic space.

The [blackboard] drawing I made is *beings;* in the middle are the Thrones; around them the Cherubim; and outermost, the Seraphim. All is essential being—beings who move and weave into one another, do, think, will, feel in one another. It is all being. Now, if some other being having the right sensitivity were to pass through space where the Thrones have established a kernel in this way, where the Cherubim have kind of circled around it, and where the Seraphim have, as it were, enveloped the whole—if a being with the necessary sensitivity were to come into this realm of activity of the first hierarchy, it would feel warmth in varying degrees—here more warmth, there less. It would all be a soul experience, and yet also a sensory experience. In other words, when this being felt warm in soul, it would be like the feeling you have when you are in a well-warmed room.

Such a united building-up by beings of the first hierarchy actually did take place in the universe; it formed what we call the Saturn existence. The warmth is merely an expression of the fact that *these beings are there.*[1]

This is the warmth that Liane Collot d'Herbois talks about when she says of darkness that it is not just one little word, *darkness.* This passage brings us close to what she meant, what she felt, and what she worked with when she painted. We, her students, are a long way from feeling this, and herein lies the extreme difficulty of painting in the way she wanted us to paint and experience light and darkness.

The story continues:

Beings of the second hierarchy—*Kyriotetes, Dynanis, Exusiai*—beings generated by the Seraphim, Cherubim and Thrones, pressed into the space that had been "formed" through the working of Seraphim, Cherubim and Thrones, formed and fashioned to Saturn warmth.... How do these cosmically younger beings work? Whereas Cherubim, Seraphim, and Thrones revealed themselves in the element of warmth, the beings of the second hierarchy take form in the element of *light.* Here we have Saturn; it is dark; it gives warmth. Now, within the dark world of Saturn, something new begins to arise through the working of the sons of the first hierarchy through Exusiai, Dynamis, Kyriotetes. What is it that can now arise within the Saturn warmth? The penetration of the second hierarchy signifies *inner illumination.* Light shines inwardly through Saturn warmth. It also became denser; in addition to the warmth element, air is now present, as well. Thus, we have the entry of the second hierarchy, coming into revelation in light.[2]

Here we have what Liane Collot d'Herbois means by *light.* The story is immense, and we cannot understand it with our intellect; other capacities

---

1   Steiner, *Rosicrucianism and Modern Initiation*, pp. 13–15 (trans. revised).

2   Ibid., p. 16 (trans. revised).

must come into play, those that Rudolf Steiner talks about in his book *How to Know Higher Worlds*. Unless some of these capacities are born in our soul, there is no chance we will understand what Liane brought to us. Moreover, if we do not make any effort to understand this, we are unworthy of receiving this knowledge, while bored readers and students just fall away and move on to simpler tasks. It is arduous to read the words just quoted, and many will skip over them. If we are to gain an understanding, a profound understanding, of Collot d'Herbois and her work, we must dwell deeply in such drama, as in this story of Saturn, Sun, and Moon:

> Those who have the requisite power of perception see the event as a penetration of light; the light reveals the path of the beings. In addition, where light enters, there under certain conditions we find, too, shadows, darkness, dark shadow. Through the penetration by the second hierarchy in the form of light, shadow also comes about.
>
> What was this shadow? It was *air*. Right on into the fifteenth and sixteenth centuries, people knew the nature of air for a fact. Today we know merely that air consists of oxygen, nitrogen, and so forth, which is much the same as saying that a watch consists of glass and silver. This really tells me nothing at all about the watch as a watch. Likewise, to say that air consists of oxygen and nitrogen says nothing at all about air as a cosmic phenomenon. We say much more, on the other hand, if we know that air emerges from the cosmos as the *shadow of light*. In fact, with the entry of the second hierarchy into the Saturn warmth, we have the entry of light and air, the shadow of light. With this, we have "Sun." Such is the way we would have had to speak in the thirteenth century.
>
> What follows after this? Further evolution comes about through the working of the sons of the second hierarchy, *Archai, Archangels*, and *Angels*. The second hierarchy has accomplish the entry of the light element, light that has drawn its shadow after it, the darkness of air, not the indifferent, neutral darkness of Saturn—simply the absence of light—but darkness that is the antithesis of light. Now the third hierarchy—Archai, Archangels, Angels—add by virtue of their nature and being a new element to this element of light, an element like our human desire, our impulse to strive or to long for something. Thus, the following occurs.

Let us say that a being of the Archai or Archangels enters *here*, and encounters an element of light, as it were, a place of light. In this place of light, the being will then receive, through its very receptivity for the light, the urge, or desire, for darkness. The angel being carries light into darkness—or an Angel being may carry darkness into light. In this way, these beings become mediators, messengers between light and darkness. As a result, what previously has only shone in light and drawn its shadow after it, the darkness of air, now begins to shine in *color*, to glow in a play of color. Light begins to appear in darkness, darkness in light. The third hierarchy creates color; *out of the light and darkness they conjure color.*

In this connection we may turn to something historical, something in written document. In the time of Aristotle, people still knew when colors come as they gave themselves up to contemplation in the mysteries. They knew that it is the beings of the third hierarchy who have to do with color. Aristotle himself, in his color harmony, declares that color signifies a cooperation of light and darkness. However, this spiritual element in human thought, whereby people knew that behind warmth they have to see beings of the first hierarchy, behind light and its shadow darkness, beings of the second hierarchy, and behind the iridescent play of color, shimmering in a great cosmic harmony, beings of the third hierarchy—this spiritual element in human thought has been lost. Nothing is left for humanity today but the unhappy Newtonian theory of color. Initiates continued to smile at Newton's theory until the eighteenth century; then it became an article of faith for professional physicists.[3]

Only with such pictures can we make the world of light, darkness and color come alive. Only in these far-reaching pictures can we come near to understanding who we are. The world of color is far reaching and only an initiate such as Rudolf Steiner can wake up the true picture in our sleeping soul and an initiate such Liane Collot d'Herbois and her initiate teacher, Ita Wegman, as well as Elizabeth Vreede (and others in the anthroposophic circles) can put it into practice.

One of Liane's paintings comes to my mind. It is of a toddler as the central figure with figures in the background. It is painted in beautiful greens,

---

3   Ibid., pp. 17–18 (trans. revised).

grays, and light blue. She wanted to represent humanity, our newborn "I." This is who we are—just babies or toddlers compared to the highly developed initiates who appear from time to time. It shows how much we have to travel toward true humanity.

Interlude

It is time for another walk. It is raining and very windy. I make a circle around Tintagel, walk down into the cliff that juts out into the ocean overlooking part of the old castle and sit there, letting my mind empty itself perhaps to catch a glimpse of bygone days. There is a strong, stern presence, a Kingly presence with blue eyes in my mind's eye. I let that go and think about the women of the age. Then another presence comes, most beautiful and tender. I let that go as well—making sure it is not me making things up—to see what else will come to me. Then I release it all, and stare at the ocean, the waves crashing on the wild coast. The scenery should be able to speak of such an illustrious past. Then I ask, why did Queen Guinevere have to be untruthful to King Arthur? What is the meaning of that? I am not familiar with these stories, so they are fresh in my mind. One cannot blame her for falling in love with the beautiful showy Lancelot and not the great King. She was young and not ready for him. King Arthur's greatness did not meet his wise counterpart, yet.

Here is what Walter Stein says about King Arthur.

Something eternal—universal—the very breath of freedom lives in this land. It stretches out, embracing the whole of humanity. It still speaks to us through the hills and the valleys, the rocks, and caves mentioned in the Arthurian legends. The winds and waves sing of it, the atmosphere is full of it. It is necessary to find contact with this invisible Power that, in only one of its forms appears as the Arthur legend. This Power in reality is the Eternal Spirit of this country that we shall meet again. Could we but realize this, a cultural element would be born again, English in its innermost depths. It speaks to all human beings wherever they live and to whatever nation they belong. The Round Table is the whole world, says the saga. Its knights still live, their search for the Grail still goes on, and the Grail as we know, is the secret spirit that must unite all humankind in love and brotherhood.[1]

I bought a copy of Tennyson's longest poem *Idylls of the King* at a Tintagel store and read the end of it. I was interested in what King Arthur had to say, and Guinevere, too, as written by the poet who walked these paths around 1848 to find inspiration for this three-hundred-page poem. He must have walked miles and miles.

> "Yet think not that I come to urge thy crimes,
> I did not come to curse thee, Guinevere,
> I, whose vast pity almost makes me die
> To see thee, laying there thy golden head,
> My pride in happier summers, at my feet.
> The wrath which forced my thoughts on that fierce law,
> The doom of treason and the flaming death,—
> When I first learned thee hidden here—is past.
> The pang—which, while I weigh'd thy heart with one
> Too wholly true to dream untruth in thee,
> Made my tears burn—is also past—in part.
> And all is past, the sin is sinn'd, and I,
> Lo! I forgive thee, as Eternal God
> Forgives! Do thou for thine own soul the rest.
> But how to take last leave of all I loved?
> O Golden hair, with which I used to play
> Not knowing! O imperial-moulded form,
> And beauty such as never woman wore,
> Until it came a kingdom's curse with thee—
> I cannot touch thy lips, they are not mine,
> But Lancelot's: nay, they never were the King's.
> I cannot take thy hand; that too is flesh,
> And in the flesh thou has sinned; and mine own flesh.
> Here looking down on thine polluted, cries
> 'I loathed thee': yet not less, Guinevere
> For I was ever virgin save for thee,
> My love thro' flesh wrought into my life

---

1 Stein, *The Death of Merlin*, p. 118.

So far that my doom is, I love thee still.
Let no man dream but that I love thee still.
Perchance, and so thou purify thy soul,
And so thou lean on our fair father Christ,
Hereafter in that world where all are pure
We two may meet before high God, and thou
Wilt spring to me, and claim me thine, and know
I am thine husband—not a smaller soul,
Nor Lancelot, nor another. Leave me that,
I charge thee, my last hope. . . .
But hither shall I never come again,
Never lie by thy side; see thee no more—
Farewell!"

    And while she grovell'd at his feet,
She felt the King's breath wander o'er her neck,
And in the darkness o'er her fallen head,
Perceived the waving of his hands that blest. . . .
                      "Gone—my Lord!
Gone thro' my sin to slay and to be slain!
And he forgave me, and I could not speak.
Farewell! I should have answer'd his farewell.
His mercy choked me. Gone, my lord the King,
My own true lord! How dare I call him mine?
The shadow of another cleaves to me,
And makes me one pollution: he, the King,
Call'd me polluted: shall I kill myself?
What help in that? I cannot kill my sin,
If soul be soul; nor can I kill my shame;
No, nor my living can I live it down.
The days will grow to weeks, the weeks to months,
The months will add themselves and make the years,
The years will roll into the centuries,
And mine will ever be a name of scorn.
I must not dwell on that defeat of fame.
Let the world be; that is but of the world.
What else? What hope? I think there was a hope,
Except he mock'd me when he spake of hope;

His hope he call'd it; but he never mocks,
For mockery is the fume of little hearts.
And blessed be the King, who hath forgiven
My wickedness to him, and left me hope
That in mine own heart I can live down sin
And be his mate hereafter in the heavens
Before high God! Ah great and gentle Lord,
Who wast, as is the conscience of a saint
Among his warring senses, to thy knights—
To whom my false voluptuous pride, that took
Full easily all impressions from below,
Would not look up, or half-despised the height
To which I would not or I could not climb—
I thought I could not breathe in that fine air
That pure severity of perfect light—
I yearned for warmth and color which I found
In Lancelot—Now I see thee what thou art,
Thou art the highest and most human, too,
Not Lancelot, nor another. Is there none
Will tell the King I love him tho' so late?
Now—ere he goes to the great battle? none:
Myself must tell him in that purer life,
But now it were too daring. Ah my God,
What might I not have made of thy fair world,
Had I but loved thy highest creature here?
It was my duty to have loved the highest:
It surely was my profit had I known:
It would have been my pleasure had I seen.
We needs must love the highest when we see it,
Not Lancelot, nor another."[2]

I had to pay homage to Tintagel's history and at least quote these touch-ing words, since I walk through here almost every day. I walk up to the old ruins perched on top of the rocky cliffs. In the empty quiet, with the wind, cold, mist, and rain, only a few souls are walking today. Then I head for the

---

2   Tennyson, *Idylls of the King*, Arthur's farewell, "Guinevere."

little church that Liane attended when many baptisms and funerals were performed. She complained that one had to walk far away from the village. It is true it is a few kilometers away, near the cliffs. Again the wind comes from the west, right into my face, but it is a soft wind and not cold. Then I head back into the village through the meadows.

Working with Our Hands

I am in my new home in Trechnow, just one mile from Tintagel and the coast. I have a lovely old house all to myself, with a little garden full of my favorite hortensia still blooming in pink, blue, and white. The tiny village is having a lantern walk, as it is Halloween, and a huge pig roast outside the decorated town hall adjacent to my house. There are roasted chestnuts and mulled hot wine. The little village is out in full; most of the people look well off, because this is their second home. I see lots of pretty mothers with their little ones and middle-aged men and women whose faces show too much drinking. I will go out later when the party is in full bloom even though I do not drink alcohol or eat pig. I feel I need to make an effort at being social, since it is my first evening here.

The next day, I walk again to the neighboring town, descending through meadows into a little forested path to where people surf. I walk far up the cliff for a hour or so and come back, then pass old abandoned farms on the top of the cliffs and wonder who lived here long ago.

It being Halloween Eve, I think a little story from this area would fit the tone of Cornwall, an atmosphere that still lives.

During the fifteenth century, there was widespread belief in Cornwall in a unique brand of little sprites, which included piskie, pranketers, caring brownies, the playful and occasionally helpful fairies, troublesome spriggans, and the restless buccas or knockers thought to haunt the mines. All were regarded as spirits of the long departed, suspended somewhere between heaven and hell, and whether they were a help or a hindrance, it paid to keep on the right side of them if possible. So when a 19 year old laborer's daughter from St. Teath claimed to enjoy communion with the fairies it raised fewer eyebrows than such an occurrence would do today. Indeed, it was taken so seriously that she was thrown into prison and subjected to the most horrifying of conditions.

It all began in 1645, when Anne Jefferies who was in service to the local worthy Mr. Moses Pitt, had a powerful vision in which she saw fairies. Mr. Pitt, who found her in a collapsed state in the garden, said that she was so frightened by the encounter with the little people that it caused a convulsive fit. The fairies, it seems, were coy about making their presence known to other mortals, for after Anne had been carried into the house she opened her eyes and exclaimed, "There they are! There they are—just gone out the window! Did you see them? Did you see them?" But no one else ever saw them. This was a prelude to a life-long association with the helpful fairies, reputedly bringing Anne not only the rare gift of clairvoyance and the miraculous powers of healing, but the ability to become invisible as well.

As soon as Anne recovered she made her way to the church. Her life was transformed; she became very devout and spent much of her time preaching, healing the sick and foretelling the future. After curing her mistress of a serious malda, word spread until people came from all over the countryside, young and old, rich and poor, with all manner of ills, flocked to her door in hopes of a cure. These were affected by the laying on of hands, and the use of wondrous potions and salves secretly supplied by the fairies. Mr. Pitt, who recorded some of these amazing events, marveled about some of the mysterious happenings around him. He described her dancing in the garden with invisible partners, and most incredibly disappearing and re-appearing.

The fairies not only supplied magical medicines, they also brought her daily bread that Moses Pitt, who once had the chance to sample some, declared to be wonderful, the finest he had ever tasted.[1]

I think this captures the unusual atmosphere of this western part of England. Besides the natural beauty, closeness to the elements has preserved something that has disappeared elsewhere. Liane was correct in saying that clairvoyance has been preserved here.

Magical powers were deemed to have passed from fathers to daughters, and from mothers to sons...[and] the son of a seventh son or a "footling" [one who enters the world feet first].[2]

---

1 Bird, *Tales of Old Cornwall*.

2 Ibid.

⁓

Now back to the mysteries.

> We have to remember that the mysteries of ancient times were of such a nature and character that in the mystery centers an actual meeting with the gods could take place.... The person who was an initiate or was about to receive initiation did actually meet with the gods. Moreover, it was actually possible in those times to discover places that by their very locality were expressly suited to inducing such meeting with the gods.[3]

This area is such a place. As I try to live in this atmosphere, it becomes clearer and clearer to me why Liane was born here. Readers may come to their own conclusions as they contemplate this.

In the lectures quoted here, Steiner talks about the Middle Ages and the encounter between a searching student and a wise man who taught the method suited to that time.

> Thus, the student about whom I have been telling you was truly brought to initiation, and he now knew what power he must exert in his soul to arouse the light of the heights [climbing a mountain] to activity, and the feeling of depths [going deep into the earth, or cave]. Further instruction was then given by the teacher, showing the student how self-knowledge in fact always consists of this: on the one hand, we perceive what is high above earthly humankind, and on the other hand what is deep below earthly humankind; these two have to meet in one's own inner being. People can then find the power of God the Creator within their own being....
>
> At a school of the Rosicrucians, the first, original Rosicrucians, the scene I have depicted—the scene between the teacher and the student, at first upon a high mountain and then down in a deep cleft of the earth—emerged.... The scene reflected there as *knowledge*. And it taught the students in that school to recognize how humanity must, by inner effort and striving, attain two things if they would reach true self-knowledge and rediscover their rightful place on Earth and finally be able in reality to become a member of the fourth hierarchy [human

---

3   Steiner, *Rosicrucianism and Modern Initiation*, Dornach, Jan. 5, 1924, p. 26.

beings]. Within the Rosicrucian school, an opportunity was provided to recognize what had taken place with pupils when they saw the Spirit of their Youth before them in bodily form—that their astral bodies, which were stronger at that moment than they would otherwise ever be in life, had been loosened. It was in this loosening of the astral body that students had come to know the meaning and significance of revelation. Again, what had taken place with the students in the depths of the Earth—that, too, was made clear to students in the Rosicrucian school. This time the astral body was seen to have been drawn back, so that it was deep within those students, which enabled them to apprehend the certainty of their own inner being.

Now exercises were found—relatively simple exercises—within Rosicrucianism. Symbolic figures were presented to the students, to which they should surrender themselves in devotion and meditation. The force and power that possessed the soul through practicing devotion to these figures enabled them, on the one hand, to loosen the astral body and become like the student on the mountaintop in the etheric heights, while, on the other hand, to become like the student in the clefts of the earth through the compression, or contraction, of the astral body. It was then possible—without the help of external environment, as before, and simply by performing a powerful inner exercise—to enter the inner being of humanity.[4]

Rudolf Steiner goes on to describe how some individuals met and worked in a brotherly way to preserve the old wisdom, centuries later.

The tradition does not, however, come directly from Greece; it comes from Asia, brought from Macedonia by Alexander the Great.

Within this little company, a deep and strikingly exact teaching was given concerning humanity, in respect especially of two human faculties. We can see there a spiritual scientist (he may truly be so called) who is a highly developed master instructing his students. The ancient symbols by which he teaches them consist of certain geometrical forms....

In particular, there was one symbol that played a large part in this little group of seekers. You have the symbol before you, when you

---

4   Ibid., pp. 34, 38–39 (trans. revised).

draw apart this "Solomon's Key," so that one triangle comes down and the other rises. The symbol thus obtained played...a significant part within this little community or school, and continued to do so even as late as the nineteenth century.

The nineteenth century

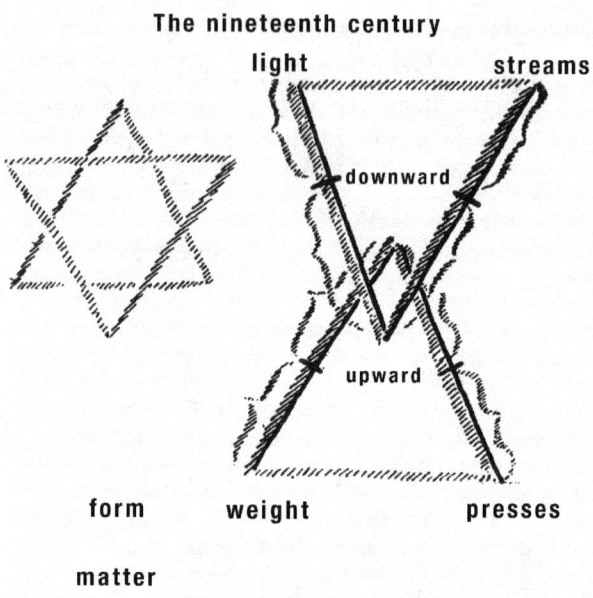

The master would then have the students assume a certain attitude with their physical bodies. The body itself had to "draw" this symbol. The master made them stand with their feet far apart, with their arms stretched out above. Then, by lengthening the lines of the arms downward and the lines of the legs upward, these four lines came to view in the human organism itself. A line was then drawn to unite the feet, and another to unite the hands above; and these two joining lines had to be felt as line of force. The student became conscious that they do really exist; it became clear that currents pass, not unlike electromagnetic currents, from the left to the right fingertips, and again from the left foot to the right. Thus, the human organism itself actually writes into space these two intersecting triangles.

The students then had to learn to feel what lies in the words, "Light streams upward, weight bears downward." They had to experience this in deep meditation, standing in the attitude I described. In this way, they gradually came to the point at which the teacher could say to them, "Now you are about to experience something that was practiced repeatedly in the ancient mysteries." The students then actually did attain this new experience; they could feel the very marrow within the bones of their limbs....

My *Philosophy of Freedom* cannot be grasped by logic alone; it requires one's whole being. In fact, you will not understand what is said in the book, which is about thinking, unless you know that people experience thought by means of an inner experience of the skeleton. People do not really think with the brain; when they think sharply defined thoughts, people think with their skeleton. Then, however, as is the case in *The Philosophy of Freedom*, thought becomes concrete, becomes real, then it passes into the whole person....

[Students] learned to experience symbols by turning their own organism into a symbol. This is the only way that symbols can be truly experienced. Explanation and interpretation of symbols really makes no sense; likewise, all theorizing about them is complete nonsense. One has to *make* them; one has to *experience* them. This is true of symbols, just as it is for fables, legends, and fairy tales; one has to identify one's being with them. There is always something in people through which they can enter all the figures of the fairy tale, whereby they can make themselves one with the fairy tale. It is the same with these genuine, ancient symbols, which arise originally from spiritual knowledge.[5]

In training the painter as taught to us by Liane Collot d'Herbois, we can see that working with the concepts of light and darkness and actually experiencing them with charcoal provides a deep experience, as Rudolf Steiner describes here through working with symbols. She developed this new way of mystery school teaching whereby we experience the light, the darkness, and the middle area where they meet in our own organism. We become the light as it pushes the darkness, or the darkness as it wants to meet the light in a warm way. In countless exercises, we live through the drama of light and darkness, and we feel it through our organism. As quoted, we turn our own bodily organism into a symbol—the light for thinking, the color for

---

5 Ibid., Dornach, Jan. 12, 1924, pp. 69–73 (trans. revised).

heart feeling, and the darkness for willing. Here again, this goes beyond theory; we actually experience the symbols.

At night, we relive what has been brought to us in the day, but in reverse order. What had been the power of the light making a space for itself by pushing away the darkness and what had been the darkness moving toward the light becomes the opening of the unconscious if the student has deeply lived in the process. It becomes the light going into the unconscious, or the unconscious taking over the light. Meaningful visions or dreams come to the students who have worked dutifully with devotion. When students are aware, they will consciously experience that entry to the unconscious; if not, dreams will be shared, and students will recognize what is happening. Here teachers are responsible for being truly aware of what they are doing. The teacher of light and darkness is not simply giving students charcoal and telling them to have fun with it.

In the modern world, being the way it is, many individuals are teaching this technique without the least knowledge of what they are doing. They do not understand the depth of the symbols and their power. They end up playing with very dangerous elements, harming both the students and themselves in the process. They are modern versions of charlatans of the Middle Ages, false alchemists, quacks. Therefore, students must be very much aware of the source of their instructions; they have to be able to rely on their intuition as to whether the instruction feels right or not.

When I started the school in the United States, Liane Collot d'Herbois was aware of how and what we taught, and we had her blessing, which meant a lot to me. Without it I would never have started anything of such a nature. She was aware of all we did and looked at photos of the students' work and at who was teaching what. She made comments such as, "Throw out that student. Tell the student to do something else. The student does not belong to this work." Or, "Let this student be a caring nurse, caring for the soul. The student lacks the spiritual capacity to do otherwise." Nevertheless, we never did; such is the responsibility of this work. Therefore, when I hear someone say that this person is a Collot d'Herbois painter or is painting in her method, I realize that some educating needs to be done as to what it means to be called a Collot d'Herbois painter therapist.

I have been reading a book by a wonderful French writer who asks this question about Christianity: "How could we have gone so far from the Message of Christ?" So much wrong has been done in the name of Christianity, and with care and love he truly tries to understand this. The same is true with any important new impulse. The person who brings it into the world is important and great, and what we do with it is something else. It comes to Earth and becomes part of our weakness unless we keep up a serious meditative life and practice. There are people who teach painting who never practice it beyond a little messy painting here and there!

Here is what we come up against:

Imagine, my dear friends, that here we have a man and that I no longer have any interest in him, but I take his clothes and hang them on a coat hanger that has a knob above here. After that, I take no further interest in the man, telling myself, *There is the man! I am not concerned about what can occupy these clothes. That coat hanger with the clothes on it is the man.* This is what really happened with the elements. It no longer interested people that the first hierarchy is behind warmth or fire, the second hierarchy is behind light and air and what we call chemical ether or color ether, and so on, the third hierarchy behind water, and the fourth hierarchy behind the life element and Earth, humanity. The peg and the hanger, on which hang the clothes—that is all.

There you have the first act of the drama. The second act begins with Kant. There is the hanger, and the clothes hanging on it. Clever people begin to philosophize in true Kantian fashion over what "the thing in itself" of these clothes, may be. They conclude that "the thing in itself" of the clothes cannot be known. Very clever; very clever indeed. Do away with the person and keep only the coat hanger with the clothes, and of course you can proceed to philosophize over the clothes; you can create most beautiful speculations. You can philosophize in as Kant did, and say, "'The thing in itself' cannot be known." Alternatively, in the fashion of Helmholtz, you can say, "But these clothes, they cannot, *of themselves,* have forms; there is really nothing there but tiny, whirling specks of dust, tiny atoms, that hit and strike each other—and behold, the clothes are held in their form."...

We are far from being ready to admit that there is no need to dream this way about a whirling dance of atoms, and that what we must do instead is return the *human being* into the clothes. This is the very thing that the renewal of Spiritual Science must now set out to do.[6]

This is the work that Liane Collot d'Herbois as a spiritual scientist brought to her students, to put life back into the emaciated world of colors. As mentioned, what we do with her great work depends on us. Whether it becomes the domain of quacks, unprepared teachers, or gifted individuals is truly our own responsibility. The knowledge has been given; now it is up to the morality of the individuals taking up the work. As Liane mentioned, the important thing is that it was brought to Earth.

As explained, we work with charcoals for experiencing light and darkness. Working with charcoal means working with our hands. We apply the charcoal with our whole hands on the large paper, and through our hands try to experience the light coming from the top, the darkness rising from the bottom to meet the light, and the middle where they interact. Our hands do the work.

Since nothing can be overlooked, we might ask: What is so important about using one's hands to spread the charcoal on the paper? Body movement or the voice and ear are used in other healing modalities. Here, everything is in the use of our hands, then, by extension, the paint brush through our fingers and arms.

Steiner gives some valuable insights about the magic behind our hands:

The etheric organs, expressed in the hands and their functions, work far more intuitively, more spiritually, and perform a far higher task than is accomplished by the etheric brain. Those who have made progress in these matters will say that the brain, with its etheric basis, in effect is by far the least skillful of the spiritual organs we bear within

6   Ibid., Dornach, Jan. 4, 1924, pp. 23–24 (trans. revised).

us because, as soon as they begin to stir in the etheric part of the brain, they quickly become aware of this foreign part of it.

The spiritual activities connected with the organs underlying the hands, though expressed incompletely in the hands and their functions, serve a far higher, more spiritual kind of knowledge and observation. Those organs can lead into the suprasensory world and busy themselves with our perception and orientation there. A spiritual seer may express this (somewhat surprisingly though accurately) by saying that the human brain is a very clumsy organ for research in the spiritual world, and that the hands, or the spiritual basis of the hands, are far more interesting and significant organs for gaining knowledge of the world, and certainly far more skillful organs than the brain.

Not much is gained on the path to initiation by advancing from using the physical brain to freely using the etheric brain. There is no great difference between what we may achieve through purified, intuitive brain thinking, and regulated spiritual work in the etheric spiritual counterpart of the brain. The difference becomes much greater between what our hands accomplish in the world and what can be done by the etheric, spiritual basis of the hands, just as the etheric brain is the spiritual basis of the physical brain. On the path of initiation, little development of the etheric brain is needed, since it is not an especially important organ. However, the etheric basis of the hands is connected with the activity of the lotus flower in the region of the heart....

This lotus flower pours out its rays of force in such a way that it builds up the organism that, at the present stage of humankind, exists in an incomplete form in the hands and their function. When we learn this fact and consider the great difference between the mere use of physical hands and all that we can acquire regarding the suprasensory world through the etheric organs underlying the hands—such far more skillful organs than those of the etheric brain—we gain a vivid concept of learning to experience initiation and all the enrichment that it means for humanity. We do not acquire much enrichment through the feeling that our brain radiates to feel its etheric counterpart. This is the case, but it is not a very permeating and significant experience. The significant experience begins when we feel that other parts are also expanding and connecting with the universe. Though it

95

may sound strange, it is true that the least skillful organ for spiritual investigation is the brain, since it is the least capable of development.[7]

This next passage about the connection between the etheric basis of the hands and the activity of the lotus flower in the region of the heart adds another dimension to this subject:

The heart poses a problem for physiologists today. It is an involuntary muscle, being striated diagonally, whereas involuntary muscles are striated vertically. The heart is striated diagonally because it is on the path to becoming a voluntary muscle. It has a predisposition for this today. In the future, when we can work from cosmic spirituality, we will be able to move the heart just as we can move our hands today.... The teacher tells us that, when we gradually attain this personal, intimate relationship to the whole world around us, when we no longer must use the physical brain, we will finally be able to understand what the Rosicrucian calls "divine blessedness," or piety, in which the independence of the human being is preserved but the highest will be felt.[8]

All these passages require meditation.

---

7   Steiner, *Initiation, Eternity, and the Passing Moment*, Munich, Aug. 26, 1912, p. 34 (trans. revised).

8   Steiner, *Rosicrucianism Renewed*, Munich, May 19, 1907, pp. 53–54 (trans. revised).

Light and Darkness, Heaven and Earth

I t is time for another walk. This time I go back to one of my favorite villages, the one in which Tennyson lived repeatedly to impregnate himself with the Cornwall elements, physical as well as spiritual and mythical, to write his beautiful long poems. I walk on the northern part, and there the view is breathless. I walk past the same crazy cliffs, high up along the meadows with grazing cows and sheep. Then I see, from the corner of the path, a beautiful waterfall diving hundreds of meters into the wild ocean. Again, I am on a path alone; no one is there except me. The rest of the tourists prefer to walk down the streets lined with shops, leaving these beautiful paths empty and quiet—all the better for me to meditate. On the horizon, the clouds are soft and gray. After a couple of hours, I walk back and once more enjoy some cream tea, and later walk through a hidden valley village, with lovely gardens lining the narrow streets atop stone walls of majestic white quartz and marble stones. Flowers abound, making everything lively and artistic. This wonderful village of Boscastle is three miles north of Tintagel. It was first discovered by a Norman from northern France a thousand years ago.

We are all mixed up. Who is English? Who is French? The Land of the Rose and the Land of the Lily. Especially nowadays, the difference is becoming blurred, which I think is a good thing. What does it matter where we come from? What matters is what we do with ourselves, wherever we were born or live. Lately, I have been wandering all over the place, and I am shocked at how similar the young people are in India, Russia, the Bahamian Islands, villages in British Columbia, or Tintagel. They wear the same clothes and talk on the same mobile phones about the same matters with their friends. We are becoming one world, and let us hope that these young people will do a better job than ignorant politicians and oblivious diplomats have thus far. I always tell young people with their backpacks in whatever country I am traveling that they are the real diplomats, the ones we need. It is tough because they have to foot the bill, unlike the "real" diplomats who waste vast amounts of the taxpayers' money.

The other diplomats are those vacationers who travel widely and live in other countries, often moving from their home country, such as the Dutch and English who live in France. The English live part time in France, Italy, Spain, the islands, South America, or India. The Indians have moved to England, the United States, Canada, and Australia, and return home to vacation. The French go everywhere, getting lost or taking up residence in some far-off place in Africa or South America. Americans get lost everywhere. Israelites travel widely, but always return to Israel. The New Zealanders travel widely, too, and return home or stay in the Canadian Rockies. Persians and Gulf Arabs are found everywhere, and people are glad to accept them and their money, especially in Paris, London, Rome, Dubai, and Barcelona, where they go to shop. The Japanese, like the rest of us, are world travelers, too, and the Chinese are traveling like there is no tomorrow, and having a wonderful time doing it, especially in Russia. The Russians have started globe hopping, especially the young people, and we can see the borders between Russia and China becoming thinner. Tourists in both countries use trains from one end of the continent to the other.

The world is becoming a far better place thanks to the millions of backpackers and other travelers on the road, moving by train, bicycle, motorcycle, airplane, sailboat, or their own two feet. This is a far nicer picture to contemplate than the doomsday scenario portrayed by the media. At least there is some progress in brotherly love when we travel beyond our own borders. I continue to advise travel, especially to the young and the retired. They are the ones on the road. I have forged friendships with young men and women and hope to make a difference in their lives. One of them, from the mountains of Columbia, will study at the Rudolf Steiner Institute in California and will, I am sure, make some worthwhile changes in the world.

These words by Ita Wegman mean a lot to me:

Here I would also like to mention something that Rudolf Steiner felt to be very important for us as anthroposophists. It was expressed this way in conversation: the Archangel Michael, the Spirit of the Age, under whose leadership we stand, will demand increasingly that we take Anthroposophy out into the whole world, and that cosmopolitanism should take the place of remaining narrowly limited within a mystery center. For individuals, too, it is exceedingly important to go out and learn something about the outer world, because, as Rudolf Steiner said, true knowledge of the outer world also makes it possible for people to understand the spiritual world in the proper way during the time between death and a new birth.

Our ability to know our own organism will also depend on the proper knowledge of the spiritual world. Thus, the next time we come down to the physical world and choose a physical body for our incarnation, we will be able to choose one that is free from inherited defects, or we will be so strong in soul and spirit that we will have the forces needed to overcome the so-called inherited body and to build up the organs with which the soul and spirit can live in harmony. Because of this, it was recommended to those in the old mysteries who were to be initiated to take long journeys and travels to comprehend the manifold nature of the world, to feel the contrast between the cold and wet regions, on the one hand, and on the other dry and hot regions, and to absorb all the intermediate conditions.

Many people today must struggle with the fact that their soul and spirit cannot always fully use their physical body. This is because between today and the time of those journeys, when the mysteries also had their period of blossoming, the Christian Middle Ages intervened with its cloistered life that limited people more to their native soil. Only where something of this ancient knowledge survived did people break through this "sticking to one's roots."

It is very important for the coming century that people once again gain the possibility of building up physical bodies that their whole spiritual being can connect to properly. Naturally, real knowledge of the outer world should not to be gained only through journeys and travels, but also by intimately and lovingly penetrating the secrets of nature. Nevertheless it is important to become acquainted with foreign lands and customs.[1]

---

1   Wegman, *Esoteric Studies,* p.101 (trans. revised).

If she could see my foreign travels this past year, she would be proud of me. I fund all these travels myself, and I travel at no one's invitation, thereby keeping my independent outlook. When someone foots the bill, you are obliged to something or someone, and thus lose your own point of view. That is why we have so few good journalists. My travels this past year have been to British Columbia, northern India, Sikkim, the Bahamas, the United States (New York City, the Midwest, Colorado, the Pacific Northwest, and New England), Iceland, England (London and Cornwall), the Canadian Rockies, Germany, Russia (St. Petersburg and Moscow). My travels in 2012 have taken me to British Columbia, Spain, Israel, Egypt, New England, Turkey, the Far East, Morocco, Tunisia, Kenya, and Tanzania.

In all these places, I meet lots of folks, young and old, and most of the time I talk about Anthroposophy, recommend books, or send them to people, such as a special young man who is a philosopher living in Columbia, whom I met in India, or a young Vietnamese woman from Australia, whom I met in Sikkim, or a young Russian woman artist living in Frankfurt. Who knows what these young individuals will do in their lives, but they certainly are bright torches of the future, and one does not find them hanging out around anthroposophic cliques. The young need to go out in the world and not remain within easy, complacent circles that do not make them work. I find that many of those young people, as well as adults, do not see the difference and want to find a job *in* Anthroposophy instead of educating themselves and bringing something *to* Anthroposophy. I am quoting these words by Collot d'Herbois again:

> Light and darkness is a spiritual experience that has to do with the incarnation of the "I." The "I" incarnates in two ways: from above and from below, along a path of light and along a path of darkness. In the soul these two opposites are active as the forces of antipathy and sympathy, in the physical body they are represented by the nerve and the blood. Remember the connection of light with the nervous system. The brain and the spinal cord with all the nerves branching off from it resemble a tree upside down, a Tree of Paradise inside us, spun of light. Its life it left behind....

The ascending light is an all-diffused light that has no center. It is a luminosity that has no space, it brings a certain spacelessness. As such it belongs to the second dimension, which in the human being can be transformed into the fourth dimension. Because in the human being this ascending light is the light of life that wells from the heart. It works in the purification of the astral body. And the more we grow from the consciousness of the head toward the consciousness of the heart, the more we grow toward the fourth dimension. In the world of color this light of life is represented by the "peach-blossom," a color that hovers between magenta and cobalt-violet.

The descending light has an altogether different quality. It radiates from a center and it carries destruction. But through that destruction it brings space and consciousness and in that way it serves Creation. In the world of color it is represented by viridian green. In the human being the descending light is related to thinking, the thinking that can be transformed into pure thinking when it comes into the right connection with feeling and will. Then it meets with the ascending light that wells from the heart and is carried by it.[2]

Here the words of Rudolf Steiner speak about the same process, but in terms of mystery school experience stemming from the old Greek mysteries. I want to show again the continuation of the presence of the old mysteries within the work brought to us by Liane Collot d'Herbois, but transformed and adapted to our modern psyche.

If we try to go out into the cosmos, we find ourselves facing the void; if we try to sink into ourselves, we find ourselves ensnared in our own will nature. This is what causes the severe ordeals that are inevitable when people, starting from their present consciousness, try to probe the mysteries of the world in either direction, about which they begin by marveling because they confront them as world wonders.

Why is this so? It is because, when we press out into cosmic space, we come into an area that... [is] the region of the upper gods, or spirits, spirits who are merely the ideas or representations of the real gods. Thus we come into a world that has no independence. It is no wonder that what we can gain from this world eventually leads us into the void.

2   Collot d'Herbois, *Light, Darkness and Colour*..., pp. 19, 25–26.

No matter how hard people struggle to gain knowledge, when they reach the utmost limits of their ideas, they themselves can come only to *ideas* of the gods; they cannot reach true reality.

If people plunge into themselves, however, into what has been built up during millions and millions of years, then they come to the acts, or achievements, of the other divine spiritual beings, whom...we have called the subearthly, the true gods. But to reach these, we must first penetrate through our own impulses, desires, and passions, through all that imprisons us, seizes hold of us, and changes us so that we are made to follow it. This leads us to egoism and cuts us off from those lower gods.... If we try to reach the upper gods, we come to the void, or world of mere idea. If we try to reach the lower gods, all thought abandons us because we are seized by the blindly raging impulses of our own inner beings, and we burn ourselves up in them. That is why the ordeals are so arduous.[3]

Here is another passage by Rudolf Steiner that approaches the subject from another angle.

From the moment human beings are observed from the other side of the threshold, they are perceived as the confluence of two spiritual realms. Basically, only a seeming unity confronts us when we contemplate the human being here in the earthly world. Indeed, human beings are not a unity at all, but the confluence of spiritually active forces from...two realms.... The forces that live in our eyes or in our ears, for example, originate from somewhere other than do those that develop when we put one foot before the other, or move our arms....

Viewed from beyond the threshold, this centripetal [inwardly directed] world is cold and icy. To experience it is to be affected by something that rigidifies or calcifies. Nonetheless, whereas it is cold and rigid and evokes chills, it is filled with wisdom and woven, as it were, from wisdom-filled thoughts. This cold, rigid world of forces holds the other [physical] world together. Human beings are not organized so that they can sense this centripetal world directly. Those who enter the realm beyond the threshold feel this chill or cold contraction. The coldness is a sign that one is actually entering with one's "I" and

---

3   Steiner, *Wonders of the World: Ordeals of the Soul, Revelations of the Spirit*, Aug. 27, 1911, pp. 182–183 (trans. revised).

astral body into the world that humanity enters each night, but without consciousness, not experiencing it....

This is an experience that can be had and it is, in fact, one that can be gained only through actual experience. Indeed, according to explanations one finds in my books (*How to Know Higher Worlds* and *An Outline of Esoteric Science*)...the region beyond the threshold must be entered, because it is as real as the sensory realm....

A spiritual world exists behind the tapestry spread out around us that contains all the sensory impressions.... This spiritual realm is a chilly, cold world.... [It] has centripetal forces that hold the spiritual cosmos together. This other realm, the origin of the forces that move our limbs, is permeated with the opposite, or centrifugal [outwardly directed] forces....

Humanity brings into this world of centripetal forces cosmic forces that dwell within the inner being. When we grasp clearly in our mind's eye what it is that lives as forces in people's inner being...it is an element that we can call love, warmth, warmth of soul; the human being carries this soul warmth into the cold domain. This is humankind's preeminent cosmic task. Human beings are the source of warmth for this sphere...inasmuch as the gods have created humanity (to put the matter trivially), they have created the opening for just this region that must hold together for them, the world that would otherwise disperse in dust....

This region is endowed with forces opposite to those in the other realm. Concerning the latter, I said that it bears centripetal forces that hold the spiritual cosmos together. This other region, the source of the forces that move our limbs, is permeated with the opposite, centrifugal forces. They are perpetually active, expanding the spiritual universe far and wide as it were. They are centrifugal forces, but you must not imagine them as you would physical forces. They are spiritual beings. In a sense, here we look into the constitution of the universe. We relate what constitutes the universe to what is within us. We trace the forces that live in our eyes, our ears, and, in short, our whole sensory apparatus. We recognize them as the forces that hold the world together. We find in ourselves the forces through which we move our arms and legs, which cause a number of other things to occur in our limb organism. We pronounce them to be forces that, if left to themselves, would disperse the universe in all directions. As human beings, we are set within this nexus of forces. Within it is found a world of the most diverse beings—beings with whom the nine hierarchies...come into relation through the human being.... The gods encounter one another through human beings.

Thus, one looks into the universe and sees the human being in a certain sense as a mediator between divine worlds. One wishes that awareness of this fact would penetrate human souls, since only such awareness can overcome the egoistic elements of traditional religions....

This world we live in, this realm, naturally has significance in the great universe. Why, then, does it exist? You see, the world we live in between death and a new birth...is another realm of the spiritual world. It is mainly the spiritual region in which dwell the beings to whom we refer when speaking of the hierarchies of the angeloi, archangeloi, and so on. Yet this world of the nine hierarchies can persist only when it enters, through physical human beings (and it can only happen through human beings) a certain mutual relationship with the world I have described here as the spiritual region beyond the sensory domain.

When you live in a house and wish to connect with the outer world without actually stepping outside, you must look through the window. When the gods of the nine hierarchies wish to communicate with this world, they must do so through humanity. They cannot do so directly, but must do it through human beings. It is a region of the world that the gods can contemplate only by means of human beings.[4]

As students work with light and darkness with charcoal and by painting colors, they are led to experience the spiritual world in a manner appropriate to modern consciousness. Of course, this is one path of development among many—a painter's path. It is a safe entrance to the world of the spirit, provided it is taught with respect, reverence, and devotion, and most of all with selflessness and humility. Otherwise, it is dangerous both to the student and to the teacher. The words cited above by Rudolf Steiner remind us of the sacredness of this work.

---

4   Steiner, *Spiritual Science as a Foundation for Social Forms*, lecture, Aug. 28, 29, 1920, pp. 168, 172–174, 178–179 (trans. revised).

Collot d'Herbois always reminded us that the ultimate healing is for the patient to experience Golgotha. We had to bring the student to an experience of Golgotha. What a task!

Now we can understand a little of what it entails to call oneself a person who paints according to the direction of Collot d'Herbois. No wonder she was severely disappointed at the end of her life, when she became aware of certain teachers and what they were doing in her name.

Again, just imagine for a moment that you are in a room with other students. You have a large white charcoal paper before you and a piece of soft charcoal. You spread the charcoal slowly all over the paper. The room is quiet, very quiet as everyone concentrates on the task. Then, after an hour or two, you are asked to bring in the light slowly from the top, in the middle of the paper—a light coming from a faraway place—then you make the necessary gestures and light incarnates, pushing away the darkness. Then you are asked to bring another movement, this time from the darkness—darkness that wants to reach the light and engulf it within. One must feel the power of that darkness and even be totally overwhelmed by it, feeling how it wants to spread everywhere and take over everything. Then the light stops the darkness here, and we feel another gesture of antipathy, sympathy. One lives with these gestures, through the hands, in the body; we feel the strength of both and as human beings; we bring the warmth of our soul into the middle and live within the interaction between the forces of light and darkness.

In the training, we work for three days in charcoal, then with watercolor painting. Liane said we should not work more than three days in the medium of charcoal, as it is too demanding on one's forces and unhealthy.

Now, as the reader, you can have a little inkling of this very powerful work, the beginning of the training of painters who will become modern icon painters or healing therapists as developed by Liane Collot d'Herbois.

Just Keep Working

By crossing the fields and following the coastal path going north, the walk to Tintagel is only about thirty minutes from my new home. This area has complicated geological features, and it was once connected with the American coastline. I learned that the mines in this area contain antimony, a substance that encourages a meditative life and makes this place suitable for spiritual development.[1]

Walking along this lonely path, these words keep coming to my mind from my morning reading.

> Even higher knowledge is dangerous.... Through it we learn that countless spiritual hierarchies have been working on us. We learn how our physical, etheric, and astral bodies in all their parts have been assembled by the hierarchies. We learn how cosmic spirits have been at work so that humanity could finally come into existence. Thus, in esoteric life, when people delve into their own inner being, they are overcome by the thought, *You are actually the aim and the goal of the gods. The gods have labored to create you.* Here they confront the great danger of falling into immeasurable arrogance....
>
> This is why human beings need so much to approach humbly the knowledge that humankind is the goal of the gods, absorbing it in humility. Otherwise, it will lead to arrogant presumption. When we recognize that the human being is the goal of the gods, we in this world have no lack of opportunities for pride and presumption. When we see the gods in the macrocosm exerting effort continually to develop the human being, we have every occasion for pride.[2]

Living with minerals that are so old, one seldom thinks about how old *we* are. In tourist shops, one can buy very interesting and knowledgeable books on geology, but nothing on our own, even older past. It takes such

---

1   See Wegman, *Esoteric Studies.*
2   Steiner, *Wonders of the World,* Aug. 27, 1911, p. 179 (trans. revised).

thoughts as these by Rudolf Steiner to wake us up to who we really are and to the great responsibility that falls upon us to be thankful for the millions of years it took for countless higher beings to struggle so we could reach this level. We still struggle, but now we can help in the process through what Liane brought to painters. How can we not say thank you?

Liane Collot d'Herbois was extremely humble: "Never mind anything Darling, just go on; keep working!" That is what I am trying to do with this little book, which is a formidable task. To explain something that cannot really be explained, but only experienced; painting is all doing, not talking. This is why I have to resort again and again to the wise, full-of-life words of Rudolf Steiner, Ita Wegman, and others. This work cannot be understood, otherwise, but just experienced when one looks at the paintings. However, if you, the reader, experience the arduous task of understanding this work, this means a great deal to the spiritual world and to those who have crossed the threshold.

Walking through this beautiful area in Cornwall certainly helps working with these more-than-life, magnificent pictures that only Anthroposophy can give. One needs to walk while living in these words; it helps to feel them. I have always been very physical, not only by walking and skiing, but also through work—hand-shoveling large piles of compost, heaps of stones for walkways, wheelbarrows full of dirt for gardens, and endlessly bailing hay to feed the animals. I attribute my ability to digest Anthroposophy to this manual work, which balances out the intense spiritual work—in addition, of course, to the artistic work through painting.

> In Spiritual Science, knowledge must turn to action, action in the whole cosmic world context.... What is practiced as Spiritual Science must be a completely different form of knowledge from the one customarily called knowledge.[3]

I feel I have enough action in my life right now, so I am not adding any more, as there is no room for it. However, one never knows with

---

3   Steiner, *Spiritual Science as a Foundation for Social Forms*, Dornach, Aug. 6, 7, 1920, pp. 7, 27.

Anthroposophy; the heart gets bigger, we feel more, and there are no limits to "Not my will but God's will," or "Not I but Christ in me."

Some of my friends who are trying to keep up with my whereabouts actually get a headache when I try to explain what I am doing these days. My friend Ann in California says it is a "force of nature" quality. I attribute it all to Anthroposophy and to painting, not to myself.

Feet on the Earth

It is raining, sometimes heavily, so my walk on the coast is a wet, windy one, but enjoyable nonetheless. As I walk in this place, I have been thinking that it would be nice to have someone to talk to about what I am doing. Yanny Mager could not come to England from Paris, where she is teaching a group of students, while other friends do not have the freedom to travel, so I am left to do this work in solitude. Then a friend told me over the phone that he knew someone who used to own an anthroposophic bookstore and lives in Cornwall. It turns out he lives in the town of Delabole, where I was for the last ten days before arriving here. What a small world! In all of England, he lives within a mile or so of where I am right now. I could cross through meadows, among sheep and cows, and probably reach his house! I look forward to next week's meeting with this older anthroposophist, now in his eighties, and his artist wife. I hope I remember which day it is, since I lose track of time living here. The world becomes spaceless and timeless— or "unearthly" is the best word—when one enters these realms deeply. That is why I need to walk vigorously to get back into the Earth. Others have taken recourse by using tobacco. Liane Collot d'Herbois smoked a cigar when I spent time with her.

She asked, "Do you mind if I smoke a cigar next to the window?" Although I cannot stand smoke, I said it was fine, though the little cigars she smoked were not bad, a little better than cigarettes. She explained that she needed the nicotine to stay on this Earth. Now I see what she means.

These beautiful words show what we are all striving for with the help of Anthroposophy and the work of Collot d'Herbois:

> When Goethe wishes to express what human beings are in the most authentic sense, and how they manifest most truly their worth and the entire content of their existence, he says: When the healthy nature of human beings works as a whole, when people feel themselves to be

living in the world as in a great and beautiful and worthy whole, when this harmony brings them a pure, free joy, then the universe, if it could become self-aware, would cry out in exultation at having reached its goal and would marvel at the height that its own being and becoming had attained.[1]

This brief meditation was given to students of Georg Kühlewind:

> *Wilt* thou be made *whole*!
> Wilt *Thou* be made *whole*! [2]

I have spoken of light and darkness, and brought in Rudolf Steiner's words on multiple worlds—the upper gods; the lower gods; the depths and the heights; the senses; the icy cold centripetal world; the warm world of our limbs spreading everywhere; the centrifugal world; the world of the hierarchies; of Saturn; the warmth of sunlight, moon color, and solid Earth; the world of the first, second, third, fourth dimensions—to grasp what it is that we do when we work with light and darkness and color. This probably sounds utterly confusing and chaotic, and so it is. Welcome to life!

---

1 Steiner, *Metamorphoses of the Soul*, vol. 1, Nov. 25, 1909, p. 100.
2 Kühlewind, *Wilt Thou Be Made Whole*, p. 80 (italics mine).

PART TWO

ON COLOR

What Is Color?

Now I will leave the world of light and darkness and enter the world of their meeting: color, the world of watercolor painting.

There is one thing we must never forget and that is that all we say about light and darkness really is: color. In the world behind the light there are all the blues from the turquoise down to the darkest violet and in front of the light are all the reds from the deep glow of purple up to the dancing movements of the yellow green.

And another thing one must always keep in mind is that all this is a picture of the human being: the light of the incarnating "I" falls into the darkness of substance and in the same instant there arises movement that is color. We are beings of light and darkness, movement and color. One has to get used to the thought that all the ramifications of all color *and* movement come from light and darkness. Light and darkness is the spiritual part, movement and color is the soul-part of it.

One has to learn to think in light and darkness, which is the most important thing any of us can do. Usually one does not like to, one likes color because with it one feeds oneself a little bit. But light and darkness are just as curative—especially with the mental illnesses, because it is a logical thing, not in words but in pictures. And it means that one is bringing light into the people, one is making a path of incarnation through letting them develop the thinking in light and darkness with logic. That form of thinking calls upon the "I" and this way of drawing brings about the incarnation of both the "I" of thinking and the "I" of will.

Light and darkness exercises work on another part of the human being than the colors. Light and darkness is a spiritual experience. It helps to incarnate and it makes the thinking clearer. One must remember that although we speak of light *and* darkness, as though the two were separate, in reality they are *one* thing. To our ordinary day-consciousness they are separate and different. It is typical of our three-dimensional consciousness to see things as fragments that are separated from each other, whereas in another, higher dimension there is only wholeness.[1]

≈

The weather is tempestuous, to say the least, and I have to be careful on my cliff walk not to be thrown around by the strong wind. The waves are crashing against the rocky cliffs, eroding the ancient slate and making caves. No one is here. I inhale the ocean air, which is thick with moisture, and I cannot see a thing. Clouds of water rise into the air from the sea and shower my face, and around me I see a dense, grayish world. The sheep are oblivious to the moisture and gently graze in the meadows. I walk past a thousand-year-old church and into the village for groceries, the visitor center for emails, and read information on this place. I learn that Rudolf Steiner visited Tintagel and said that this place had been a center for mystery school teaching.

I walked through similar wild places on the coast of Iceland this past summer. The monasteries here were established by Irish monks who traveled through the islands in that area and far into Europe, bringing Christianity as they set up their places of learning. Here in Cornwall, they say that monks established some monasteries, but the feeling present in those faraway ruins of Icelandic monasteries is different. There you could feeling the monk's presence in some ways, while here it seems there was something of the wild elements celebrated, a strong Druidic presence, exalting a communion outdoors with the cosmos and the elements rather than in a small enclosed chapel.

Returning to the different movements, Steiner repeatedly tells us that the air is the element in which our astral/feeling body lives, and our feelings develop in the element of air. Within us, the movements that the soul makes are colors. Conversely, with meditative work we create the weather of the future by controlling our lower impulses. If that is the case, then we can look forward to having fewer storms, or perhaps deluges, and massive earthquakes or volcanic activities from the look of what is happening in

---

1 Collot d'Herbois, *Light, Darkness and Colour...*, pp. 32–33.

the news. That is why Liane always told us that we are making "future weather"!

> What is it, what does one see in the movement and the mingling of color? The movements and the encounters of spiritual beings, the will, and the deeds of the angels and of still greater beings. In all that a great cosmic force is at work—cosmic activity, cosmic will, cosmic love. That is your background when you work with color....
>
> One must realize that thoughts are color. At the center of one's thinking there is color. That is given as part of our spiritual being. From another point of view one could say that colors are thoughts that are not in the head but in the heart. The world of color is the world of the heart and it gives the "I" a connection with the will—and through the will with the Earth. One has to cultivate that world of thinking that is in the heart and one has to carry it within oneself and never leave it for any reason whatever. And in the daily painting-exercise it all comes together: the concentration of the waking consciousness of the head, the thinking of color that is in the heart and the act of will that is in the actual activity of painting.
>
> Painting in veils is then a very useful technique: one works at a picture from day to day and so one is able to take it with one into the night where the colors work deeper into one's being. And so painting becomes more and more an activity in which the "I" is involved.[2]

After struggling with light and darkness, the reader can have a bit of relief and enter the world of color. In these pages I could not have entered this world without having put the reader through what the painter has to go through at the beginning of this schooling. If you have read thus far, then you can now enjoy the world of colors, and some of the insights I have gained as a painter and student of Collot d'Herbois.

Trying to understand what stands behind light and darkness is an experience in itself, one that brings grounding and a strengthening of the "I." By struggling with this part of the book, you strengthened yourself and now you can experience the warmth of the colors. In this world of color, you can go a bit outside yourself more safely and not get lost, as this is not allowed

---

2   Ibid., pp. 43–44.

in the schooling of light, darkness, and color. The whole schooling is training in observing the colors without getting lost in them. Even when you become the color you are experiencing, you must maintain yourself firmly on the ground, on the Earth. Otherwise you might think you are an angel, and an angel does not have a body.

If you skipped the first part of the book or other earlier parts because it seemed too boring or difficult, then you have not earned the right to read the second part of the book. This means that you need to work more on incarnating your "I." You must be on the Earth and not lost in the clouds! You need to go back; otherwise you are intruding. One needs to earn something, not just take it. One needs to struggle to understand *Light, Darkness and Color in Painting Therapy*. When you struggle with some of the content, you add your understanding to the world and make it better. When you do not, you take something and make it worse. Your effort to understand is what counts. Making an effort to understand does not mean the results will come immediately, but what counts is the effort itself, rather than skipping what is difficult. So, if you skipped some parts, go back!

> Two, duality, is the number of appearance, of manifestation. There is however, no revelation save that the Divine rules behind the scenes. In this way, unity is hidden behind every duality. Therefore, *three* is nothing but two and one—that is, the revelation and the existent divinity backing it.[3]

Color is three; light and darkness are one and two. Color is revealed through the meeting of light and darkness. It is our soul, and our soul is a meeting ground for spiritual beings, as quoted earlier.

> There is still another reason for thinking in color and that is that in our time we tend to lose the possibility of seeing in color. Color-blindness is not only something in the eye; it is something in the soul too. Perhaps one could call it an atrophy of the soul. One cannot take in color anymore. Moreover, when one does not perceive color one sees the

---

3 Steiner, *Occult Signs and Symbols*, p. 34; see also Georg Kühlewind, *Wilt Thou Be Made Whole? Healing in the Gospels.*

deadness of the outer world. That is something that will happen more and more. We too are too much in the light today; our nervous system is too brilliant and too overworked. Western civilization tends to make the human being cool, calculating, aloof. When one is too open to all such influences soul-qualities like enthusiasm are easily lost. . . .

It is a well-known fact that when color blindness comes, the first color to go is red. The person is then not able to distinguish red from green. These colors disappear from consciousness. One may not be aware of it, but to the soul that is a loss. And to the soul *world* that is a loss.

The colors are there, they are living reality. When one wants to work with color one should not just look at them, but look and *see* the colors. Besides one's inward work with regard to color one should always be conscious of it, wherever and in whatever form one meets it. Because then one can do something. Such conscious observation is a creative deed in the soul-world, whereby one does something for the whole environment.[4]

Much has been touched upon to try to understand this work. Liane Collot d'Herbois here talks about painting, painting as a sacred ritual. This is where we see that her work is that of the mystery school. Therein lies why it is so incredibly difficult to understand—or easy to misunderstand!

The preparation of a painter is more than a serious act; it is a duty, a calling like the priesthood, medical work, or other service. It follows, as I have tried to show, the process of initiation work as explained by Rudolf Steiner, the Rosicrucian Path with its seven stages.

To paint in the right manner is the striving to come into connection with the Cosmic Soul. In order that one can overcome one's subjectivity and reach objective truth, the area beyond one's individual feeling must be discovered.

The first step is the knowledge and the experience of color. That is dependent on the individual human being as a THREEFOLD being.

When one sees color or uses color, then as Rudolf Steiner says, one's "I" and astral body *are* color. But we must be clearer in what that

---

4   Collot d'Herbois, *Light, Darkness and Color. . .*, pp. 43–44.

really means. We must first distinguish between "I" and astral, by realizing that it is the astral body speaking when one says *I wish; I want; I must; I will.*

Our "I" is bound up with thinking—without an "I" we wouldn't even know we were thinking. We make pictures, really, of our "I." But the deeper impressions of our "I" come very rarely. Here will be a stronger impression, there weaker, here none, and so on. We could not bear in this state of consciousness to have a full awareness of our "I" for it is so radiating and so light. It would be an unbearable experience for us.

But if we know that when we experience color our "I" and astral body are *in* color and *are* color at this moment—then we begin to understand to what great experiences color can lead.

To cultivate one's soul in the dreaming world of one's feelings could be done perhaps through the mysticism or monasticism of the Middle Ages, but does not belong in any way to this age.

To meet the Cosmic Soul with only soul qualities is not appropriate for our present time. Today, it has to be conscious. This calls, on the one hand, for the complete absolute knowledge of 1) the LAWS OF COLOR; 2) then, a much greater step that leads one very far, to the FORCES and PROCESSES OF COLOR; 3) and eventually, in heightened consciousness, to the BEING OF COLOR. Those are the three steps that must be taken in our time as conscious painters.

The conscious concentration on individual colors is an exercise toward making the feeling more conscious. When one does this, one is able to experience one's own thinking more and more intensively— thereby bringing life into thinking.

The control of feeling is very, very important. One learns to control the feeling even as one learns to control the colors while painting. This is dependent on the impulses that come from willing.

From one point of view, our willing can be said to be divided into three parts. It has the essence of goodness and the essence of evil, both. Between is an emptiness, a space wherein the highest hierarchy can work....

It depends on the force of our thinking and the luminosity of our concentration how conscious we can make our feelings, how far they can be illuminated. Knowledge of one's motives and making one's feeling conscious leads toward freedom.

Rudolf Steiner has so clearly explained and described the impulsing activity of the angels in the sphere of thinking, and its movement from thought to thought; movement akin to the movement of color to color, woven by the angels between light and darkness, from darkness into light, giving rise to the resulting colors having all nuances from lightening to an opal. This process is emphasized by our conscious feeling.

The consciousness that we can radiate upon the dream world of our feelings leads eventually to a purification of our feelings and a transformation takes place through the activity of our "I"—a transformation into "manas."

Outwardly it is dependent on the knowledge and experience of the laws and then the processes and forces in color. This knowledge and experience of color can be supported by painting. The reason of painting is not simply painting per se—but is inner development in a certain direction. Painting can be concerned with *anthropo-sophia* and the whole conception of thinking, feeling and will bound together in the threefold human being. Then the concept of the threefold human being connects with the threefold cosmic being of: LIGHT-COLOR-DARKNESS.

Our thinking is a reality and a creative force; and color, inner planetary color and inner light are creative forces. Therefore it matters a great deal that our work is not subjective feeling only.[5]

---

5   Collot d'Herbois, *Colour*, pp. 62–64.

Confidence

My walks take me to the moors about twenty-five miles from here. I walk through the area's highest hills to a small village with a beautiful, very old Celtic cross, an old church and farms scattered here and there. The same cows graze happily in the faraway fields. There is an old forest that seems to echo former horse riders traveling through it. I am amazed that this part of England is still pastoral, lovely, and untouched by pollution. In the afternoon, young women collect their red-cheeked children, who run around happy and content, far from the cities. Here the population has not abandoned the countryside as people have in France; they actually live here and do quite well. I go to two nearby little towns, and find them full of life. I peruse an organic store where I find the same things as are available in a village in British Columbia, Canada. There is a kind of green revolution that is definitely touching everyone, and here it is very much alive. The farmers still make their own cheese, and the butchers will still provide some special cut if you want it. It is still an agrarian society, but it is not without elements of culture. The arts thrive here: drama, film, writing, poetry, and painting. History is very much a part of the area, yet people seem to be moving forward into the future, thanks to all the little children. The English are definitely reproducing, unlike the French or the Italians for whose demographics show population at a standstill, a problem for the future.

I see a grandma taking a baby for a walk in a red pram, bright geranium red, with a tote bag hanging on it that is just as red. I could not buy those deluxe prams when I had children, as they were too expensive, although they would have been awkward for me anyway because I always lived in the middle of nowhere. Usually this kind of expensive pram is dark blue, gray or black, but one can see this one coming for miles.

The houses are surrounded by beautifully tended flower gardens, so here there is no fear that people will lose their soul since, thanks to the old gardeners, they are certainly living with colors in their surroundings. If only people worldwide could have simple lifestyles that include gardens, or if they could simply tend gardens, even flowers in their apartments. Then the world would be a better place. Instead of bombing our enemies, we could shower them with gardens, orchards, or simple vegetable plots instead.

This area was not always so peaceful, as we gather from history. The knights who were sent out all over the world have certainly done their work—to subdue wild instincts. And it is from this area that they were sent. Perhaps the harmony I feel here throughout these villages is the effect of these dedicated horse riders of the past who, with spear in hand, literally fought the wildness of humankind. Now our wildness has become internalized. The battles on the outside have become battles on the inside of each and every one of us. And the battles on the outside from the past ages have created the peaceful setting that I observe now. What we gain by fighting our inward battles will show in the future, in the outside world. How much peace and harmony we can acquire in our inner life will be the shape of the Earth in the future.

So when we discuss such important work as *Light, Darkness and Colour in Painting Therapy* that stems from Liane Collot d'Herbois's work with Anthroposophy, we are actually talking about having a hand in shaping our world of the future. And that is the main point of doing this kind of work as opposed to other kinds of painting. Here we are aware, or should be aware that *we do make a difference.* In this manner we gain more confidence about ourselves and have a strengthening of our Will. By strengthening our will, we become more energetic. We rid ourselves of obstacles that stand in our way when we feel we cannot do anything—apathy. With the awareness of our power, we become involved in the world and become active.

To enter the world of "light, darkness, and color" is to become active and alive. We rid ourselves of the trapped energies that Georg Kühlewind mentions in his books on Consciousness. The trapped energies of the lower self are the ones that make us lethargic and feel dead or soul dead. Working with colors and light and dark releases these lower energies, or trapped energies, so that we can become who we were destined to become before we were born. It is not that we do not have energy, but that our energies are caught up in negative ways. Think of our energy as being sucked out into nonsense—wasted—and then there is nothing available to use when we want it. Without those negative energies one becomes more alive.[1]

As I sit working on this tremendous task, I hear the words Liane Collot d'Herbois wrote to me on a small green card with her lovely handwriting before she died: "You must paint as you do mathematics, and you must have confidence in yourself." She also said something that I did not understand until a few years later when I ran the school: "You must learn to be nasty, and start with your husband!" Even more to my surprise, Liane went on and added something to the effect, "For you, if you are looking for a mate, marry an older German or a younger English man." Not a younger German man, or an older British man, but a younger English or older German! I wondered where that was coming from, as she knew that I was already married with two children. It seemed that she was totally oblivious to my married state! She could certainly be straightforward, and I loved that about her.

"You must have confidence in yourself." I need to remind myself of these words. Even though I have confidence when I am teaching, traveling, and living my daily life, I have always had doubts about my work in art, writing, or painting. I find myself thinking self-doubting thoughts: *I can't be this; I can't be that. I am not as good as the others.* I always have the feeling that I do not know enough right now and need to know more and more and more. Then, at one point in my painting work, I came to a conclusion: *This is the way I paint and I accept my imperfections. I will still work hard, but this is what it is right now, and it is not any worse than anyone else.*

---

1 See the books by Georg Kühlewind in the references section.

Since then, I often see that others have not put forth a fraction of the effort I have, and it shows. I have concluded that it was worth saying, "No, it is not good enough yet," but at some point it must be good enough. That is what Liane meant when she said, "Now you must have confidence in your work." And I agree; otherwise I would not be writing or painting.

Turner, Pioneer of Watercolor

I am taking another walk in Boscastle to see the beautiful waterfall far above the cliffs. The wind is blowing the falling water into a great misty cloud, getting me wet. I touch the beautiful rocks lining the path and say hello to a tiny, minuscule yellow flower growing between the rock walls. Everyone loves stones here, and they use them to decorate their walls. Walking down the narrow valley lane from the moor down to the ocean, I touch the big crystal stones that line all the stone walks. The big stones sit like kings and queens among abundant flowers. The little houses look like dollhouses, with blue painted windowsills or other bright colors. Lace curtains line the windows, and I glimpse an old woman sipping her tea inside.

Everything here is cared for, and I think that, because of the Earth's richness here—amethysts, crystals, coal, granite, slate, and all sorts of semiprecious stones and veins of metals—it must have some effect on the people who appreciate and include this bounty in their daily life. They see and walk past these stones every day and touch them tenderly because they are so special and beautiful. They recognize something, and if you grow up as a child like Liane Collot d'Herbois did in these surroundings, something happens to your soul. I am sure it strengthens it, like growing up with a garden and the beings that live there. As painters, we use rocks that are pulverized to a fine power and spread on the paper. We watch those colors as they mingle and create beautiful tones. This helps us bring out something from the hidden world. Stones spoke to Liane Collot d'Herbois from an early age, helping her meet her destiny as a powerful painter, teacher, and healer.

The great teacher, Rudolf Steiner, reminds us who these rocks truly are.

> You must get used to the thought that we may meet very high and exalted beings in the things closest to us, things we often regard as very lowly. It is easy enough to say about the solid element that it is

only matter. Some people may be tempted to say that it is no concern of the spiritual investigator; after all, matter is of little importance. Why bother with it? We rise above matter to a spiritual level.

Anyone who thinks like this is ignoring the fact that, through countless ages, lofty spiritual beings have been working in such discredited substance to bring it into this solid state. Actually, if we were to penetrate in our feeling life through the elemental covering of the Earth to what has made this crust solid, it would be natural to feel the deepest reverence and greatest respect for the exalted beings we call the spirits of will, who have labored so long in this earthly element to build the solid ground upon which we walk and that we ourselves bear within us in the earthly constituents of our physical bodies. It is these spirits of will we also call the thrones in Christian esotericism, who have in fact constructed (or rather condensed) the solid ground upon which we walk. The esotericists who named what the spirits of will created within our earthly existence called these spirits *thrones,* because they did indeed build "thrones" that always support us and give us a firm foundation, upon which all other aspects of our earthly existence will continue to be firmly and solidly "enthroned." These old expressions have an essential quality to which our feelings can respond with the greatest respect and admiration.[1]

≈

As I walk in these surroundings, I am reminded constantly of the hierarchy of thrones. Perhaps that is why I am always in a thankful mood when treading on these beautiful rocky and muddy paths. Will, strength, will power, tremendous will power!

Talking about strength, might, thrones, and will, one of the greatest British individuals with these qualities who came to this wild coast to paint was J. M. W. Turner. To the world of watercolor painting, he was one of its fathers. Turner was one of the greatest painters to visit Tintagel and paint this wilderness. He certainly was a monumental human being and at one with elemental forces. Watercolor was first accepted as a medium because of him. Before Turner, it was considered a medium only for amateurs. He

---

1   Steiner, *Genesis*, pp. 79–80 (trans. revised).

changed that. His paintings became more and more simple, and some of his most famous and admired works are his ethereal paintings. I have looked at his paintings in several museums, and I am in awe of his larger-than-life talent. He is one of the first and one of the few who struggled with and painted according to Goethe's color theory. One can see the careful study and great power with which he painted the sea, using the laws of light and darkness—wonderful plays of shadows and light, darkness in front of the light, a dark form in the foreground, refracted light, or an enlightened background reflecting the light. Colors are painted according to the great cosmic laws—something most people never appreciate.

Collot d'Herbois told us that Turner was one of the fathers of our work, and that we should study his paintings and honor what he brought to us. Whenever I have the opportunity, I go to a museum to see his paintings first-hand, even if there is just one. I am always reminded of how powerful a painting can be. He was experiencing what Rudolf Steiner tried to explain in his exercises on color, when he said we should try to lift the color out of the object and live in the color itself. That is what Turner does in his later paintings—he simply bathes himself in the color. However, it was not just any color thrown on the canvas: he had studied Goethe's color theory and thereby experienced the morality, the moral beings behind the colors. He was trying to reach something beyond what his contemporaries had achieved.

> Today, in the fifth post-Atlantean age, painting has assumed a character leading to naturalism. Its prime manifestation is the loss of a deeper understanding for color. The intelligence employed in contemporary painting is a falsified sculptural one. Painters see even human beings this way. The cause is space-perspective, an aspect of painting developed only after the fifth post-Atlantean period. Painters express through lines the fact that something lies in the background, something in the foreground; their purpose being to conjure an impression on canvas of spatially formed objects. However, in doing so, they deny the first and foremost attribute of their special medium. True painters do not create in space, but on the plane, in color, and it is nonsense for them to strive for the spatial.

Please, do not think that I am so extreme that I would object to a feeling for space; in the evolution of humanity, the development of spatial perspective on the plane was necessary; this fact is self-evident. Nevertheless, it must now be overcome. This does not mean that painters in the future should be blind to spatial perspective, only that, while understanding it, they should return to color perspective, employ color perspective.

To accomplish this, we must go beyond theoretic comprehension; the artistic impulse does not spring from theory but requires something more forceful, something elemental....

In nature, we see objects that can be counted, weighed, and measured; in short, objects with which physics is concerned. They appear in various colors. Color, however...is spiritual....

We see both mineral and plant colors properly when they stimulate us to see the gods' primeval activity in nature.

This requires one to live with color artistically, which involves experiencing the plane as such. If someone covers the plane with blue, we should sense a retreat, drawing back; if covered with red or yellow, we should feel an approach, pressing forward. In other words, we acquire color perspective instead of linear perspective, a sense for the plane— the withdrawal and the forward surge of color. In painting, the linear perspective that tries to create an impression of something essentially sculptural upon the plane creates a falsehood. What must be acquired is a sense for the movement of color, *intensive* rather than *extensive*. Thus, true painters who want to depict something aggressive, something eager to jump forward, use yellow-red; something quiet, retreating into the distance, requires blue-violet. Intensive color perspective![2]

This is what Turner achieved through his paintings. We can see how he slowly abandoned the classical painting style of linear perspective to enter the spiritual more and more. Two-dimensional, planar paintings are the real domain of painters. We love his large paintings of color that play with the color perspective; they are fascinating to look at when we think how innovative it was in the 1850s to leave behind the world of oil paint for the more transparent, flowing world of watercolor. It started a great

---

2 Steiner, *The Arts and Their Mission*, Dornach, June 2, 1923, pp. 31–32, 35 (trans. revised).

British watercolorist movement. At the time, the French were creating the Impressionist revolution, which we all love now. They both show human consciousness changing, as demonstrated by Turner, one of the greatest painters of the nineteenth century. For that matter, we could say the same for the world of words. We call them the Romantics. Owen Barfield speaks about this in a masterful way, in his book *Saving the Appearances* and *Owen Barfield: Romanticism Come of Age*. We are still dealing with the same problems with words and color—to enliven the dead words and bring life into colors.

Turner begins by painting what Goethe started, and Steiner's Anthroposophy allowed Liane to develop it much further, both artistically through her paintings and therapeutically through her work with Ita Wegman. With Liane's work, we can once more make a bridge between artistic, religious and scientific work. Through painting in a scientific manner, we can reach and meet the world of the gods, and create a work of art worthy of the whole human being. It used to be all one activity; there was no separation between the artistic and the religious. With this new beginning we can slowly enter this new realm of wholeness. Then what is created is healing. It is both religious, artistic and scientific because it is based again on wholesomeness, on a view of the world that is whole, Anthroposophy.

Turner once asked to be tied to the mast of a boat as he was crossing the English Chanel so he could feel more a part of the elements, feeling the strength of the ocean waves as they crashed over him. He wanted to be part of that ocean, not separated, becoming one with the elemental force of water. He painted out of that elemental strength. When we look at his enormous body of work, we see that he became a force of nature himself.

By choosing birth in such a place on Earth, Liane Collot d'Herbois had this elemental strength from the beginning of her life. As we look at some of her paintings, we see that she went beyond what Turner brought for the first time in his use of color. In her technique, which she developed scientifically, we notice the precise gestures with which she observed natural phenomena.

Here is how Liane talks about beginning a painting: "In the chapters on the separate colors, there are descriptions of painting exercises that one can do." Those are the exercises discussed at the beginning of this book, all of which I reproduced when I first got her book, because I found them so exciting!

The best thing to do is to study with someone who is experienced in this way of painting, but for those who do not have the possibility to take lessons we give here some very vague general rules.

Before you are going to paint, think a light and darkness for yourself. Know where the light is coming from, what is the preponderance of the darkness in relation to light. Is there much light or only very little light. If there is much light, it will be viridian green. A weaker light may be a cobalt blue or even a violet, or on the other hand it might be orange, going into golden hue. All the other colors will then be much darker.

It is always very important that one tries not to be too complicated. A picture must go from the initial simplicity to complication and then end with simplicity again. That is the way in which the plant grows. Nature and art obey the same hidden laws of creation, the laws that also rule the etheric body. So keep your painting simple, it will then have far greater working than when it is complicated.

To begin with one just puts on flat washes of color—a bare statement of the color. The color has not life, yet it is simply beginning to be there. Every color is always accompanied by others. Often one sees on the white paper next to it the so-called complementary color. But one need not paint that in, one can work very well with the colors that are in the color scale on either side of the initial color.

Now one has to give life, feeling to the color. Suppose one's first color was turquoise. Then one paints some indigo and violet near to it. Now the colors awaken each other to life and movement arises—in this case the movement from violet or indigo to turquoise. When one looks at it from a distance one can see between them a beautiful cobalt blue. One did not paint cobalt blue in, but it arises in the interval of the movement from violet or indigo to the turquoise. When color meets color both are given life and new colors arise between them.

No color exists on its own. The only place where a color does exist alone is in the sky: sky blue is the greatest in space and it lasts the longest in time. And even there it is darker in the zenith and lighter on the horizon. It changes hue. It might even go over into ochre on one side and into greenish tint on the other side.

In cobalt blue and indigo the darkness is not moving much, therefore we do not show the movement of the blue with a hard line, but let it merge into its background.

In the first veils of blue that one puts on the paper one can leave little openings of white in the movement of the blue. These will show through the veils that one paints over them later and that will help to make the movement of the color visible. In the blues the light is on the inside of the color

One need not stay with the first lot of colors that one has put on the paper, because colors are always moving. The only thing in a painting that is constant is the light or the direction of the light. When the light is in front of everything one has an entirely blue painting. But as soon as some darkness moves in front of the light the whole atmosphere changes and one has to change one's technique a bit.

The colors in front of the light [the reds] show themselves on their edges, against the light. The greatest concentration of colors is in the center, where the darkness is most concentrated. Toward the outer edge the color becomes lighter, because the mass of darkness is thinner there and the outermost edge can be nearly, or even completely white. That is because the darkness is so thin there that it is completely lit up from behind, like the silver lining one can see around heavy clouds.

One must always keep in mind that the world of color is an endless space and that there are great distances between the colors. One can have vermilion, orange and yellow in a picture—that is then one great, moving mass of darkness in front of the light, but the place where the orange comes into being is so to speak two miles further away from us than the vermilion and the yellow is again further away. And that these distances are there is shown by the lighter patches of color, where the heaving crests of darkness catch and hold the light for a moment before they move on and metamorphose into another shade of color.

The colors have to change in order to show the movements. When one just makes one color darker and darker one paints a pattern, not a movement. To give an example: a brilliant yellow can go over into a raw umber, then change into magenta and from there to ultramarine. The radiance comes out when one puts the darkness in. And one has then made a movement from in front of the light to behind the light.

In any exercise either the part in front of the light or the part behind the light is active, shows movement. One cannot have activity in both parts, because that makes the picture feverish and disharmonious. There should always be a place where the eye can rest.

Two things one should always avoid: horizontal layers of color and symmetry. They stop the movement and make a picture dead, uninteresting. One must always be able to see that a movement comes from somewhere and that it goes in a certain direction. And it helps to bring out the movement when one has the contrast of a light foreground against a darker background in one part of the picture and dark foreground against a lighter background in another part. That will help one to stay away from symmetry....

When one sees color and the variations in color one's soul makes the same movements that the colors make. Because what is paint on paper in the physical world, is in the world of the soul living beings, moving and interacting in an infinite space.[3]

Reading these directions, one can appreciate the scientist in Liane, and looking at Turner's paintings one sees exactly what Liane is talking about, except that she went further in developing the exact movement of each color. That is where she says, "Darling, you must paint as you do mathematics."

Newton's theory is demolished by the laws of light and darkness and color, which are based on life rather than the abstract deliberations of a dry intellectual dualistic scientist. In this type of painting, you gather that one has to change dramatically and actually enter a different realm, the realm of the etheric forces that Rudolf Steiner discusses. When one enters that world, then one is in the same realm as life, and thereby the elemental forces that accompany that realm. It is life, life giving, and of course healing.

As one followed Liane's directions, one was constantly moving from this color to that color, and one's soul was making the movement constantly.

---

3   Collot d'Herbois, *Light, Darkness, and Colour...*, pp. 48–51.

Nothing was ever stagnant, but always wonderful movement from here to there. This is the healing aspect of color therapy, learning how to move a patient's soul from where he or she might be stuck and unmoved to more movement and thereby changes, changes in which the person becomes more alive in the soul, and that affects life directly. That is the medical aspect of this work. But we must not forget, Liane always emphasized that one can heal through the soul feelings (regular color painting, the Hauschka method, and the like), but one can heal through willing and thinking (light and darkness, with charcoal) much more powerfully.

In 1946, Liane met Francine Van Davelaar.

When I first met Francine, I did not like her.... Someone took me to visit her in The Hague. She was in a room with a big window and a fireplace. She asked me, "Why have you come, really?" I said, "I was interested to see you and what you do." It was a very cold reception. I was snippy; she was snippy. I was glad to leave because I did not like her at all. I thought, *That was it, then. I do not see anything marvelous about her....* Afterward, someone brought her to me. It was my turn to play the game in which the normal way to receive people was to ask why they had come and what did they want (which she did to me when I visited her; cold indeed). We were so polite and so very cold to each other! And I was glad when she left.

Then I met her at a dinner that somebody gave. Francine was so nice and so funny that I thought, *She is not bad at all once you come to know her.* She was more or less the soul of the party. She laughed and made other people laugh....

Actually, I did not write the book *Colour* myself. Francine was always taking notes during my lectures to the Magenta Painters group, and she wrote and rewrote them. Then she made me correct what she had written. I sat in my studio, and Francine sat at her desk in the next room. Whenever I had tried to write something, I would cast it over to her. Then she would correct it: "No, this is no good," and send it back, and I would scribble something else.

Francine did not want her name in the book, did not think it necessary. As a group Magenta was in no way involved in the writing at all....

The years I spent with Francine were a very nice time. Life was easy; I could work a lot. Since she died in 1983, things have been different, more difficult.[4]

Francine van Davelaar was a great artist herself, and she gave up her own work as a glass engraver and painter to dedicate herself to Liane and help bring down to Earth this important impulse. Without her, we would not have Liane's two books, and that was a great sacrifice. She was the one who took it upon herself to do the difficult job of protecting Liane from troublesome people so that she could work in peace, or nursing others when they were offended by Liane Collot d'Herbois's very direct ways, or when the students had problems when entering into the process of light and dark and needed a warm understanding heart to soothe them. When people start doing this powerful work, they shed tears and Liane did not deal with that, but left it all to Francine. Francine died early and we must be forever thankful for the silent one who stood behind Liane Collot d'Herbois from 1946 to 1983. When she died Liane painted a whole series on roses, beautifully painted roses of pink and yellow. When I visited Liane in Holland, I had the opportunity to look at some of Francine's own beautiful work.

Students need a warm, knowledgeable guide when they enter the world of self-knowledge, which is the path expressed in *Light, Darkness and Colour in Painting Therapy:* Liane showed this path, and her dutiful helper Francine was there with a helping hand when the going became thorny, as students dive into and face their own darkness with great courage.

Self-knowledge would be much more common if people were not so timid and so afraid of getting to know themselves. But the awareness of what rules in the depths is already suppressed in the unconscious levels of the soul because people have such unconscious fear and inhibition and anxiety about confronting themselves in all their manifoldness and complexity. And when it does surge up, what comes glowing and gleaming from out of the depths really does make a sphinx-like impression. The experiences of others who have really felt such things in their own soul can be deeply moving.

---

4   From the author's notes on conversations with Liane Collot d'Herbois.

The following literary passage expresses beautifully how the human depths can appear to us from the surging dreams of our soul life. We must imagine someone who has laid down to rest after the toils and the burdens of the day.... Here is how a Polish poet Jan Kasprowicz once described it:

> And in the secret magic of the night,
> There, before my palace,
> My dreams took hold of the ghostly mists and built
> Unimaginable blossoms with dead eyes
> That formed a balefully grinning Medusa
> In the moonlight drenched with dew,
> And she waxed monstrous.
> As the moon streamed into my chamber
> And lay across the bed of my exhaustion,
> I was roused from sleep by lecherous,
> Monstrous desires
> That shuddered on my stammering lips
> And sent hot fires of fever streaming from my eyes
> Toward creatures that were yours!
> Mea culpa, mea maxima culpa!
> My guilt, my most great guilt![5]

With the world of color we can learn about ourselves. It allows us to dive into the depths and reach the heights in a safe loving way. The beings behind the colors teach it to us. When we try to paint the colors in their true movement, in their transparent beauty and clarity, they bring us much healing power. When the therapist is faced with a muddled mass of disturbing colors on the paper coming through the paintbrush of a patient, the work begins. Bring order, clean up the mess, enlist the help of the masters—the beings of color who so readily give us a hand.

Steiner repeatedly mentions the fact that we need to enter the elemental world, think with our heart, and become more alive in our thinking. What does this actually mean? It means very simply what it says, that we become more energetic and elemental ourselves if we have not lost the meaning of

---

5   Steiner, *The Riddle of Humanity*, pp. 68–69.

what stands behind the word. Steiner is asking us to partake in the Elements, forces of nature, air, wind, fire, and earth, and then we literally become like the wind, the air, fire and earth. It means: we think, become enthusiastic in our feelings, and then we act. Now we act without thinking, or we feel our way through things with no thinking. When we achieve the balance and harmony between the three, it is the coming into being of the philosopher's stone, the diamond of the Heart where thinking becomes willing, and willing thinking. This is a powerful combination that we will need in order to face the challenges the future will bring.

If all the words stay in our head and do not become part of our bodies, then what is the use? The words must become part of ourselves and we join the elemental beings, because when we live with the words of Rudolf Steiner we have life. If our life does not reflect that, then we are not doing what Steiner worked so hard to teach: become more alive and act. Stop the endless chatter about "What can we do?" that we hear so often. Act! Do! Liane never asked herself what she could do. She acted!

As we share in the world of the Color Beings, they give us their strength. I remember one summer when I was painting a very large work. I had given up the small format as I felt I needed bigger, larger surfaces. I was using the warm colors and working with one of Liane's own paintings as an inspiration. It was full of vermilion, and red colors with some viridian, but for the most part I was living in these red colors all day and all night for days. Then I began to ask myself, "What am I doing living in these more than powerful colors, beings?" I slept less, and was so full of energy that I was working in the garden for hours, painting for hours, reading and studying up at night for hours. Then I realized that I had been working all day with mighty beings. I knew because it is the nature of this work, but I became even more aware of the enormous powers in the Color Beings when working with these reds. Steiner mentions that we have to become aware when we are touched by higher beings.

We start with a blank page, decide on some colors, or as Liane stated, we decide where the light is coming from, far away or close by, and this will determine the painting. No subjects are mentioned; the subject comes into being like a plant. We the painters provide the opportunity for something new to arise out of the determining factors. Where is the light? Far or close? Are we choosing to be in front of the light, the reds, or are we choosing to be behind the light, with the light behind us, the blues. This and only this will determine what incarnates in the picture. We can always change our minds, and change all the colors. We can begin with reds and end up with blue if we wish. This might not be obvious to non-painters. Here is Liane's explanation as she talks about the light, about thinking and about the interval.

> In our head, with the activity of thinking is a self-contained world, absolute, making the Ego ["I"] itself both subjective and objective, and giving the possibility of rising above concept and percept. Thinking views the past with certainty, but when it observes an immediate experience, destroys it, letting it flow over into the past. From this most conscious element of man radiate the forces of antipathy: analyzing, carrying death, forming and finishing. The concepts are molded into ideas, the pictures arising are finished; to paint an already finished picture, that is in one's head in this way, was done until roughly the end of the last century. One began a picture with an already completed concept, a form was "thought out" and the form was then colored.
>
> This was done at a time when the accepted path to the worlds of spirit was through feeling, as expressed in the mystics and in the monastic orders of the medieval centuries. Then paintings were permeated with intense subjective feeling, expressed in the world of form, with color, then applied.
>
> Today the process is reversed, through the step that is taking place—and has already taken place—in our inner theatre. This same path can be pursued in the full light of our consciousness based on our *thinking*, whereby through recognition of the laws of light, darkness, and color, these laws lend themselves as instruments to the hands of the human being to be used again through him, in the process of creation.
>
> With this knowledge arises the longing to paint not the finished pictures from the formed concepts, carried from the head into the hand, but to take part in the creative element of color by using instead the laws of light, color and darkness.

We can put it thus: until the twentieth century, out of dreaming feeling, through the head forces, to form—and out of the form, to color. At the present time: out of conscious thinking through and out of color, to form.

Therefore today painting can take part in a process of becoming (*Entstehen*) through the building up, veil by veil, in accordance with the all-pervading enlightening laws of light and the impulse of darkness: a spiritual experience, and of moving color: a soul experience.

One observes a cosmic threefoldness, with color revealing itself in the sense-world as a moving interval between the unseen creative activities of light and darkness....

A process that can be likened to the growth of a plant born out of ponderable darkness and dying into the imponderable light....

This method of painting with color veils takes patience for reflection, patience in doing; then at the end of the last hour, content can appear, arising out of a mood of color, now created.

The same laws appear in the inner life of feeling—a dreaming rainbow-world existing in the immediate present, a subjective sphere incapable of being shared with conscious certainty by another "I"-being, moving between sympathy and antipathy, moving in rhythm between air and liquid, a balancing interval.

"We taste the colors and smell the intervals," Rudolf Steiner said. Without the intervals there would be death: no room or space between note and note, between pillar and pillar, between star and star. An interval is "that which breathes between": for instance between emerald green and fire-red springs a new fragrant color; between green and purple again there is a new interval of color. Only in watercolor, slow transparent veil by slow translucent veil, can intervals organically emerge as entities, not projected by thinking, not subservient to the head (as in the case of most other mediums).

This is also the reason for painting in watercolor with veils, wherein the most evanescent moods can be portrayed. This was used to a great degree by people living amidst the play of water and air continually intermingled, mood chasing mood, shadow chasing light, light permeating air, air penetrating air, air penetrating spray, spray flashing with evanescent color in the foam of waves.

On the Western coasts of the British Isles out of the weaving of the elements came this technique—and there the technique of veiling had been used long before, for instance by Turner and Cotman, but applied to form.

Stress is placed on what one can call "quality," which is achieved through perfect technique of stroke under stroke for one veil of color so that the liquid above runs down over what is below, never touching till it is dry, repeating with different colors, sixty or more times; a brown has more "quality" when composed of a layer of green, of red, of violet than ever just: brown. This technique takes practice.

It becomes no longer merely a question of naturalism or abstraction, which is after all an end product, but a question of living in one or more moods of color and an immersion in the essential nature of color itself. This is not only a subjective experience for one has the possibility of going beyond subjectivity by using these laws of light, color, and darkness, into a world of greater objective significance.[6]

The magic word, *interval,* is the space between—between objects, the empty space that Liane had asked me to look at and focus on. This is where the meeting takes place. It is not a world that can be measured, weighed, or counted; it can only be felt, like the silence in between words among good friends, or the meaning in the silence. Here we create these new spaces between colors, they come into being and beings come. That is the realm Turner touched upon when he painted his large seascapes with reflections and darkness in front of the light. He was trying to reach the realm of intervals, but it was too early to enter that realm. We can see with what monumental strength he tried to assail the heavens. That is what we love about his paintings. They are larger than life, reaching something far out. I think that if he could have, he would have created paintings that were 100 feet tall!

What he was after, Collot d'Herbois practiced, and she led the way to a new art of painting: The emergence of the intervals in painting.

---

6   Collot d'Herbois, *Colour,* pp. 16–18.

Entering the Land of Red

I have mentioned the Thrones, the beautiful stones, the elemental strength of Turner, the will. The will is the realm of the red colors, so now I will enter the world of the beautiful icon, to which I have always been attracted. And as you will see, it involves the reds and Russia.

Before coming to England, a few weeks ago I traveled to Russia to see the icons in their original settings and experience their power. I went to St. Petersburg and proceeded to see as many icons as I could. Then I went on to Moscow and did the same. My other reason was to see where Soloviev had lived, because he is one of my favorite writers and I wanted to pay homage to two sacred sites.

In one town to the north of Moscow is Sergei Posad Monastery, the theological-orthodox center of Russia, a large complex with a school in icon paintings. The other place, in the Southern part, five and a half hours by bus from Moscow, is called Optina Pystin Monastery. It was a center also for the mystical path of stillness and repose, called *Hesychasm* (for silence and the endless repetition of a prayer, see my book *Deliverance of the Spellbound God*).

Thousands of Russian pilgrims visit both of these places every year. The icon is at the center of these monasteries and at the center of much more than I thought before traveling there.

In Russia we enter the realm of red. (They did not name it the Red Army for nothing, but we will only deal with its positive aspects and forget the army for now.) When one looks at icons, one sees that the color red, along with gold, is in the background of most of these sacred paintings on wood. The oldest icons are the ones that interested me.

The first thing one notices about icon paintings is that they are painted without spatial perspective. That says something right away about what we have already discussed. The Russian soul had not entered into the life of the three dimensions, which is the realm of space here on Earth, while the rest of the Western world had. The paintings are flat and two-dimensional. This, we said, is the domain of the painter, not the sculptural element of three dimensions. So the icon still lives in the real world of color. The viewer of the icon is not thrown into Earth space, but still lives in the realm of the soul-spirit.

The following is by St. John of Damascus, who lived in his monastery of St. Abbas in Palestine around the seventh century amidst raging persecution, while writing, and defending the right to use images, or paintings.

> What more conspicuous proof do we need that images are the books of the illiterate, the never silent heralds of the honor due the saints, teaching without use of words those who gaze upon them, and sanctifying the sense of sight? Suppose I have few books, or little leisure for reading, but walk into the spiritual hospital—that is to say, a church—with my soul choking from the prickles of thorny thoughts, and thus afflicted I see before me the brilliance of the icon. I am refreshed as if in a verdant meadow, and thus my soul is led to glorify God. I marvel at the martyr's endurance, at the crown he won, and inflamed with burning zeal I fall down to worship God through His martyr, and so receive salvation. Have you not heard the same of the Holy Father, at the beginning of his sermon on the Psalms, when he says that "the Holy Spirit, knowing that the race of men is lazy regarding righteousness and stubborn to follow leadership, set the psalms to tuneful music." What do you say to this? Shall I not bear witness to the martyr both by word and paintbrush? Shall I not embrace with my eyes that which is a wonder to the angels and to all creation; painful to the devil and the terror of demons.[1]

This fervor to worship the sacred image, the icon, is what lives in Russia, and it is very much alive in its tradition. St. Petersburg is a gigantic city of awesome proportion, with very large avenues and immense buildings. Russia is colossal; there is greatness there. Even the subway is a work of art, large and special. Russians are truly living in an element that is larger than

1   St. John of Damascus, *Three Treatises on the Divine Images*, p. 39.

life. I am reminded of these words from Steiner, which did not make much sense when I first read them, but they do now.

What once lived in the East, what once vibrated through Eastern souls, survives in its final results where it is no longer understood, where it has turned into a superstitious ritual.... A direct line runs from ancient India to these formulas of the Russian church ritual, which are now only rattled off to the multitudes in the form of lip service. For this whole inclination that thus expressed itself, which bestowed on the Eastern soul its imprint and also does so today in a suppressed form, is the potential for developing a spiritual state of mind that guides the human being toward the prenatal, to what exists in our life before birth, before conception. In the very beginning, the nature of what permeated the East as a world conception and religious attitude was connected with the fact that this East possessed a concept that has been completely lost to the West.... The West has the concept of immortality, not that of "having never been born," or "Unbornness."... This implies that in our thinking we continue life after death, but not into the time before birth. On the other hand, the East possessed that special soul inclination it had that still included Imagination and Inspiration in its thoughts and concepts. By means of this particular manner of expressing the conceptual content of its soul world, the East was far less predisposed to pay heed to the life after death than to that before birth....

This life, this mood of soul, is particularly fitted to turn the human soul's gaze to the spiritual, to fill humanity with the suprasensory world....

What has this remarkable development in the East led to? It has led the people of the East to employ the holy inner zeal they once utilized to foster the impulse for the suprasensory world and to apprehend the spiritual in all its purity, to accept the most materialistic view of outer life with religious fervor. Even though Bolshevism is the most extreme consequence of the most materialistic view of the world and social life, it will, as it moves further into Asia, increasingly transform itself into something that is received there with the same religious zeal as was the spiritual world in former times. In the East, people will speak of the economic life in the same terminology once used to speak of the sacred

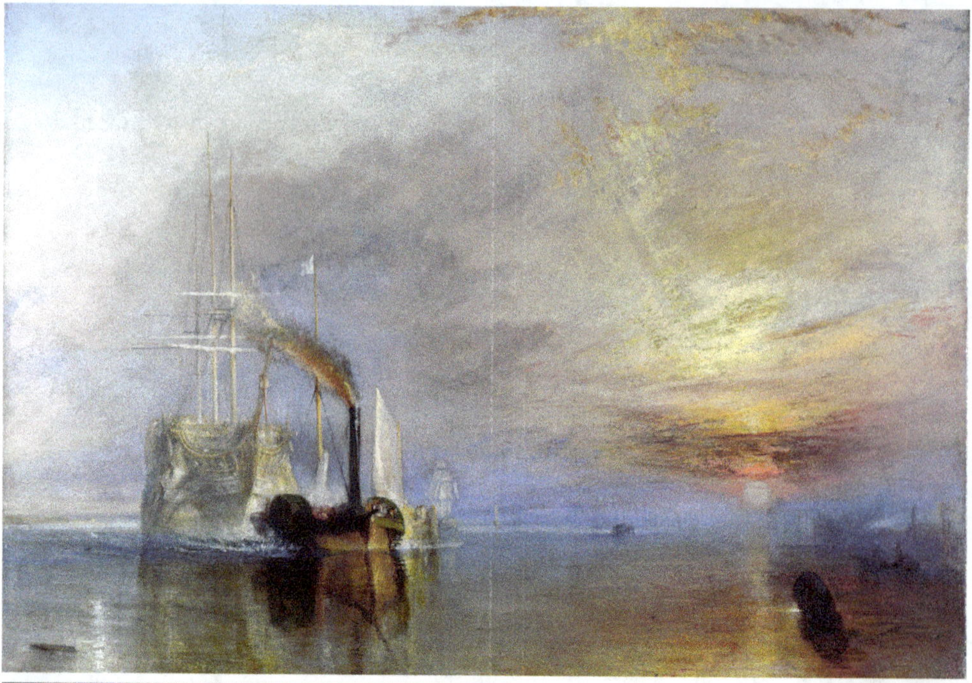

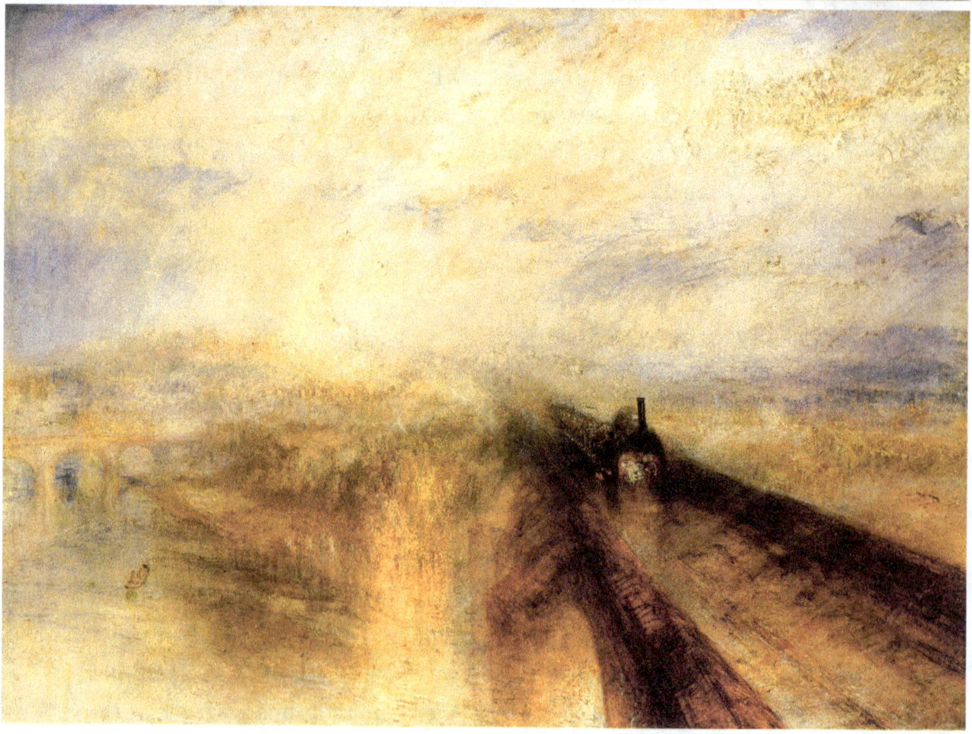

William Turner was the first major painter to use Goethe's work on color;
top: The Fighting Temeraire Tugged to Her Last Berth to Be Broken Up (1839);
bottom: Rain, Steam, and Speed—The Great Western Railway (1844)

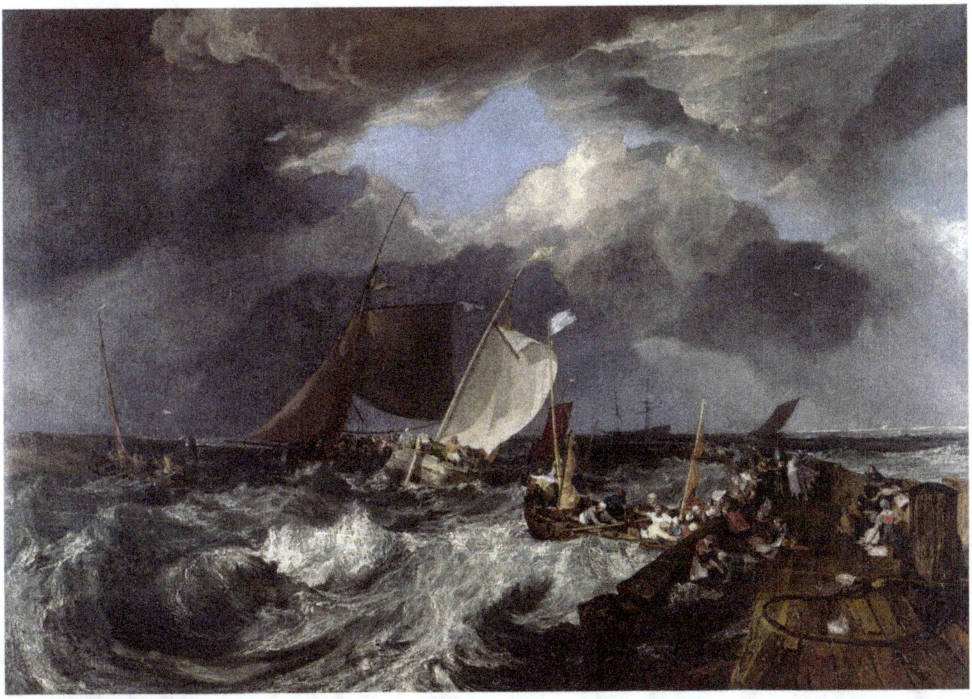

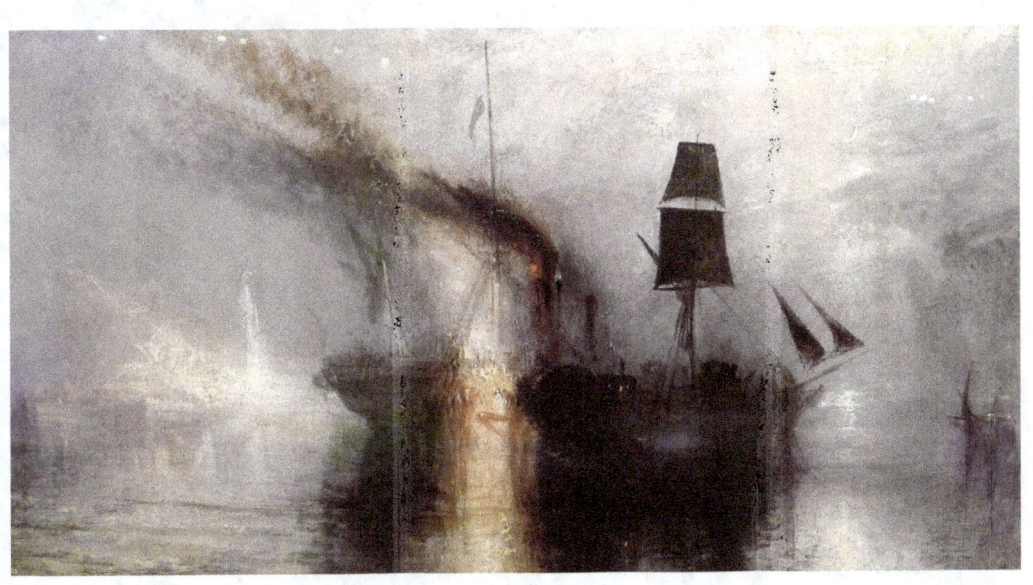

*William Turner: top: Calais Pier (1803);
bottom: Peace—Burial at Sea (1842)*

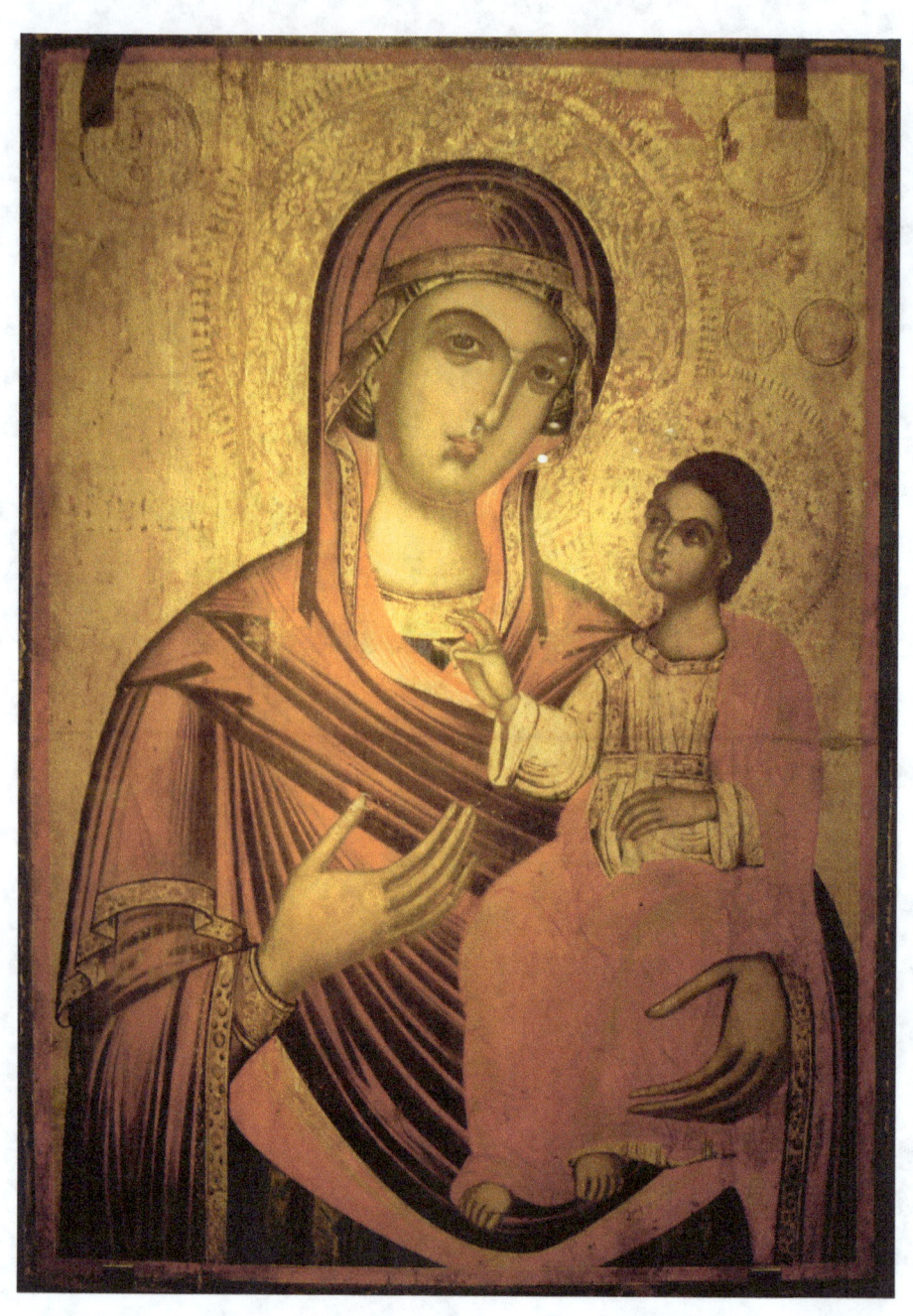

Red and Gold are the important colors in Russian icons.

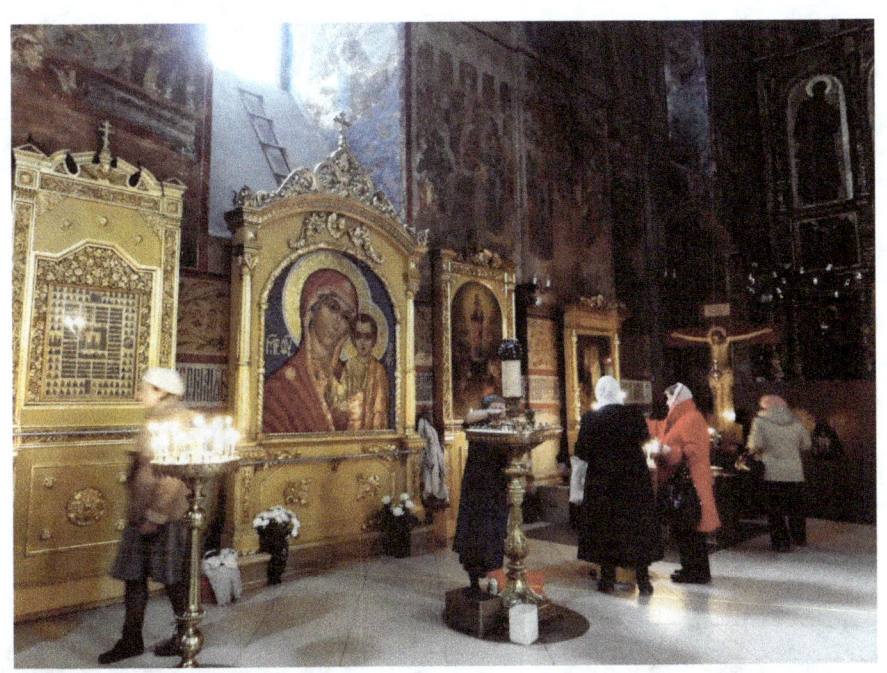

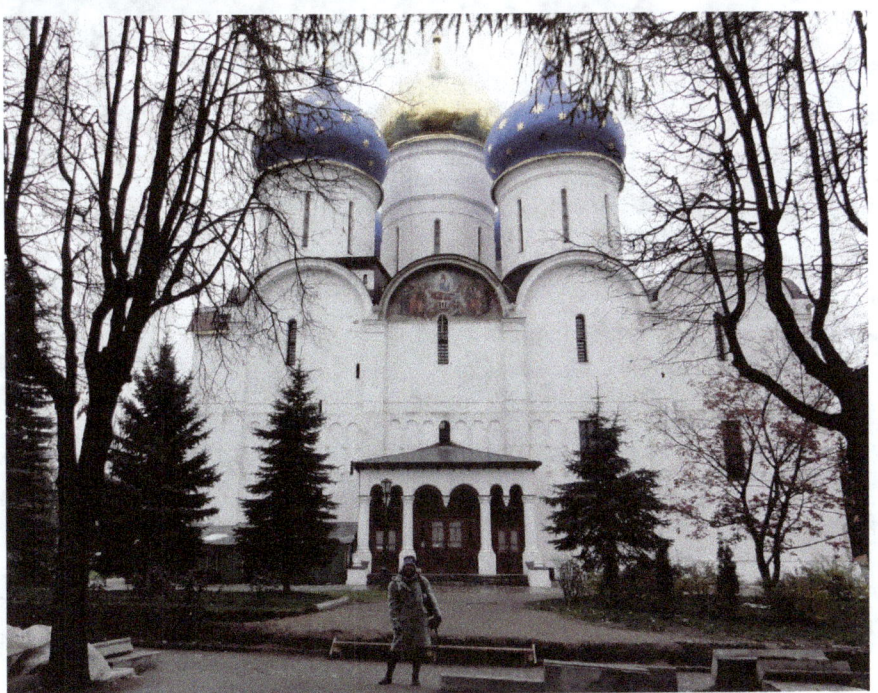

Trinity Monastery of St. Sergii in Sergiev Posad.

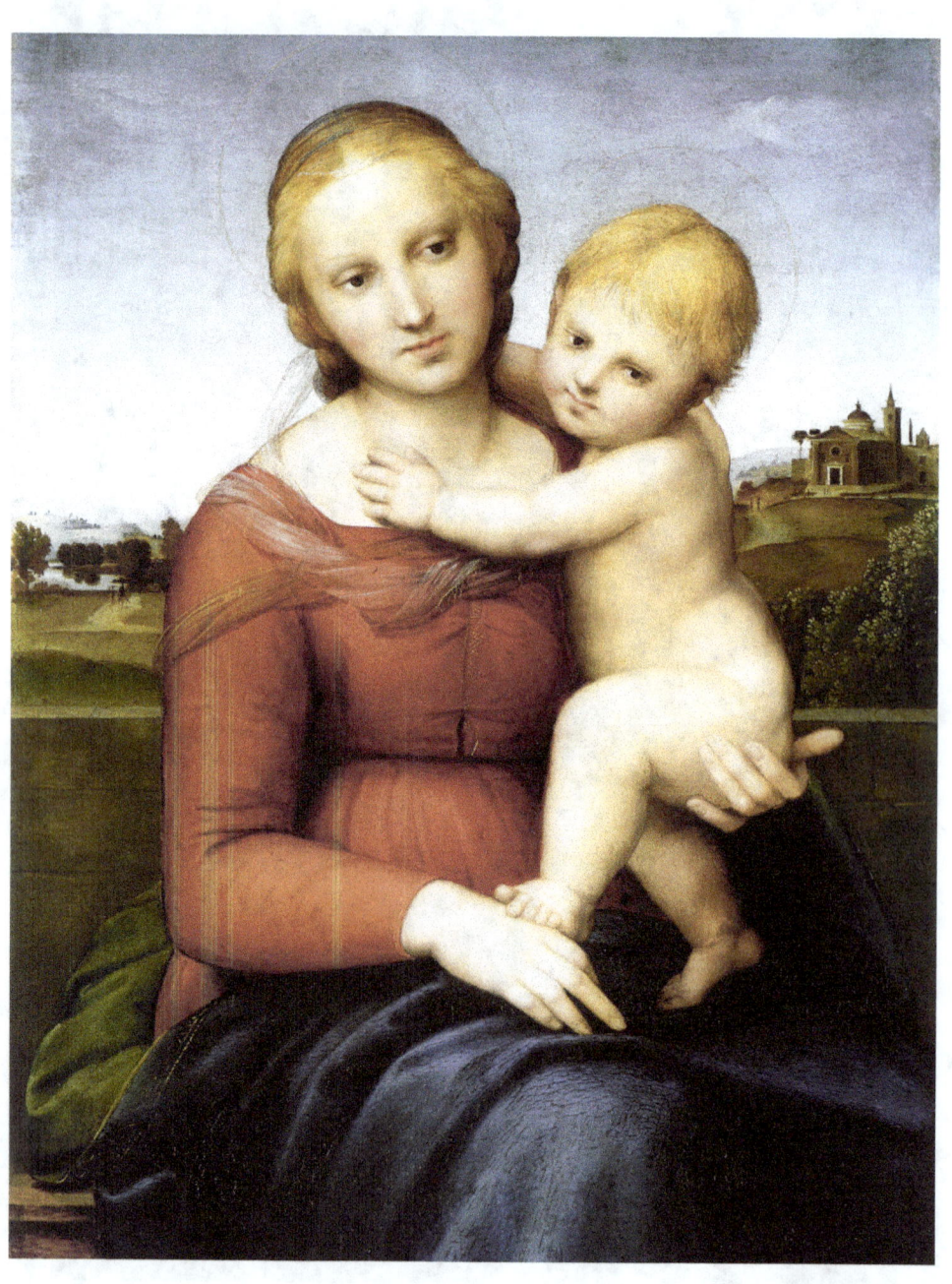

Magenta: newborn, Unbornness, dissolving.

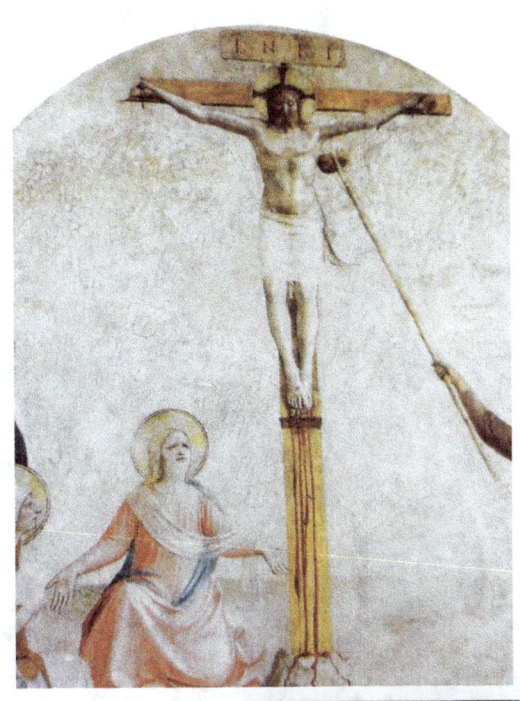

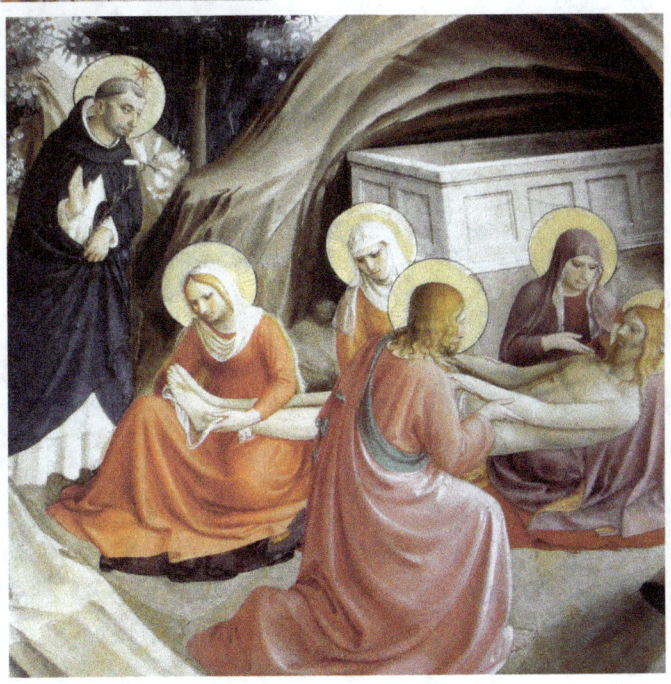

Vermilion: Mary Magdalene; transformation, crucible.

147

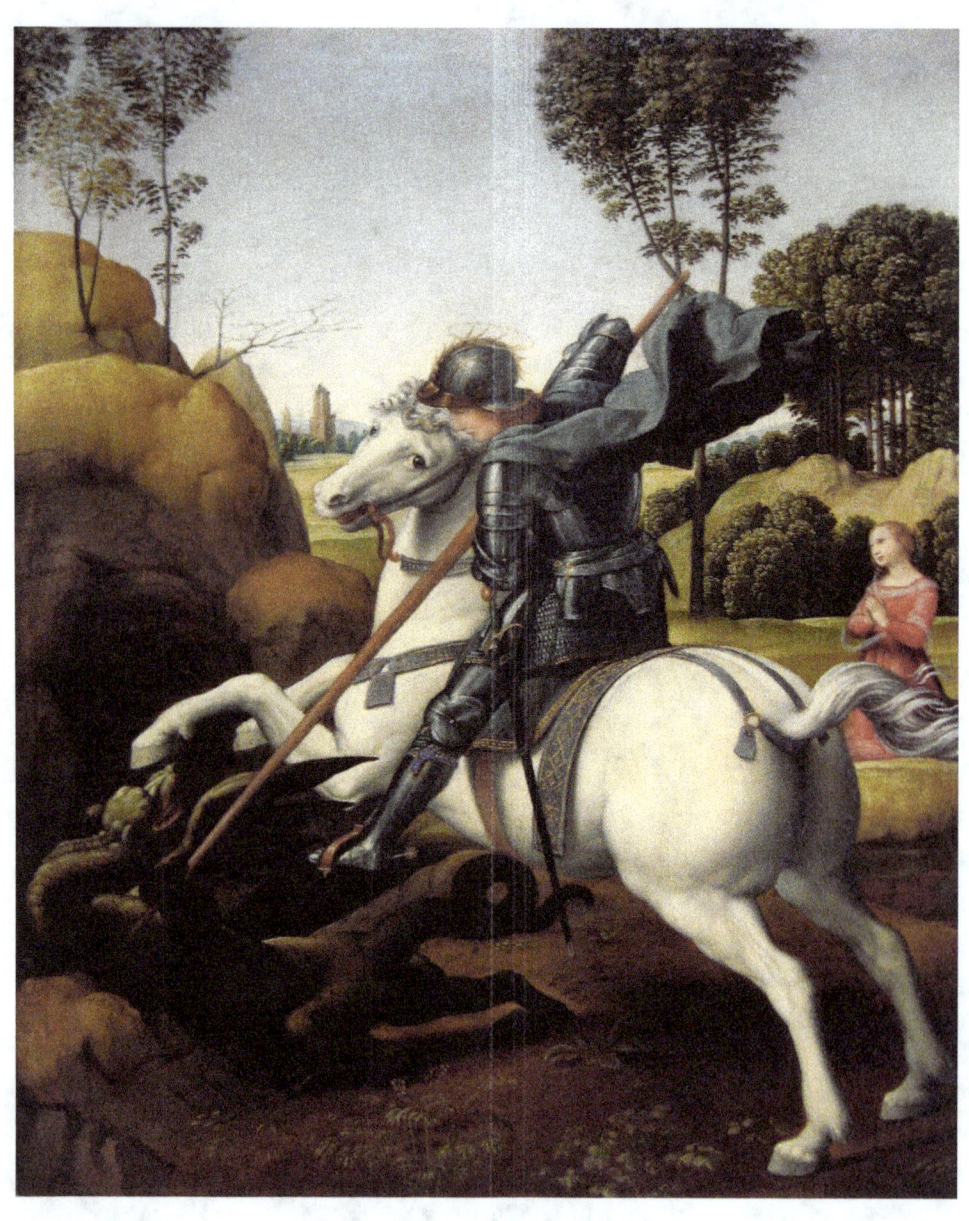

Yellow-orange: Raphael: Saint Goerge and the Dragon (1504–1506)

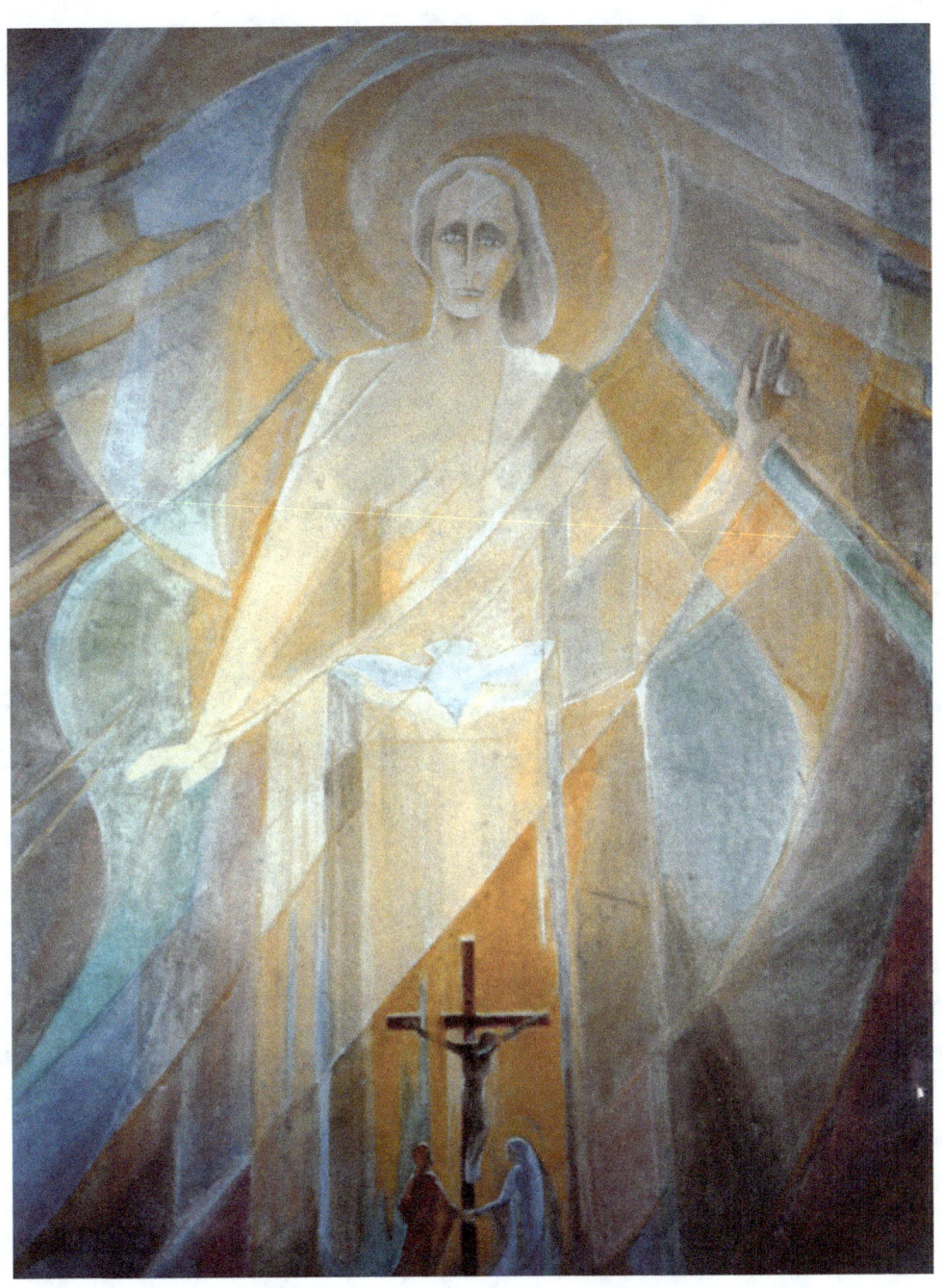

Green: Most healing color, often used to paint the Christ; color of the precious stone chrysoprase;
Easter, mural by Liane Collot d'Herbois for the Ita Wegman Chapel, Brissago, Switzerland
(see page 255 for the artist's comments on making this fresco)

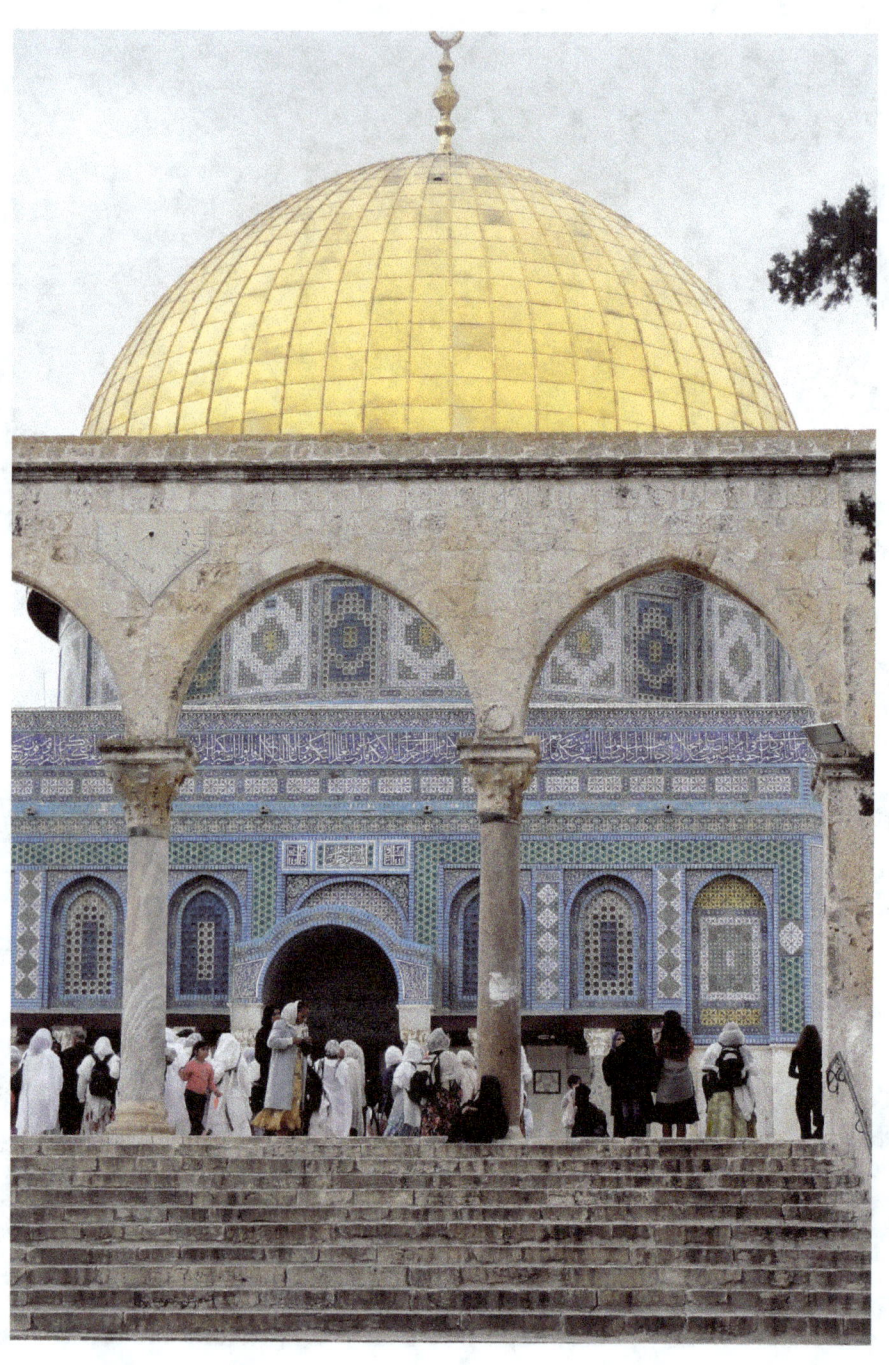

Turquoise: Al-Aqsa Mosque, Old Jerusalem; clarity, finished forms, severity.

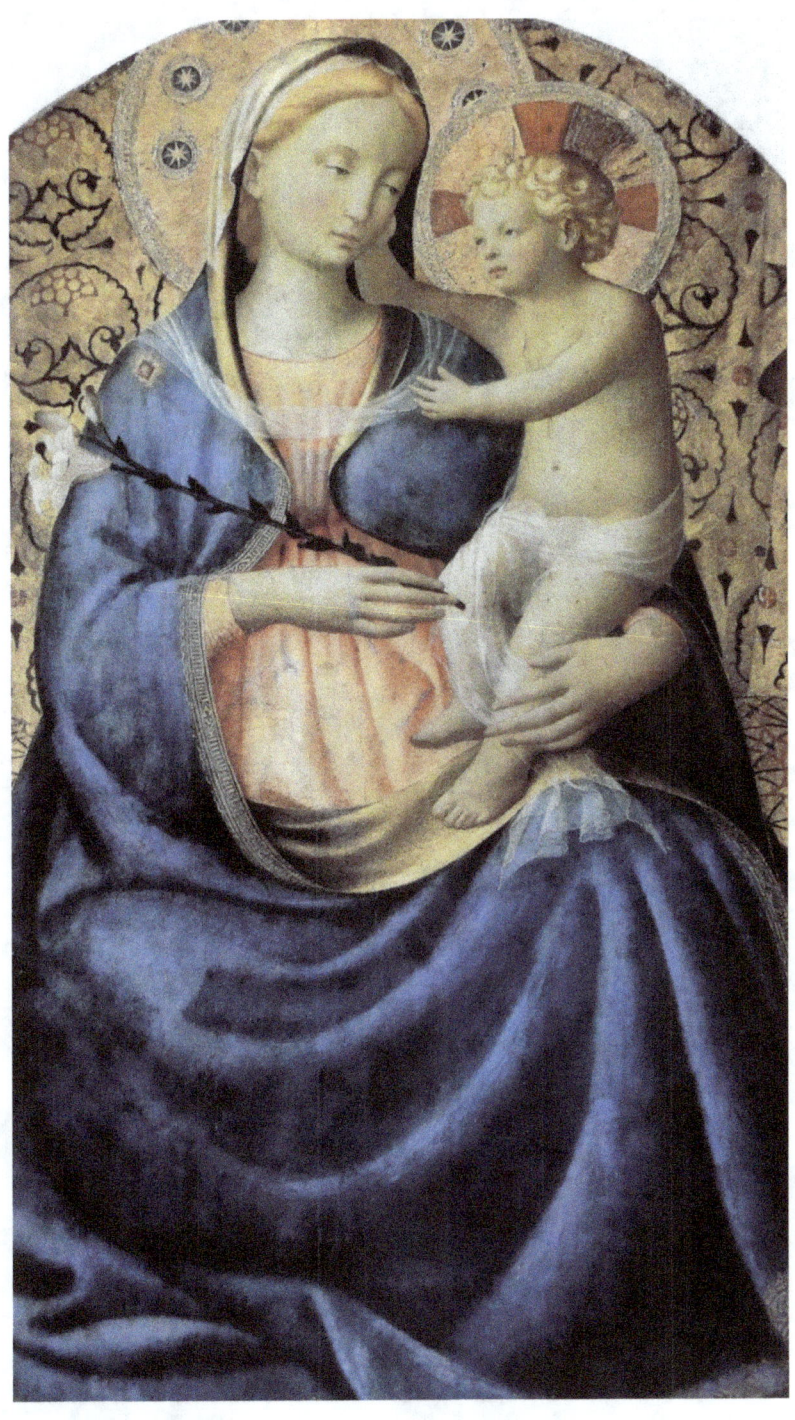

Cobalt blue: Madonna; boundaries, warmth, birth of space, inner and outer.

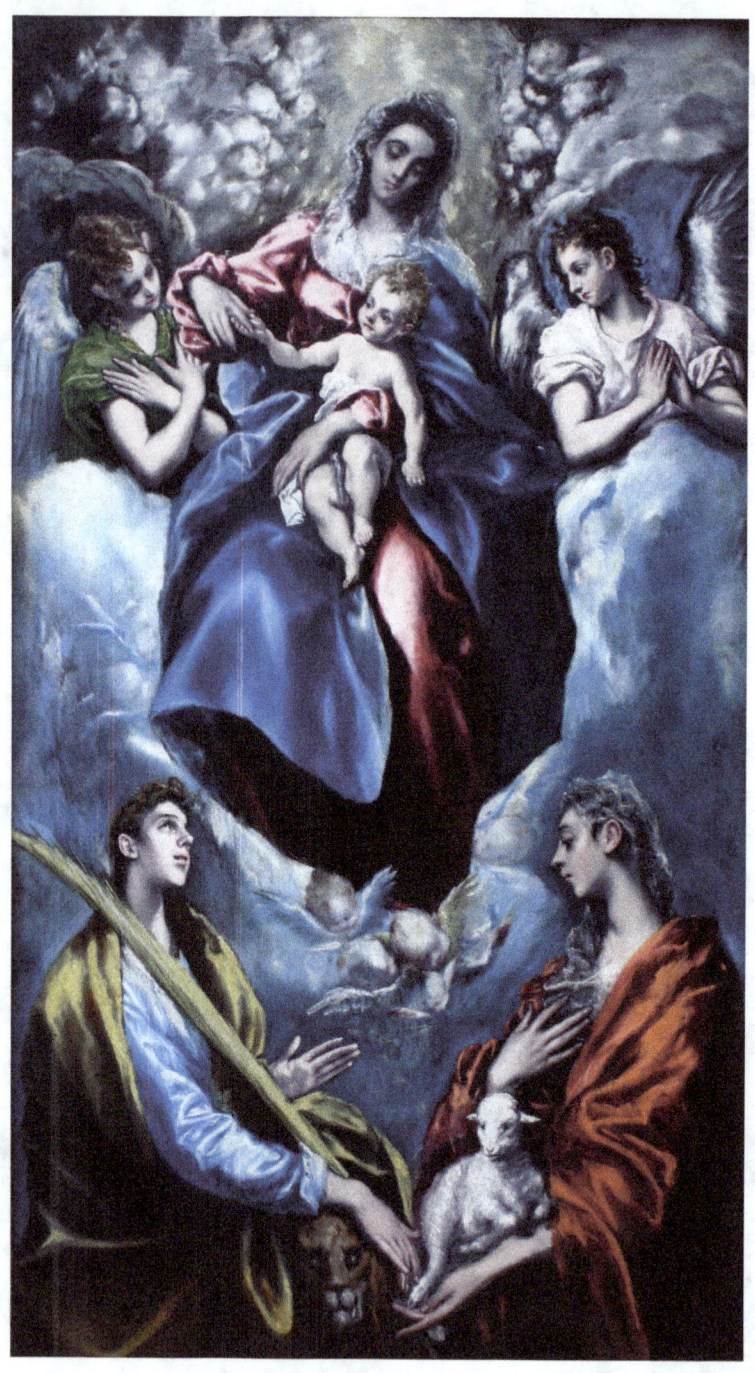

Indigo: El Greco's use of indigo: Virgin and Child with St. Martina and St. Agnes *(1597–1599); boundaries, warmth, birth of space, inner and outer.*

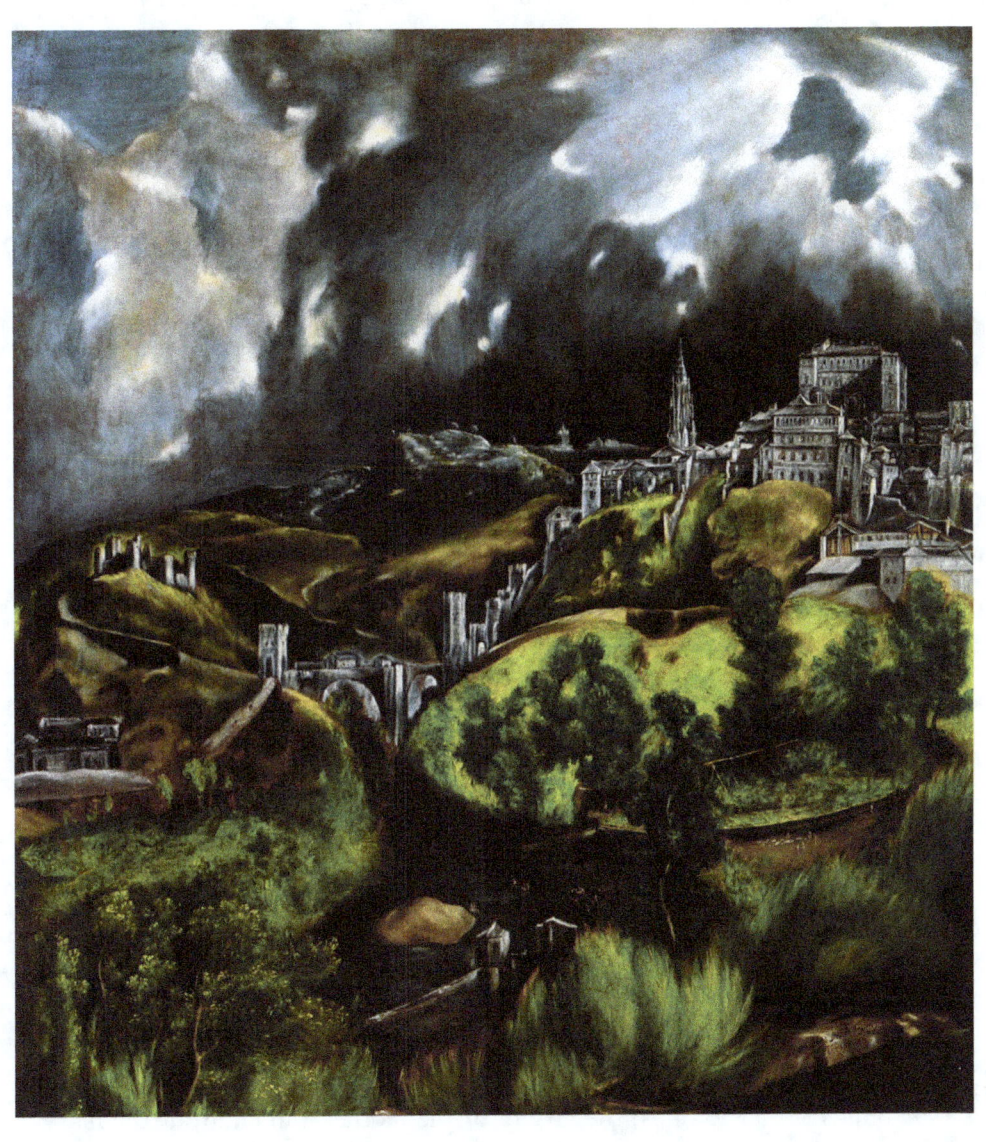

Indigo: the color of the consciousness soul, suffering, and entering darkness; intense warmth,
mother of pearl, and the quality of sacrifice;
El Greco: **View of Toledo** *(1596–1600).*

Brahma. The fundamental disposition of the soul does not change; it endures, for it is not the content (of the soul) that matters here. The most materialistic views can be approached with the same fervor formerly used to grasp the most spiritual.[2]

And what does this have to do with the color red, with icons, and with the feeling that I had when I first walked in the streets of St. Petersburg and in its churches? The Russians were forced for many years to tackle their economy with "religious fervor," and hence the immense programs, cement factories, armies, and so forth. This is reflected in Soviet literature and Soviet art that I had a chance to see in museums dedicated to Soviet paintings. Everything there seems immense and this religious fervor, taken in the materialistic sense, is reflected in this largeness and colossal greatness. Now this material element has finally cooled, and I could see, feel, and watch the religious fervor coming back as I entered many churches and saw Russians of both sexes and all ages coming to worship. Russia is back on track after this terrible diversion.

As I traveled around, what the Russians suffered and went through as a nation was never far from my mind. That degree of suffering is really not conceivable in the West. I feel that it could not have been endured if the people had been more awake. This suffering in turn has incarnated the Russian soul, but what a way to incarnate!

Now Russian souls gaze at their favorite icons, still painted two-dimensionally, although the new ones have a trace of the three-dimensional in them and access to the spiritual realm and its healing power. For the most part, the icon still retains its real function as a window to another world.

The color that one notices right away is the vibrant red. The red that surrounds the Theotokos, the virgin, or the mother and child, or the martyrs envelops the soul of the viewer with its warmth. One sees this warm red everywhere in large frescos or very large wooden icons, triptychs, panels, and walls.

---

2 Steiner, *Spiritual Science as a Foundation for Social Forms*, pp. 110–112 (trans. revised).

In color perspective, the carmine color that surrounds the Russian icons is a gentleness that comes from magenta. Magenta is the color of birth, of coming into the world from the spiritual world. After magenta we move slowly into carmine, the beautiful color of the rose.

Let us take again the journey into colors as we did at the beginning, just to remind ourselves of the space we are entering.

Imagine that you are floating in an endless space. All around you is a nebulous atmosphere that is dark and warm. At first you don't see anything but darkness, but you feel that you are being carried by this warmth that is there and that it carries you along with it in very slow movements.

After a while you begin to realize that you must be moving toward light, because in front of you and all around you the darkness dimly begins to glow with a beautiful purple, the color we call magenta. The magenta envelops you and still you feel that you are being carried, but now by this color and by its warmth. Gently it moves you on and the darkness gradually becomes a little lighter. The magenta seems to glide away to the sides and in front of you the color changes to a deep carmine. You are beginning to vaguely discern the movements that the dark atmosphere makes, pulsating, rolling, coming together and dispersing again, but all still hardly perceptible. The movements carry you with them. They become quicker and stronger and you find yourself traveling through a world of vermilion. To your left and to your right the atmosphere is a little denser and there the carmine still lingers. The movements gain more speed, taking a more upward course and now you come to a world of orange, the vermilion receding on either side of you. In front of you the orange suddenly opens itself, moving aside, and you feel that you are being pulled toward the yellow that you see there radiating in front of you. Here the movements are almost linear, pulling you along forward and upward to the point where they are split up by the light into small fluttering patches of yellow-green that accompany you till you stand in front of the splendor of the light itself. You feel drawn toward it, toward that pure unveiled light that has the color of a clear emerald. It takes you into itself and you can look through it, gazing out into ever deepening depths of blue. You step out of the light, leaving it behind you and you find yourself in the geometrical movements of the turquoise. On either side they soften to a cobalt blue. Here the atmosphere is no longer warm and nebulous, it is clear, crisp, crystalline. As long as you had the light in front of you the darkness carried you toward the light, with movements that were gradually ascending. Now, with the light behind you, you are being borne away from it by retreating movements that go gently downward. Here the darkness allows itself to be pushed away by the light. You come to the cobalt blue that envelops you, carrying you down to the uncertain movements of the indigo. The light grows weaker, reflecting softly on the hesitant movement of the darkness. Then you come to the mysterious violet, where the movements are still slower and almost horizontal. You realize that if you would still go further you would come to a great boundary where the light finally dies out.[3]

When we talk about magenta we talk about the Old India Epoch that is mentioned in the Rudolf Steiner quote above, the old Indian epoch still surviving in a few of the old church rituals.

At the first dawning of human consciousness the first color to be observed outwardly was a kind of bluish red...magenta. This dawning consciousness was a dream consciousness....

Magenta is a color that is very close to the world of the etheric, to the world of the soul, so close that one might call it a reflection of the second-dimensional....

It comes from behind you. From the realm of sleep, from the regions before birth it sweeps into the world of day-consciousness. Behind one it unfolds itself, flows around one and to a certain extent carries one. It brings mercy. One can imagine oneself in a river of mercy and peace, walking along its stream. Then one sees a very light jade-green in front of one as a promise of the future incarnating Ego ["I"]....

That is the world of "Unbornness," the world of magenta is the world we come to when we leave the spiritual world. Then we gently move into carmine with softer movement but we are still in the realm of darkness, of warmth, of creativity.[4]

3   Collot d'Herbois, *Light, Darkness and Colour...*, pp. 17–18
4   Ibid., pp. 70, 73.

For a gentle image of magenta, we can picture a newborn, because most of us have seen or been around a newborn child and remember the feeling; it is a smell, a beautiful fresh smell, untouched, still lovely and new. Liane calls it a "bloom of magenta." Try to live in that atmosphere for just a few seconds; stay there and bathe yourself in that space. That is the space which belongs to magenta. It has a strength all of its own. Remember how the little one captivates your total attention. It comes from far away, from another world. In former times in ancient Greece and Rome, only Kings and Priests were allowed to wear that color. They were born to the purple, to the magenta color. Anyone else could be killed for wearing it, and it was worth its weight in gold. Gold and magenta were for Kings. The soft color of magenta is the first dawn of being in our world, an entrance into the darkness of our world. Birth happens in the warm darkness of the reds and slowly moves toward the light of consciousness.

> In the beginning of our human evolution... one was so united with the Gods, that when one breathed in, that was the wisdom of the Gods one breathed in, and when one breathed out, that was the will of the Gods; so united and so unified one was with inner and outer creation.
>
> That is one of the qualities of magenta, that it is of an all-pervading mood; magenta is more a mood than a color. It was always the representation of ... the All-Highest.[5]

Now we move further away from "Unbornness" toward the light, entering into the beautiful carmine, red-rose color.

> Carmine is the color that belongs to our early childhood, to the time when we were not yet fully conscious... people began to love the Earth... people could be aware of other human beings, not through thinking or feeling, but through what they did, through the expression of their will. Their whole existence was carried by an all-enveloping life-air—the atmosphere of carmine. Slowly the senses awakened....
>
> Carmine has a warmth, a gentle soul-warmth that is deeply connected with the faculty of will and with the Earth.... The warmth of carmine is akin to the feeling one has when one feels at home.... The

---

5   Collot d'Herbois, *Colour*, p. 54.

pleasure one has in incarnation…a contentment, a satisfaction. It is something connected with being human and with being on Earth. And when one becomes aware of that, walking over the Earth becomes a kind of communion, as it used to be to the Old Persians. They knew: I am here and there is the Earth and with the system of my limbs I divine the Earth because I am part of it.…

Perhaps one can understand now that carmine gives back to us a certain connection with the Earth, that it gives us warmth, that it gives us life. And because of this connection with the Earth it gives us a certainty. It is an all-enveloping, all-binding element. It is a colored air. But from it water appears. That is one aspect of its working: it is like water poured over a plant. When you look at Carmine you pour water over your ideals.[6]

We become aware as Westerners that the Russian people (not those in the wealthy class) are not incarnated as fully as we are. The first place to see that as yet they are not fully of the Earth or have a real feeling for being on the Earth, and that they are coming down slowly to the Earth is: One does not see many gardens, an awareness of the plant world, of the surroundings, or animals. They are still dreamy. Poverty is not the reason, because I have been to other parts of the world that are equally poor, if not worse, where small flower gardens were carefully tended. They do not really care about working bathrooms, or the efficiency of the West. They have other interests. The color carmine is the color in which they are at home. But it is the darkness, the creative darkness, the immense power of the darkness that one can feel everywhere in Russia. As I entered countless churches, little ones or big ones, I was stunned by the religious fervor of the Russians. The Russian's soul is totally absorbed in the picture; the icon has a palpable life for the believer. They all have their favorite icon and often set one up in their homes in a special place for worship. There is no thinking involved. We are not in the consciousness soul there as we are in England, America, the West. In Russia as one travels one sees the poor living condition of the countryside is in stark contrast to the opulent cities

---

6   Collot d'Herbois, *Light, Darkness and Colour…*, pp 86–88.

with their former large tsarist estates. The houses are thrown together with pieces of wood gathered here and there or tar paper and they are tiny. There is no plumbing and rarely electricity. Houses have no attics—that would be a waste of space—and instead there are bedrooms on the upper floor. Most of the roads are dirt. The village community life as Steiner mentions is still a real village community.

The Russian soul is still sleeping; it has not awakened from its dreamy carmine mood that is the mood of childhood and is preserved through the icon. The childishness of the religious faith is heartwarming. If the West had only one bit of that fervor, we could go a long way, but we have lost that. Young men standing with religious fervor praying intensely, prostrate before the icon of the Mother of God, or at a famous Mother and Child, or a saint, or the Christ is a common sight. That religious warmth and strength is something to reckon with. It reminds me of the biblical saying: "Unless you change and become like little children, you will never enter the kingdom of heaven" (Matt. 18:3).

Try for a moment to feel that carmine yourself, carmine as coming from magenta, the realm of birth and before birth, a gentle coming unto the Earth realm. Seep yourself in its warmth. Picture the rose and sink into that color with your feeling and become this color. If you have a picture of an icon, look at it. If not, look at a plant, a red flower, and feel it. That is the feeling that one receives as one gazes at the perfect carmine painted on all the icons as a background to the Theotakos, Mother of God, and other sacred paintings.

> When one stands in the carmine-atmosphere one knows that one has magenta behind one, almost like a far echo of what used to be. There is still much darkness here and in that darkness there is warmth. In the sphere of magenta one had hope...but here in carmine one gets a feeling of certainty. And it is all centered around this picture the darkness gives of what is human.... When one paints, it brings about a most harmonious interweaving of that interval where so many illnesses lie, it creates harmony between the physical body and the etheric on the one hand and the astral and the "I" on the other. And carmine can

do that because it has so much to do with creative darkness (darkness as it lives in the metabolic system). It works more specifically on the etheric and physical body. Through the etheric it works on the blood and thereby it can move the blood. It is a color that can "feed" the heart. It can give a picture of what human love can be....

It works as all-connecting; it is all-embracing, all-permeating, all-penetrating. It binds together the members of the fourfold human being, especially there where one finds the great interval between the upper and the lower man, between the astral and the etheric body. That is one way in which carmine supports our being human.[7]

Russia has enormous forces of warmth and creativity that the West has lost. When I travel I always stay in youth hostels because I can't afford hotels when I leave home for several months. But there one meets the travelers, as I mentioned before. And I have noticed that many French men and women, young and old are flocking to Russia. And they simply love it, and when they leave they can't wait to return. France, the country of the Age of Enlightenment, I am afraid has lost the carmine. They are forever in the land of duality with fragmented minds and souls. They consume many new drugs designed by industry in order to stay sane. They have lost that warmth by being cold thinkers with cold intellect. Therefore, if they can afford it, or follow their intuition, they come to Russia and bathe themselves in the icons, the churches, the people, and then go home feeling a bit better. But we will get to that later on in the realm of another color.

Slowly, as the younger generation in Russia travels, it is catching up and bringing in some awakening. In Moscow I went to a Sunday service at a very modern church that was built only recently. I think Russia is the only country that has built a church as enormous as this, with lots of marble, cupolas, and icon paintings from top to bottom. This gargantuan task was carried out in just a few years. The church was full of believers praying in all corners in their own way. I was reminded of the world of the East, because the service did not have the formality of the Catholic service

---

7   Collot d'Herbois, *Light, Darkness and Colour*..., pp. 88–89.

where you merely sit and must wait patiently until the end. Here no one sits, but stands before God. Here people pray, sing, talk, leave, and come back as they please, while others around them may be in deep contemplation before their favorite icon, bowing very low with no concern for who is watching. They are totally absorbed in their religion fervor. I can see again what Steiner meant when he said that their religious fervor had been taken by the Soviet economic plan. Now religion is again back in its rightful place. I must have looked at a few hundred icons, one more beautiful than the other. In each sacred piece I could see the beautiful carmine at work, the lovely jade green and gold.

My next expedition was to the monastery of Sergie Posad, which had several churches on the site. I could not visit the icon school because I was told, "They need to work in silence, and it is a holy place." I understood because that is how I work myself, and I do not allow visitors when I am working either. If by mistake someone comes in when I am working, it gives me a jolt that is hard to manage. It feels extremely uncomfortable to come back from another world so suddenly. I always tell my family or friends to knock first, to give me time to switch gears, so to speak.

> For spiritualism to establish links only with the spirit is not enough; the material world must be conquered—we must learn to recognize the spirit in matter.... [Spiritual Science] leads one to discover new connections, such as the unique place of aesthetic humanity in Earth evolution. To a certain extent, aesthetic humans lift themselves above the stream of development and enter a different world. And that is important. The aesthetically inclined person and the person who works in an aesthetic field do not act in a way that is entirely appropriate to someone on Earth, but rather their sphere of activity is in a certain way lifted out of the Earth sphere. With this discovery, aesthetics leads us to some profound secrets of human existence....
>
> In aesthetic experience, the etheric stream circumvents the "I" and flows directly into the astral body, giving one the impression that the "I" hovers in the etheric that surrounds the head. People who feel and respond a little to beauty do not need to be very clairvoyant to

experience how they seem to live in a space that surrounds their heads while they are contemplating a work of art....

To etheric observation, this green hovers in the immediate vicinity of our head. The "I" lives in it, and alongside the "I" are found the elemental beings of the myths and sagas. There they are called elves, fairies, and so on. When we enjoy something aesthetically, all that is hovering around our heads.[8]

We will return to this process later, but for now we can begin to understand why artists do not like to be disturbed. They are not the only ones to be disturbed; a whole army is being disturbed!

≈

The old monastery had several churches and chapels, and all of them were full of old icons to delight in. I was bathed in their luminous light, and the intense gaze of the Madonnas touched my heart in some mysterious way. I lit beeswax candles throughout for all my friends, I lit candles to the Madonnas for the living, and candles to the Christ icons for the departed ones or departing ones, especially to my friend Rose Edwards who was going into the spiritual world. That is what a lady I met there gently told me to do. The Russians, young and old, were lighting a vast number of candles. There were many old women standing by the most revered icons, the ones that had the most lit candles in the little corners, or in the middle of the church, and they gently and continually cleaned the wax to make room for more candles. Reflecting on this mood of reverence, prayer, and devotion assures one that Russia will be fine in the future.

After that I visited the other monastery, Optina Hermitage, near Kozelsk, southeast of Moscow, and off the usual tourist track. After a long bus ride through valleys and large birch and pine forests, I finally arrived in this almost mythical place. It has been visited by many illustrious writers—including Gogol, Dostoevsky, Khorniakow, Soloviev, Tolstoy—in search of a "spiritual father" to lead them into the spiritual world and

---

8 Steiner, *The Riddle of Humanity*, Dornach, Aug. 15, 1916, p. 124; Aug. 6, 1916, pp. 59, 62 (trans. revised).

initiation. One of my very favorite writers, Paul Marshall Allen, wrote about this famous spiritual enclave in the center of Russia:

> Optina Pystin had become increasingly famous as a spiritual mecca for Russians of every class for some fifty years at the time Dostoyevsky and Soloviev visited it. Inspired by the example of the famous Staretz Paisius Velichkovski of Mt. Athos, some of whose pupils had revived ancient mystical practices at Optina at the end of the eighteenth century the spirituality of the monks and Elders had attracted a whole series of famous men in the first decades of the nineteenth century, among them Ivan Kireyevski, who increased the fame of the monastery by advising the monks on publications, including their remarkable series of translations of the writings of the Fathers of the Church and outstanding works on Hesychasm, the mystical "path of stillness and repose," the way of initiation into the Divine Mysteries.
>
> The Elders of Optina taught and practiced meditation on "the uncreated Light" manifested at the Transfiguration of Christ on Mt. Tabor, which, though present in everything enveloping all things within itself, is hidden from men until through spiritual training, they are able to perceive it.
>
> One of the most significant aspects of hesychast mystical training as it was carried out at Optina and in countless other holy places in Russia, concerns the Prayer of the Heart, which begins as a verbal expression, "Lord Jesus Christ, Son of God, have mercy upon me, a sinner." Eventually after long practices this sinks into the Heart as "praying without ceasing," whether asleep or awake.[9]

Both monasteries were the sites of mystery schools in the past. This monastery is quite small and has younger monks in training. I found out later on that there is still an old monk who is very much a remnant of the silent meditation tradition. He is a *staretz*. He is not one of the monks with a black tunic and long beard, but is a simple cleaner with a broom. He carries within himself a power well known among these old monks to see in the other world and to awaken one who needs it with a gesture or a look, so deep is his meditative life. The monks live a life of prayer, repeating over

---

9 Allen, *Vladimir Soloviev*, p. 134.

and over again the same words, such as *"Kyrie Eleison, Lord Jesus Christ"* thousands of times a day.

If one were invisible, here is a conversation that one might hear between a monk and his "spiritual father," or *staretz* (Старец).

During a whole week, I did my prayer exercises dutifully in the solitude of my garden following exactly what my "staretz" had told me. At first all seemed to go well. Then I began feeling a certain weight fall upon me, a laziness, boredom, sleepiness, and thoughts fell upon me like a mass of heavy clouds. I went to the *staretz,* full of sadness, and explained what was happening to me, he greeted me with great compassion and said to me:

—Beloved brother, This is the fight that the dark forces of the world is leading against you, because there is nothing that they hate more than the prayer of the heart. They are trying to upset you, and to give you a distaste for prayer. But the enemy only acts according to the will and approval of God, only in the measure for what is necessary for your development, not beyond your strength. You must again suffer and become more humble: it is too soon for you to attain the goal by such excessive zealous activity of your heart, you risk falling into total spiritual avarice, or becoming a "spiritual gourmet."... The more one pursues spiritual work, the more one is dedicated to God, the more one will be confronted with the forces of the darkness, the enemy that will give a merciless fight to remove the dedicated one from the right path....

Shatun [Satan] in Hebrew means obstacle; while a desire for union with Christ or God awakens up within us, at the same time, there awakens within us the great obstacles that will prevent such a union. Within the Judeo-Christian thought, *Shatun* is not a god facing another God, as in the dualistic world view of the power of evil and darkness opposing the forces of good and light. *Shatun* is a creature whose function is to shake us, confront us, to tempt us, so that we can become stronger or simply allows us to become aware of our strong faith, and trust in God.

The desert fathers used to say, "Without the demons and the multiple obstacles that they throw on our path, we could not make any progress."[10]

---

10 Leloup, *Writings on Hesychasme*, pp. 128–129 (trans. by author).

The grounds of the monastery were full of small gardens, well tended by the monks. I could see these monks dressed in their long black robes sweeping the fall leaves off the ground with their little brooms. The bookstore was very well stocked with many books on various religious and spiritual topics, art books, icons, and candles. White-haired elders walked, in intimate conversation with women or men, down the paths, gently trying to heal their souls. This monastery, too, was full of beautiful icons that I looked at with veneration and thankfulness. They certainly have the power to move one's soul.

I arrived back in Moscow late in the day completely exhausted. The next day I went into the large new Church and had a peculiar feeling that I was dedicating my life to some future thing. The Saints that I had been gazing at for days now had somehow delivered their silent message. It was a realization that here my *total dedication is needed*. It must be absolute dedication with nothing holding me back, nothing! It felt like a kind of message from the old Saints who were saying, "Nothing of yourself can be left behind. You must dedicate your whole self, no more and no less. Here in Russia we know sacrifice, and it can't be any other way." I also had the feeling that I would incarnate in Russia in the future along with many of my friends. This cognitive feeling is the sphere of violet, which we will encounter later. Violet is deep religious devotion and future consciousness. This truth was almost palpable in Russia. The landscape was screaming for loving attention; it needed gardens and people who were more incarnated in order to work. The Russians had done all they could to survive their last devastating holocaust, and now they needed the power of individuals to come and help.

Here, I end the world of carmine, the world that is as close as we can get to "Unbornness" even though for me Russia served as a beginning. Much more could be said, but it is beyond the scope of this book. As color must be experienced rather than talked about, so, too, Russia deserves our attention. My first visit will not be my last. Here is the morning meditation of the Elders at Optina Pystin, which they have prayed for centuries:

Grant that with peaceful minds
 we may face all this new day is to bring;
Grant us grace to surrender ourselves utterly to
 Thy divine Will:
Instruct and prepare us in all things
 for every hour of this day.
Whatever tidings may come to us this day,
 may we accept them tranquilly,
  firmly convinced that everything that happens to us
  fulfills our divinely-willed destiny.
Govern our thoughts and feelings in everything we do or say,
 granting us the wisdom when to speak
 and when to remain silent.
When unexpected, unforeseen things happen,
 let us never forget for even a moment
 that everything comes from Above.
Teach and guide us that we conduct ourselves in all sincerity and
 reasonableness toward every other human being,
  helping us that we bring neither confusion,
  doubt, nor sorrow to anyone.
Bestow upon us, O Lord, strength to endure the weariness this day's
 labor will bring, and give us the courage
 that each of us may bear his full share
 in all its tasks and events.
Guide Thou our willing, teaching us to pray, to believe,
 to hope, to bear, to forgive and—above all—to Love.[11]

≈

My walk today takes me in a circle around Tintagel. I want to find the area where Liane lived as a child. She said that the water used to come up to the house. I see cliffs everywhere hundreds of feet above the sea, but there aren't many places where there is a house by the water, none I can find. They are all up on the cliff, so I take a walk on a rocky valley carved out by a river coming down into the ocean. It is in the forest where there is an old mill where I find a wall of the cliff facing the mill and the river. On it are two

11 Allen, *Vladimir Soloviev*, p. 135.

beautiful carvings in the granite, two beautifully formed labyrinths dating from at least 3,500 years ago. Meditating on these and the mystery of who the people were from ages ago who carved them is powerful.

I walk down to the wild coastline where the little river meets the raging waves. It is high tide and I sit on the rocks and observe the relentless waves crashing on the cliffs wearing them down with time. I walk back to the village up on the cliff paths. It has taken me about three hours round trip on this lovely sunny and windy day. Many more walkers are enjoying the day, sitting on rocks looking at the far horizon, or walking. I stop at another café for yet another try at good coffee and then head for home after another beautiful walk in these glorious surroundings.

> You could say that we are still just within a period when the responsibility for holding together the different members of which a human being is composed has not yet been turned over to humanity itself....
>
> The time will come when people will experience how complicated they are, a time when people will require knowledge to hold themselves together. However, everything in the future has to be prepared, and the stream that carries a spiritual-scientific worldview has the task of preparing the development of earthly culture for the age when people will have to know how to hold together the various parts of their being. [12]

The world of carmine has, as you have read, a warming, holding-together quality, and Russia has that, the icon, to keep the country together until they slowly awaken. As I spoke to many different Russians, they mentioned that they routinely enter churches at any time, look at their favorite icon, and then go on with their day, drawing on the strength they have received. What does the West have? We have everything under the Sun, a wealth of stimulation to which we are subjected that makes one unable to concentrate. You name it, we have it. We are never left alone to create our own space. Our lives are filled with nonessential stuff that, after a while, rules us, and we can no longer keep it under control. Addiction, emptiness, and depression set in. We act without thinking, going from one stimulating

---

12 Steiner, *Riddle of Humanity*, Dornach, Aug. 7, 1916, p. 71 (trans. revised).

thing to another, never spending time in solitude. In the West we have a fear of being alone, fear of what comes into that hollow space.

For many in Russia that space is filled with the power of the icon. Others who are not so intuitive fill it up with other things; there is much drinking and sexual pornography in this country.

Nevertheless, the West has Anthroposophy, which it has not as yet adopted seriously. This holding together of the human race is already breaking apart if one listens to the news. Human feeling, thinking, and willing are being torn apart, and strong "I" forces are not in place to keep us together. This means that emotions and feelings take over and we act without thinking, leading to subjective and emotional deeds that bring lies in their wake, or thinking takes over without feelings. We see the latter in modern medicine and health care systems that treats the body as if it were at a mechanic's shop. We see it in our economics and defense industry, to name a few examples. Finally willing takes over, and acts are committed without any thoughts or feelings whatsoever about the out-come. The papers are full of these kinds of acts: rampant murder, useless malls being built, a glutted housing market, among other things. No one asks who is in charge; only Rudolf Steiner dared to talk about it.

Look and you will see the life of the West being torn asunder already. In the holistic field people are making some progress but they do not go deep enough! Until now an anthroposophic view is the one daring enough to penetrates the depths of the human being. This path of painting is one way to keep the human being whole, to experience the human being holistically and to penetrate deeply into our darkness, and shed light via the Beings of Color. Experience what is there. If the West continues to dissipate and scatter itself in all directions, this is one of the consequences:

> Those who rush about everywhere in search of sensations and want everything they learn to come from outside of themselves would be in danger. In their next incarnation, they would be in danger of arriving in the world with a head formed from a body that had transformed very little. It would have an animal-like appearance, as that would be

the fate of those who had not accumulated much in the way of formative forces.[13]

Now is *not* the time to ignore such statements and sleep through life.
When one is totally dissipated by outside events of various kinds, one does
not have the force to consolidate the "I." It becomes so weak that whatever
impulses come into the thinking/head are obeyed without thought. People
act from whatever impulse reaches them, and they blow here and there like
a feather in the wind. This means serious trouble for the individual as well
as for society as a whole as Steiner pointed out.

13 Ibid., p. 76.

Vermilion

Now we will enter the world of vermilion. We traveled through magenta then on to carmine. Now we leave the realm of carmine, pick up a bit more speed going toward the light, enter scarlet red, and then vermilion. But more needs to be said about the journey of human consciousness that I have mentioned before.

In the schooling of painters, the changing of human consciousness can be seen and experienced through colors. By that I mean the nature of human beings' relationship to the world of the senses, the Earth, and how it changes has developed over thousands of years. For the Collot d'Herbois therapist or painter this is studied in terms of color. We learn how we came from the past, birth, and how we are facing the future—all in terms of color.

When coming into the world from the world of "Unbornness" (before we were born), we enter the world of magenta, the world of the Indian epoch that Steiner talks about.

> The world as the dream-consciousness perceived it was flooded with magenta. It was a reality with no hard outlines, formless, dreamed of. One was only aware of variations of light and darkness, perceived, not through the senses but through another part of one's being—partly through the feelings (the heart), and partly through the will (the limbs). One felt carried by creation, one felt wrapped in a cloak of mercy.... All existence was one great outpouring of mercy in which one was carried, in which one lived.... So it was that period of evolution of mankind that Rudolf Steiner calls the Old Indian Epoch.[1]

This is a world that is all encompassing, dreamy, the world of the newly born child. There we have a dream consciousness and nothing is separated, therefore the use of that color in therapy is to unify a dissipated

---

1   Collot d'Herbois, *Light, Darkness and Colour...*, p. 70.

soul. Then we move on to the world of the ancient Persian epoch, the world of carmine, a slow entrance into the earthly world that we experienced in the previous pages.

Carmine is the color that belongs to our early childhood.... That state of consciousness corresponds to the one that was prevalent during the Old Persian epoch that lies in prehistoric times. The human being for the first time... "began to love the Earth" Rudolf Steiner says....

The Old Persian people began to experience a certain circumference and to have an awareness of movements in the atmosphere around them. Before in magenta, there was no such movement, but now it begins to occur because of the slow approach toward the light. It is the light that brings that darkness to movement. People began to be aware of variations of light and darkness. They did not see the Sun, they saw a sphere of light. It was not necessarily round because their eyes were not crystalline and focused like ours. For them the Sun could easily have been a glowing oval. However, they did discern a direction of the light.

It is important to remember that all these changes are accompanied by great changes in the physical body. There was for instance the gradual closing of the great organ of clairvoyant perception and this was later followed by the focusing of the physical eyes....

We now stand in the period of time that marks the transition from the Old Persian Epoch, which was bathed in carmine, to the Old Egyptian Epoch that flourished in all the shades of orange and burnt sienna. In his consciousness man begins to separate himself from the surrounding, which was then the world of the gods. This separation was not something that was thought or seen, it was something that was felt with the heart. In a dreamy way it is the beginning of a separation between inner and outer. There is a certain withdrawal from the outer world and man becomes slightly self-centered for the first time in evolution. That is what scarlet can do: it gives the beginning of a reliance on oneself.

In magenta the human being was carried from outside and he was part of an all-encompassing, breathing world. In carmine all was harmony in all directions. In scarlet it is man himself who breathes. He moves away from the certainty that he is an integral part of creation and now he begins to feel a bit uncertain. That is the beginning of what later, in the vermilion, grows into fear.

The physical body changes because the soul-body has changed and also the relationship between the two. Man no longer dreams. On the other hand…he is more clearly awake in his day-consciousness…. With the awareness of the difference between inner and outer there comes the feeling of having possessions. Before that was an utter impossibility, because one lived in an all-encompassing oneness. (Man could not possess the Earth until the Roman time. In fact he did not even possess his thoughts until a late time in Greece. Modern man derives his sense of being from his possessions.)

The awakening to day-consciousness brought with it a greater consciousness of the physical body and all that concerns with it. And so man began to suffer its illnesses. Before the physical body could be ill, but man would not be so aware of it, it would not mean much to him. Now, in the scarlet, he has so to say left the heavens and his consciousness begins to be focused in the physical world. It is then that illness becomes a source of suffering.

All the processes described above were carried further and intensified in the dawning of the vermilion at the beginning of the Old Egyptian Epoch. Vermilion brings with it the concept of morality. It is the time of the Old Testament. In fact the whole of the Old Testament is steeped in vermilion: man's struggle to be a truly moral being and his awe and fear of the Father God. Even today vermilion faces us with the judgment and the wrath of the Father God….

I want to give you a picture of still another aspect of this color: one might say that the Whipping, the second step in the Christian Initiation, lies within the realm of vermilion. And at the same time this color gives an intense strengthening of the soul. When one can bear it, it leads one to a greater life, because it can lead one to that which is imponderable. It can bring greater life to one's thinking, because vermilion works more strongly in one's imagination than it does when one sees it in the outer world. And apart from that it can lead one to a greater equilibrium to stand the Whipping and that everyone must have because we are going to be whipped over the threshold whether we want to or not. And so this color is for mankind the greatest blessing.[2]

2 Ibid., pp. 86, 101–102.

For an experience of vermilion, I would like to introduce a work of art, a very special one. I have always loved the painting of Mary Magdalene by Fra Angelico that is in one of the cells of the St. Marco Church and monastery and also in several Renaissance paintings. Mary Magdalene is painted in a beautiful light vermilion as she looks up to Christ, or is weeping on the body of her beloved teacher. She stands in powerful colors. The Mother of Christ is close by enveloped in her blue cloak and her carmine robe with her hair covered by the robe, but Mary Magdalene is in vermilion with her hair uncovered and flowing. She is engulfed in deep sorrow because she has lost her "Raboni," her master. She is not the mother, but the disciple. She is left alone to face the future.

Why was she often painted in vermilion? Here we will look at the properties of this most lively color. As mentioned above, vermilion is a powerful color and painting it is not so easy. One needs to withstand its power. As Mary Magdalene stands by the Christ being, one can imagine what power one needs, and she is present. She is also the one who comes to the tomb first. Thereby she had soul/spiritual qualities that can be portrayed in this vibrant, powerful vermilion.

> Vermilion is the most substantial, the most heavy of all the colors. It has a love and a desire for substance and it has the possibility of digesting, of transforming, of bringing substance from the ponderable state into the imponderable. And that is its greatest quality....
>
> Of all the colors, it makes the quickest transitions between one sphere and another, between one color and another—for instance from orange to violet. The making of transition is one of its functions, it is a carrier. Transition is always accompanied by warmth, be it physical warmth or soul-warmth....
>
> Vermilion can be called the revelation of the Divine on the threshold of consciousness. If the whole world would be vermilion one would be thrust back upon oneself and have to come to the recognition of a being outside oneself, that is greater than oneself. And one comes to prayer. That is what vermilion does to the soul: it breaks through one's self-occupation.[3]

---

3   Ibid., pp. 104–105.

That is how she is often painted. She is going from one world to the other to follow the Christ being. What better color to paint her in, than vermilion. Then she prays. Mary Magdalene is also the one who first sees the empty tomb at Easter, and recognizes the Christ; no one else is able to do so. Again we experience this scene with the color vermilion in mind. As quoted above, it makes the quickest transition between seen and unseen, a revelation of the Divine. Mary Magdalene was in another state of consciousness, due to her preparation as a devotional, loving, meditative soul, unlike Martha who was the busybody, who had not acquired the necessary quietness, the deep well of rest.

That is my reason for choosing Mary Magdalene in her vermilion robe to portray this color. The rest must be left unsaid. One can write another book on this topic alone, but it is up to the reader to meditate on it further by looking at some of these masterpieces and live into the vermilion. Experience the being of Vermilion and who Mary Magdalene was in relation to it.

Here we have another wonderful quality of the Vermilion being. I often use this color in therapy.

> People who are constantly occupied with the past and the wrongs done to them, who always speak about the past and blame others for their misfortunes, need this force of the vermilion. It digests the past and thereby opens the way for the future. It can make the blood rush around like a mad horse and that is very good for some people. One has to break that fearful chain of the past. Nursing the wrongs of the past is a way to develop cancer.[4]

As a matter of fact, since I have had to live in vermilion for the last couple of days in order to write these words, I need to have something for lunch. Usually I skip lunch! As was stated, vermilion does activate one's system and, coming really down to earth, it is good for people who have a sluggish digestion or constipation. In the schooling, the students are often amazed at how hungry they get when they work deeply with certain colors and how quickly it affects their systems!

---

4   Ibid.

One detail for painters: there is a most beautiful vermilion that one can buy from Da Vinci Paints. When painted very light, it is a beautiful apricot color, and when used in veiling, with 50 or more layers, it has a most vibrant warmth that does justice to vermilion-scarlet.

> If the whole world would be vermilion one would be thrust back upon oneself and have to come to the recognition of a being outside oneself, that is greater than oneself. And one comes to prayer. That is what vermilion does to the soul: it breaks through one's self-occupation.[5]

Here I must talk about the importance of vermilion as far as cultural epochs are concerned. Liane talks about magenta and the Indian Epoch, carmine and the Persian Epoch, and vermilion as the epoch of Israel and the Jewish people. Recently I had the opportunity to spend a month in Israel and I spent much of it observing people praying at the Western Wall in Jerusalem. It was a revelation to me, to live and experience the fervor of the people praying; there were men and women, young and old from the many nations of Mother Earth gathered there. By witnessing the intensity of these prayers, of giving oneself up entirely to prayers with such strength, I understood the power of vermilion and what it means to live in the intense warmth of this color. One needed to totally abolish oneself and look up to something greater and mightier. At the Western Wall in Jerusalem, I could actually see that. The everyday world was gone for all the people who were praying. There was nothing but the experience of recognizing what is greater than oneself and then bowing and praying. I was very thankful for having observed this holy site in this marvelous city that is so full of paradoxes. In this city in terms of color, one had the Wall with its vermilion atmosphere and color and, immediately on the other side stands the great mosque, the world of turquoise. The in-between, which is just a wall, there is the green—unseen but felt—but that is for later in this color adventure and will be the subject of my next adventure in writing, *Beyond the Blood*.

Our Earth, when seen through these insights on color, is an amazing experience. One cannot but love its paradoxes. In Jerusalem, one confronts

---

5   Ibid.

the different atmospheres daily as one moves from a vermilion environment to a turquoise environment to the Realm of the Green. Totally different worlds live side by side. It is movement at its utmost, as Itzak, a writer and inventor living in Tel Aviv, said, "There has been so much war and confrontations, for ever and ever. We live with it!"

Yellow-Orange

There was stormy weather here all night, with high winds and changing clouds. The cliff walk will be very wet and slippery. Yesterday, I looked at my favorite Hortensia flowers. The bushy flower that looks like a huge globe grows everywhere here. It cascades from rocky walls and touches my face as I walk in the narrow alleys. These blossoms come in beautiful blues, lilac, white, or light pink and as they die into the winter they become brown, light brown, and greenish. I have gathered many bouquets of them. I could never grow them in my garden at home, as they need the moisture of the sea and gentle temperatures of England or in Brittany, France, where they also grow profusely. I always try to live into color, especially when I am not painting. One needs to maintain a relationship with the Color Beings at all times when one's work is painting. Walking back through the fields I pass tiny yellow flowers having a last look at the world before the winter sets in. They are valiant little beings, untrammeled by the cows or the sheep. I breathe their lightness in and walk on to the towering cliffs. The sunset colors were absent since it has been a rainy, very gray day. I miss the vermilion and the crimson colors of the sunset.

≈

Now our journey continues through the colors. We have slowly traveled through magenta, carmine, vermilion, and now comes orange and yellow. As you travel through the substance/world/atmosphere that is the meeting of the darkness advancing toward the light, the speed increases. After vermilion, the substance of the darkness becomes lighter as it encounters the light. In orange it speeds up toward the light, meets it, then goes back a bit, and then goes forward again. For this color, I have chosen the wonderful imagination of Michael fighting the dragon, the great Archangel who means so much to the students of Rudolf Steiner, but also to the West. In all these countries there is not one place—hospital, school, university—that does not have a church, tiny St. Michael chapel, Iglesia, or monastery and some islands have a cathedral on them, sometimes an enormous one. There are many statues of St. Michael and paintings of him and the dragon. We see him as we enter churches and he welcomes everyone with his stern look and sword as if to say, "What are you doing for me? I am waiting, look!"

The Archangel Michael is everywhere to be seen. We can't forget him in the West. He is our icon. But regretfully I do not see many human beings enthralled by his presence as the Russian people are when they meet him in countless icons in which he is surrounded with gold and enveloped in a red cape. His colors are between orange and golden yellow.

Here we leave the realm of the red, of the icon, and enter the realm of orange, yellow, as we prepare to meet the realm of the Great Being in the green of viridian. Vermilion is in-between as we have seen; it gives us the strength to go through the threshold, the realm of the Israelites, the Ten Commandments. And to our aid comes the Archangel Michael.

We will look at some facts about orange and golden yellow.

Imagine that for days it has been raining. It is late afternoon, the rain stopped. You look out and you see a whole sky of astonishing brilliant yellow. You still hear the dropping of water everywhere and everything is glistening, shining: the roofs, the streets, everything. Below near the ground there is a thick atmosphere, you cannot see very well through that. In time the Sun comes lower and begins to set. And that yellow color then becomes an orange.... The whole landscape, with trees, houses, animals is bathed in that orange and you see them as though you have never seen them before. It is a mood that is so incredible that you become aware of having senses. Not only the ordinary day-senses, but also the sense for the "I" and the sense for life that one otherwise is not aware of. This orange mood at the end of the day does not last long, usually not more than a quarter of an hour.

Orange is a color that moves very quickly. It has no center, it has no circumference and it is continually expanding. It does not come to a definite end. One could say that in it there takes place all the time a fight between light and darkness, a continuous fight.... It is transparent and concentrated at the same time. It has its greatest concentration of color against the light, there the color is heaviest. It has on the one hand a love for the light and that gives it movement. On the other hand the darkness in it tries to rise against the light and that gives it its fullness....

Try to imagine that you are standing in the middle of that orange atmosphere. See the quick movements, the flashes of light, the glowing of the darker movements. Feel the warmth of that all that activity. Maybe you can have a feeling then of the force and the enthusiasm, the energy and the certainty this color brought to the battlefield of the War in the Heavens. And maybe you can also understand that orange is such an essential part, such a very necessary part of our soul for this incarnation, where everything, all over, goes against the soul. The brilliance, the transparency, the movement and the courage that orange can give are necessary for today. Therefore Frau Dr. Wegman always spoke of it as the... "light of Michael."

Orange creates an enormous sphere.... Orange is inexhaustible. The colors in front of the light all have a love for the tendency toward substance. Therefore they have this fullness and this warmth and this lack of form where the darkness becomes stronger....

This whole sphere from orange to violet is something very special and has a very deep connection with us and with our evolution. Remember that orange was the color that was outwardly observed by the Egyptians, in the epoch of the awareness soul. From that Egyptian civilization we have something in our soul that has given us an inner basis. The Egyptians were the first materialists—there orange deepened to burnt sienna [color of red earth].[1]

And here are a few words about the Archangel *Micha-el*:

Let us therefore turn our gaze to the whole series of these archangelic beings: Gabriel, Raphael, Zachariel, Anael, Oriphiel, Samael, Michael. As we look to these beings, we may characterize the relation that exists between them and the loftier Spirits of the Higherarchies somewhat as follows.

---

1   Ibid., pp. 116–117.

I beg you not to take these words too lightly or too easily. We have but human words to express these sublime realities. Simple as the words may sound, they are not meant lightly. Of all these arch-angels, the number of whom is seven, six have, to a very considerable extent, though not entirely—Gabriel most of all; but even Gabriel not completely—six, as I say, have to a very considerable extent resigned themselves to the fact that human beings face Maya, the great Illusion, because their quality no longer accords with their original predesti-nation, because in fact they have descended from their original stat-ure. Michael alone,... Michael is the only one who would not give in. Michael, and with him even those who are the Michaelic spirits even among human beings, continues to take this stand: I am the ruler of the Intelligence. And the Intelligence must be so ruled that there shall not enter it any illusion or false fantasy, nor anything that would restrict the human being to a dark, vague, cloudy vision of the world.

My dear friends: to see how Michael stands there as the great-est opponent in the ranks of the archangels is an unspeakably uplift-ing sight—over powering, magnificent. And each time a Michael Age returned, it happened upon Earth not only that...intelligence as a means of knowledge became cosmopolitan, but also that intelligence became such that human beings were filled through and through with the consciousness: "After all, we *can* ascend to the Divinity.[2]

We also need to mention another aspect of orange. It takes us to the Egyptian Epoch when the human being slowly arrives on this Earth.

From the Old Persian epoch there came two streams of development. One blossomed along the borders of the Euphrates and we call it the Chaldean civilization. It had a certain spiritual, cosmic character. The other one we know as the Egyptian civilization and this is one that has a more soul-quality. The awareness soul played a great role in it.

The consciousness of the people living in these times was such that they were aware of the colors magenta, carmine, orange, and burnt sienna. To them the atmosphere was not clear, it was a thick mist of colored air. They felt themselves bathed in a glow of orange, of burnt sienna and later also of yellow. They did not see the light in the way we

---

2   Steiner, *The Archangel Michael*, Dornach, Aug. 1, 1924, p. 261.

do, for them it was something that appeared and disappeared rhythmically. The priests in the temples could see more light than the average person could. The whole landscape with the river, the fields, plants, everything was bathed in the golden atmosphere. Everything was seen in tones of orange, ocre, and gold, the colors of wallflowers. The rising and the setting of the Sun brings variations of color in the thick golden atmosphere....

> In the later part of the Egyptian period Akhnoton saw the Sun for the first time and that was a tremendous event. He had the Sun depicted with rays, sometimes with hands on the ends of the rays.... But the majority of the Egyptian people did not have the faculty of perceiving a clear light—that only dawned in the Greek period. The Egyptians had a veiled light, they lived in a colored atmosphere. For them the air itself was color.[3]

For the therapist, orange is one of the leading colors that we use.

> People who need courage, who have no certainty of decision, who can be very nice but have no inner movement of any kind in their thinking—those people need orange. Because it gives warmth, enthusiasm to one's thinking. Because of its movement it is not to be caught in by anything.[4]

Now for yellow. When one paints a Michael painting, it is orange and yellow and of course other colors as well. These are the most difficult colors to paint; they give one the most challenge. One has to maintain a balance between transparency, darkness and movements seen through a delicate sap green. It is exquisite but demanding. One experiences the intense fight in this realm of orange when one paints it, especially on a large canvas. Now, however, let us enter the realm of yellow, which is also part of Michael.

> Yellow is *not* the light itself, neither is it the lightest color there is.... It is called into being in the *second* veil of darkness in front of the light and however bright and radiant it may look, yellow *belongs to the world of darkness....*

---

3 Collot d'Herbois, *Light, Darkness and Colour...*, p. 115.
4 Ibid., p. 118.

One of its aspects is that it has to do with the past, with that which has been formed and is now finished. It can give one an awareness of long stretches, long distances of time.... It can even carry us back to the beginnings of time, when the whole of creation existed in the minds of great spiritual beings, as thoughts, full of wisdom. One might call yellow the shadow of these thoughts in the minds of the arch-creators. In our times their wisdom as it were shines on creation from outside.... The light yellow is so strongly permeated with light that it therefore has a connection with the past, with that which is finished, which has been created through the thoughts of the gods. But as soon as yellow becomes intense, deeper, stronger, it has a certain warmth and joy. Therefore we can have this extreme love for yellow, thinking it is light and warmth. But what is not understood is that the warmth comes from the darkness....

Another aspect of the yellow is that it is a very objective color. Because it has so much to do with the light it has a certain amount of antipathy in it. In the human condition this aspect expresses itself in the process of consciousness that belong to the nervous system....

The outer yellow has to do with the past, with that which is formed and finished and it is the carrier of intelligence and wisdom. But there is another yellow that has to do with the immediate present, with the continual now, and we can be conscious of it with our heart. That yellow has to do with the archangel Michael who brings to us the Sun-intelligence. One might call it a "resurrected" yellow. It is something we know in our innermost being, but we are hardly ever conscious of it. When one reads what Rudolf Steiner has written in his "Michael Letters,"[5] one can come to an understanding of it. In this Michaelic yellow one can experience the longing for wisdom we all have. One has to see the picture of it clearly before the mind's eye when painting yellow with a patient—not of the outer yellow that is connected with the past. The living Michaelic yellow is a golden yellow, a kind of fluctuation between yellow and orange. All the colors that are not fastened to matter are in a state of movement and fluctuation and that is the way we have to picture them inwardly

In the human being the living yellow represents the aspect of joy and directed thankfulness. It is not an air of gratitude in general, but

---

5 The "Michael Letters" accompany Steiner's *Anthroposophical Leading Thoughts*.

it is actual faculty: that one can feel thankfulness, that one can give thanks—over against life, over against destiny.[6]

Yellow has another quality as well.

Yellow is a color that moves quickly, goes quickly over into another color. It contains much light, therefore it is very straightforward, knows no compromise....

When it is directed it can breaks through things....

Yellow pushes away without giving. It makes open. In painting it can act like a knife; when there is an abscess or a blockage of for instance the glands, yellow can break that.

The Sun-like yellow can be used to open up the rigid thinking.[7]

Now you can picture to yourself in your mind's eye the great imagination of Michael fighting the dragon with the great sword of light yellow thrown straight into the dragon's mouth. Make your own painting, more powerful than one on the wall. Make it alive in your soul!

You can now feel more for the colors of Michael, the great Color Beings of Orange and Yellow. They are here to help us, armed with the courage and enthusiasm of orange, in our own fight against our own dragons, to pierce through the darkness with the uncompromising sword of light yellow—clear thinking.

Since yellow is the carrier of wisdom and intelligence, here are a few words about intelligence, cosmic intelligence.

In very ancient times people did not produce their thought from out of themselves; when they thought about the things of the world their thoughts were not the product of their own inner activity. The faculty of thinking, one's own activity in the forming of thoughts, has only unfolded since the fifteenth century, since the entry of the Consciousness Soul into the evolution of humanity. In older, pre-Christian times it would never have occurred to people to believe that they were producing their own thoughts out of themselves; they did not feel that they

---

6   Collot d'Herbois, *Light, Darkness and Colour...*, pp. 130–134.

7   Ibid., p. 135.

themselves were forming their thoughts, but rather that thoughts were revealed to them from the things of the world. They felt: Intelligence is universal, cosmic; it is contained in the things of the world....

Thus human beings were conscious all the time that their thoughts were revealed to them, were inspired into them. That is, people ascribed Intelligence only to the universe, not to themselves.

Throughout the ages, the Regent of Cosmic Intelligence, which streams like light over the whole world, has been the Spirit known by the name of *Michael*. Michael is the Ruler of Cosmic Intelligence.[8]

Before ending our discussion of the Michael imagination, I would like to mention again an aspect of Collot d'Herbois's work that shows her brilliance. Part of the training of the painter/therapist is to know the healthy, correct movement of the color and then see the fallen down aspect of that color. With this in mind, Liane Collot d'Herbois always mentions the healthy aspect of a color and then discusses its unhealthy aspect and how as therapists we can help people by seeing and experiencing a color's duality. In the passage below she discusses "too light orange." In it one recognizes the genius of Liane Collot d'Herbois, her incredible insight into the human being. When she speaks about the medical aspect, she actually sees, knows in Imagination the organs, the liver, spleen, and so on. She sees these things through her clairvoyance and through her knowledge of Rudolf Steiner's words; her work embodies wholeness. Here we do not have medicine, then art, then religion. Liane Collot d'Herbois works with all these aspects as a whole. Here is a glimpse of that fascinating, powerful work. We can see through these passages her long apprenticeship in anthroposophic medicine with her masterful teacher, Ita Wegman. When she started this book, from which I quote very heavily, she wanted the therapist to partner with a doctor to discuss all aspects of the work. One was not allowed into the seminar unless one was working with an anthroposophic doctor. Even to be present during the discussions, one must have already been a painter and a therapist and have a knowledge of anthroposophic medicine along

---

8   Steiner, *The Archangel Michael*, Torquay, Aug. 21, 1924, pp. 271–272 (trans. revised).

with general anthroposophic knowledge. This was not work for anyone who thought they might want to merely play around with colors. This was serious schooling to Liane, and admittance was not for everyone, just as not everyone is accepted to medical school, and for very good reason. Just because one likes to paint does not mean he or she can automatically work in this demanding manner.

Imagine for a moment the certainty, the enthusiasm and the spiritual energy of the healthy, balanced orange. One is almost not to be overcome. Behind one there is veil upon veil of colors that are bathed in gold. Jupiter has a deep connection with the Sun and the other way around. Therefore what the orange gives can be almost Sun-like, but it is warmer. It has a soul warmth that one does not find in the world of the senses.

Suppose that a person has not got that in him, something that can happen easily in our times. He shivers a little, has a certain fear. He avoids what is called today "a confrontation." Therefore a certain possibility of communication is not there for such a person. The next thing is that his faculty of concentration goes away, because the people of the too light, dirty orange cannot catch hold of their will. Their will is lame. They can have wonderful ideals that they talk about for hours, but they never do anything.

Another problem they have is that they have a very uncertain connection with the outer world, because they do not use their senses. When they do use them it is in a very erratic way. One could almost call it hysteria; it is not hysteria but it has a certain affinity with it. There is the same uncontrolled sanguinity. They want to do bits of everything, they start all sorts of things that they never finish. They have periods of extreme nervousness. The nerves eat the blood, the tablet of the blood so to speak becomes broken.... Then there is the kind of patient that has too much awareness of soul. They have not made the step to the consciousness soul and they suffer accordingly: they have problems with the lungs.

It can also be that the intelligence soul is too strong. Then the kidneys suffer, because they were the instrument that the "I" used in fulfilling its work on Earth in the period of the human evolution in which the intellectual soul was paramount; that was before the fifteenth century.

From intelligence soul to the consciousness soul (from the kidney to the liver) is one of the greatest steps and often mental illnesses occur where this step has not been accomplished....

The planet Jupiter is connected with the liver, but also with the brain. Rudolf Steiner says that earlier in evolution the liver was a kind of "preliminary stage" of the brain. The connection between the two still exists and so what happens to the liver happens to the brain; when the one organ swells the other swells and the reverse. When we are using our day consciousness our way of thinking is influenced by our liver. When a person repeats himself continually that is very often a too large liver. When a person makes big jumps in his train of thoughts that often is an indication of a too-dry liver.

The people of the too light orange have no warmth in them. They cannot form. The liver may be too dry and the functioning, the working of one lobe on the other, is disturbed. They cannot use their senses properly and that may cause them to have certain illusions. Their nervous system, their astral body wears them down during the day. They become very tired and they cannot catch hold of their will and therefore they have no connection with what one could call the sphere of orange. In the normal healthy situation the etheric during sleep builds up again what the senses have worn down during the daytime. But with those people it does not go that way and there is no rejuvenation at all in the nighttime. Their nerves are misformed and they misuse them and there is nothing to counterbalance that.[9]

Here we will see how she observes the illnesses of the yellow:

The illnesses of the yellow are illnesses of the nervous system and it is usually said that they start in the astral body [emotion body]. Personally I am of the opinion that they in the first place originate in the way of thinking a person has, because thinking is a light process. Whether one is a confirmed materialist in one's way of thinking or not makes a great difference. When one concentrates all one's light on outer materialism and all the soul-qualities connected with it, the astral body is affected. Thinking and light are the same. In such a case the light has become enclosed and the thinking has become fixed,

---

9   Collot d'Herbois, *Light, Darkness and Colour...*, pp. 120–121.

hornlike, in a way dead. It is confirmed and supported by the senses only. Those people may be too strongly attached to their past, they cannot leave it behind. All these factors together have robbed them of their inner mobility. And because of that they have no interest or enthusiasm. They are left with a finished intellect and a certain coldness. It is dead thinking that they have. And has to have *life*! One way to give them life is to arouse their interest in the play of colors in the atmosphere... It can affect their breathing in a wholesome way. It is all a play between the blood and the nerve. The blood can give life, can build up the etheric. But looking at colors in the sky and painting is for these patients not really a healing, it is merely a stopping the getting worse. The one true healing for these illnesses is a connection with the Mystery of Golgotha, because there is an absolute renewal of the human being, an absolute rebirth. Where yellow has so much to do with the past one may assume that many of these illnesses (except neuritis) are from the past. The people brought the tendency with them. And to cure that they need to renew themselves.[10]

Liane Collot d'Herbois specifically lists the following illnesses of the yellow: Encephalitis, Neuritis, Infantile paralysis, Parkinson's, and Multiple Sclerosis. As we observe these illnesses of the orange and yellow we can also understand the powerful healing action of the Michaelic Imagination, its importance in our contemporary life, and what a painting of that Imagination can bring to a home, this as well as reading, studying, and meditating on the many lectures given by Rudolf Steiner. Here Liane discusses this process of pure color, washed out color or color that is too dense:

We look at the human being from the point of view of color: we shall look at the organism as an organism of color, at the processes that take place in the organs as processes of color. Each life process is here regarded as a process of *pure* color, each illness as a corruption of that pure color: the color can either become too light, too thin, faded, grayish, dirty, or on the other hand it can become too dark and dense and then it is dirty again. The pure color is luminous, full, rich. It has life

---

10 Ibid., pp. 135–137.

and it is in continuous, rhythmic movement. It can go to a lighter or darker hue and still have all the qualities of pure color. But when it becomes too light the color so to speak loses its substance and thereby its richness. It becomes pale, lifeless, lightless and it loses its rhythm. The movement can almost come to a standstill or it can speed up too much and become frantic. On the physical plane such a too light color process often becomes manifest as a mental illness. When the color becomes too dark its substance as it were clutters up so that light can no longer penetrate it and it becomes heavy, dirty, dull. The color can even become so dense that it becomes immovable. In the end this process becomes manifest as a physical ailment.

It is important to keep in mind that in this book everything that is said about color is at the same time said about the human being. The reason why this can be so is that colors can be looked upon as a representation of the great entities who since the beginning of time have ceaselessly worked at the creation of the human being and of all the realms of nature. And those entities of color were called into being by the great spiritual creative activity that to our (human) consciousness manifests itself as the polarity of light and darkness.[11]

---

11 Ibid., pp. 55–56.

Yellow-Green

Now we will go on to experience, again, slowly leaving the worlds of magenta, carmine, vermilion to enter the realm of orange, of yellow, toward the light of consciousness. Human beings are leaving the world of wholeness in approaching the light, which cuts through the darkness. Humans are losing the quality that kept them together. Now in the realm of the second veil in front of the darkness, yellow, humans are very close to light, intelligence. Intelligence allows people to have their own thoughts, to think for themselves. Entering this realm is the very beginning of being able to think for oneself, but this does not happen right away. In the realm of the yellow-green, the dancing, the breaking up of yellow into the light, we enter the last veil before the light. This is experienced in the lightness of the acrobats, the dancers in Crete. Yellow-green is difficult to paint. One must feel the lightness, the dancing, but have total control of the movement as the graceful and swift acrobats had total control of their physical bodies.

One can think of a sanguine person. A person of that temperament is full of movement and joy, looseness and lightness. He is able to have a certain control over the quick movement of his thinking and the heat and cold in his body are well organized. That has to do with the healthy functioning of the kidneys. It also stands in a relationship to the lungs. Sanguine people have a gaiety that lights up their surroundings. When a sanguine person comes into the room the atmosphere there changes much more than when a melancholic person comes in.

All these qualities of joy, looseness, lightness and movability are given to our soul by the yellow-green. For many people who are unable to incarnate properly and who therefore cannot have a relationship with the world of breathing and of inner light over against outer light, yellow-green, painted in its purity, can be a great help, because it gives a certain radiance. It can feed the soul. It gives promise, it gives youth, it gives a joy and a certain confidence in life—aspects of soul that too easily fail in our days....

Yellow-green is the color of youth, of innocence and joy.... It can give back the innocence, the confidence in life and the feeling of promise that we take for granted when we are young, but that leave us when we grow older.[1]

For a picture of this feeling of yellow-green, I have chosen a young man who is dressed in fashionable colors one sees these days on the ski slopes. The outfit includes beautiful yellow-green pants and ski jacket to match. The young man has longish hair flowing in the wind, and he is skiing down a steep beautiful white slope with the grace of a bird, a dancer, with the wind gently touching his face. The new powder is wetting his face and he is free, gently gliding on the virgin snow, happy and light as the snow, the yellow-green rapidly dancing down the white wall of the mountain. He has left all his troubles behind and now only lives with the element in total concentration for a few minutes. He is light and joyful, confident on his legs, moving through the steep terrain with grace. At the bottom he stops with his friends and looks at his beautiful sinuous track on the white mountain wall, laughs and stares at the Sun, thankful for such a day.

Yesterday I enjoyed the coastline walk to the nearest village south, Port Williams. It was stormy again and the elements mingled: the warmth of the wind was churning up the sea, the foamy waves crashing against the cliffs full of caves. Descending steeply 800 feet or more down from the high cliffs, I went to the small hotel facing the sea where there is a small beach for windsurfers. I had a wonderful warming up with coffee and from distant tables I heard talk of farmers losing their farms and committing suicide. Perhaps it is not as lovely here as it looks. They were saying that a hotline had to be established for the farmers to call because it has become a real problem. Again this brought me much sadness. We are not addressing the issue with our economic model that bases everything on having to make

---

1   Ibid., pp. 142–143.

money. If it does not make money, we get rid of it. So the farmers do not make money; they are not a profitable lot, and we let them disappear. And they do. They turn to the last resort, leaving this world in this terrible manner, unable to face leaving their beloved land and farm.

I walked back to Tintagel on the northern coastline by King Arthur's Castle this time. The storm was raging. I could see the black clouds in the distance, and decided that if the going got really rough I would just sit quietly against the stone wall and wait. But the gale passed by, although it soaked me completely. I went to Tintagel to buy a few things and then walked back on the road this time, since I was getting cold from being drenched. A few other adventurous souls like me were out walking in their full rain gear.

Here are more words from Rudolf Steiner when he visited this area around August 17 or 18, 1924. They remind me of the strong pictures that flood my mind from my walk in this area.

> In earlier epochs, people strove for intelligence, *not* by developing the faculties of the head, but by seeking for the inspirations conveyed to them by cosmic forces.
>
> An example of how humanity sought cosmic intelligence in earlier times in a way that it is no longer sought today may be found when one stands...at the place in Tintagel that was once the site of King Arthur's Castle, and where Arthur and his twelve companions exercised a power of far-reaching significance for Europe.
>
> From the accounts in historical documents, it will not be easy to form a true concept of the tasks and mission of King Arthur and his so-called Round Table. This is possible, however, when one stands on the actual site of the castle and gazes with the spiritual eye over the stretch of sea that an intervening cliff seems to divide in two. There, in a relatively short time, one can perceive a wonderful interplay between light and the air, as well as between the elemental spirits living in light and air. One can see spirit beings flowing toward Earth in the rays of the Sun; one can see them mirrored in the glittering raindrops; one can see what comes under the sway of earthly gravity appearing in the air as the denser spirit beings of the air.

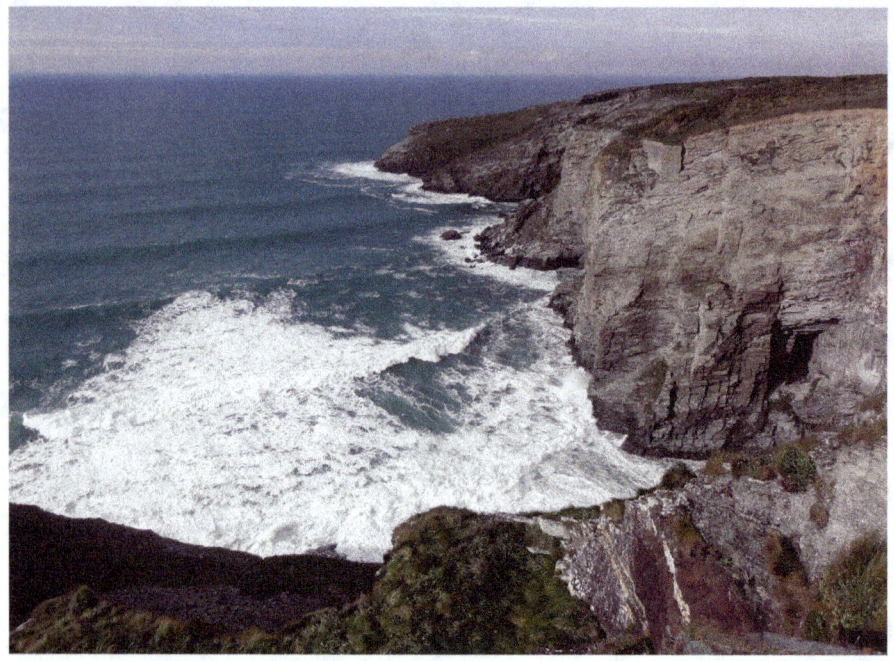

Again, when the rain stops and the rays of the Sun stream through the clear air, one perceives the elemental spirits intermingling in quite a different way. There, one witnesses how the Sun works in earthly substance, and seeing it all from a place such as this, one is filled with a kind of pagan piety—not Christian, but pagan piety, which is something altogether different. Pagan piety is a surrender of heart and feeling to the manifold spirit beings at work in natural processes....

This interplay between the Sunlit air and the rippling, foam-crested waves continues to this day. Over the sea and the rocky cliffs in this place, nature is still alive with spirit. Nevertheless, to take hold of the spirit forces at work in nature would have been beyond the power of a single individual. A group was needed, of which one individual was inclined to represent the Sun at the center, and whose twelve companions were trained so that, in temperament, disposition, and behavior, together they formed a twelvefold whole. Twelve individuals, grouped as the zodiacal constellations, surround the Sun. Such was the Round Table, with King Arthur at the center, surrounded by the twelve, with a zodiacal symbol displayed above each, indicating the particular cosmic influence associated with each knight. Civilizing forces went out from this place to Europe. It was here that King Arthur and his twelve knights drew from the Sun into themselves the strength to set out on their great expeditions through Europe to battle the wild, demonic powers still dominating large masses of the population, driving them out of human beings. Under the guidance of King Arthur, these twelve battled for outer civilization....

The whole of configuration of the castle at Tintagel indicates that the twelve under the direction of King Arthur were essentially a Michael community, belonging to the age when Michael still administered the cosmic intelligence.

This was in fact the community that worked longer than any other to insure Michael's dominion over cosmic intelligence. At the ruins of King Arthur's castle today, the akashic chronicle preserves the pictures of the stones falling from those once grand gates, and those falling stones become an image of cosmic intelligence falling and sinking away from the hands of Michael into human minds and hearts.[2]

---

2 Steiner, *The Archangel Michael*, Torquay, Aug. 21, 1924, pp. 274–276 (trans. revised).

Green

Now, we go on to the most healing of colors, viridian green.

In its evolution, humanity has traveled long distances through the world of color and we shall see that its entrance into green has been a very important step. We started in the magenta; in that color there is no circumference at all. In the carmine people got a consciousness of the using of their limbs, there was the rising of the will. And in that red there came the first glimmers of a circumference, even though this happened more in the consciousness of the priests than in that of the ordinary people. It was not a static circumference but a changing one, maybe one should say that there was a suggestion of a boundary that showed itself and disappeared again. This consciousness grew during the Egyptian Epoch in the orange and burnt sienna, becoming stronger toward the end of this period. With the Greeks there came a circumference that the people could see: very far and promising. They had a longing for it and a tremendous wonder and joy. They felt that the Earth has to do with them and they had a deep gratitude for it.

The Egyptians depicted Osiris with a green face. Green did not yet belong to the consciousness of the people, but even as today there are beings amongst us incorporated who are preparing the consciousness of the future and who are able to see colors that we do not yet see, so one can imagine that the Egyptian priests could see green at that early time. And they had to give Osiris a green face because they realized that he was the embodiment of pure intelligence, the living intelligence of an entirely different state of consciousness. And they saw it as a pure green with a little gold in it.[1]

Describing her early struggle to penetrate the spiritual world, Johanna von Keyserlingk told Rudolf Steiner, "If I were to describe my earthly path up till the present...I would compare it to the picture of having

---

1   Collot d'Herbois, *Light, Darkness and Colour...*, p. 150.

to cross the globe barefoot with bleeding feet, and being told on arrival that I was to repeat the performance, not once, but more than once. To break through into the spiritual world I had to possess the amount of energy equal to that which would be required to walk around the world three times—abandoned to every danger and obstacles and only supported by my own spiritual forces."

Resolution came in 1907 with a "Damascus Experience." Critically ill, she was filled with the thoughts of death. Death approached. She would have accepted it gladly, for she always yearned for the light behind the phenomena. The doctors said they could do no more. She knew she was about to meet the Christ. Enveloped in white starlight. She knew that if she could see Christ she would be healed. Then, as she told R. Steiner, "Powers whirled around me and a pillar of fire appeared by my bedside. Such a mighty force streamed forth from it that I thought I would not be able to withstand it.... I felt as if I would burst and I heard the words, "Depart hence, your faith has helped you."

"Who was the pillar?" she asked R. Steiner. "That was Christ," he replied.

From that moment on, she and her whole household were dedicated to Christ's service.[2]

With these powerful words by Countess Johanna von Keyserlingk, I chose to introduce the realm of green, viridian green, and the hundreds of greens we can see in the beauty of nature.

The pure viridian green is *the* healing color. It is an independent color. It is the carrier of the spirit and that gives it its objectivity and creativeness.... The kidneys are the organs for which the viridian green is particularly wholesome. Typical for the kidneys is that they have a deep connection with the astrality [our emotions]. Therefore they react to and suffer from emotional disturbances, such as nervousness, fear and shock. Some people wet themselves when they are nervous or when they have a fit of helpless laughter: the astral in the one case contracts, and in the other expands, and in both cases the person loses control....

Figuratively speaking the kidneys are light submerged in darkness. And all health and harmony in the organism depends on whether that

2   "The Women around Rudolf Steiner" (unpublished manuscript).

light comes up or not. When that inner light fails or gets closed down, the kidneys suffer. They get inflamed and become too soft. Then viridian green and turquoise will have a wholesome effect....

Traditionally green has always been looked upon as the color of healing. The German mystic Hildergard Von Bingen (1098–1179) writes about it extensively in her book on medicine. She distinguishes between the working of green in the plant-world, in the world of the soul and in the realm of the spirit. To Hildergard green in all its aspects is the manifestation of the Resurrected Christ. It is the creative force and it is the power of healing that restores and nurses life. And, she says, in the human being green is the color of intelligence or thinking and of conscience. All the powers of the Holy Spirit are green....

The color that is connected with the Risen Christ one can approach in painting by viridian green and a slight tinge of light yellow. Viridian, the chromeoxide green, is very cold, it can even be bitter. It needs just a tiny bit of soul-quality added to it. But only so little yellow that one hardly notices it. It takes a lot of careful painting to bring out the real quality of this particular green.

In the human being the processes of intelligence, the various thinking processes show as various shades of green. Exact, mathematical thinking goes more toward the turquoise.... Ordinary thinking, which always has a certain soul quality, goes more toward the yellow-green, the processes of average intelligence that are connected with the brain usually being yellow. Pure thinking, a faculty that is very rare at the present stage of human evolution, is a color that we are not yet aware of. Rudolf Steiner describes it when he speaks about the aura of the brain and of the spinal cord.[3] I think one could picture it as a movement from light green into viridian, fluctuating with magenta and finally going over into a sap green—a whole scale of color with the greatest emphasis on the viridian green.[4]

This passage shows clearly the path of the painter as a spiritual scientist. How do we work so that we develop these beautiful paintings that reflect the entrance of pure thinking, though in our case the use of substance, of mineral substance? It cannot be done unless we think, not the little thinking,

3   Steiner, *An Occult Physiology*, Prague, March 20, 1911.
4   Collot d'Herbois, *Light, Darkness and Colour...*, pp. 156–157.

but the thinking as experienced in *Intuitive Thinking as a Spiritual Path: A Philosophy of Freedom*. This color that is a mixture of viridian, light green, a touch of yellow, sap green, magenta, and flowing back and forth, is actually a realm that one enters as one paints. This is just as I mentioned earlier regarding the word "thankfulness" as an actual world-space, so is this a world of *pure thinking*. It is the world that can live or be on the canvas. This pure thinking allows the painter to approach the painting "The Resurrected Christ" or "Dove Coming Down." If one does not have that cognitive-feeling, there is no painting to speak of, but just playing with colors. The touch of the spiritual comes through the Path of the Green. When we paint this color, it is painted in veils so that it shows a vertical motion, from up to down. The other colors have some horizontal movements in them, slight curves dependent on the color, rounded forms, or more vertical/horizontal forms, showing movement. With green, the movement is down, vertical, like our spines are straight, the coming of the "I."

With green we leave space—space of the warmth of the darkness meeting the light; here the spirit and time enter space. It is a breaking up of the darkness, of this endless world of red moving toward the light. It meets the light of green and that is the incarnation of the "I." We now stand on our own, no longer moving in the warmth of the darkness, the reds. We are in the Light.

In Greece, where the pure green came into the consciousness of the human being, logical thinking came into full blossom. The foundation for this development had been laid during the Egyptian culture-period, when in the consciousness of the yellow the incarnation of the nervous system had taken place. Gradually people had learned to "feel" their way into their physical body and so the nervous system was prepared for the development of thinking that took in Greece....

The beginning of the Greek culture-period is a repetition of the development that took place on Crete. There is the same quality of lightness, the same radiance, the same shine over everything. The color of the sky was now seen as a greenish yellow, honey-colored one called it.

To the early Greek, the universe was filled with beings, divine and very holy beings and beings of a lower rank, more connected with nature. All these played a part in human life, they could help or hinder the mortals. Among them there were the Furies—fierce beings that followed a man who had done something wrong until they had sufficiently punished him.

In a relatively short time there took place a change and after that the Greeks were no longer able to perceive these beings, they no longer saw the Furies, they no longer could see their thoughts or the original ideas. Instead they began to see the outer world, the world of the senses, in much firmer outlines. The atmosphere became more clear and they saw a light-green Sun in a yellow-green air and atmosphere. A change-over, a tremendous change. There came now a very definite frontier between the outer world and the inner world. The human being who had done something wrong was no longer pursued by the avenging Furies, but he suffered pangs of conscience and remorse. His conscience was now part of his inner world and it was no longer contained in beings outside him. The Greeks were the first to become aware of the third dimension. One only has to cast one look on an Egyptian painting or bas-relief to see that it is all in two dimensions. But the Greeks began to see the third dimension and they loved it, to them it was an adventure, a great discovery. And they still were carried with the lightness that had been part of the Cretan time. At a certain period of the year it was to them as if light radiated from the Earth. Then there was love and light in the atmosphere. The Sun not only radiates the forming principle of antipathy, it also does the reverse, it attracts. And that was what the Greeks experienced so strongly in this green light. The Earth could be a yellow green and there would be a light-green Sun over it. They did not see green before they could think inwardly. The early Greeks who saw the Furies did not yet see the actual green. The seeing of the green began when the inner world shut itself off from the outer world. Then one saw green. It was then that one could become conscious of one's Ego ["I"].[5]

In the green we are in the light. As you gather from reading this book a painter has to live in colors all the time. In my homes I always paint the walls according to what is living in the family and what it needs. A few years ago I had painted my dining area with a glorious peach-orange as seen in the conch shells in the Bahamas, a very rich color. Then one spring

---

5   Ibid., pp. 150, 156–157, 150–152.

I repainted the whole house in a wonderful green with a touch of yellow from top to bottom—kitchen, entrance, stair hallway, bathrooms—except for the library/sofa room that was a deep magenta. I felt wonderful living with this lively green. The entire downstairs of my home in the Canadian Rockies is painted in a flamboyant vermilion red. I live very much in a color world. The clothes I wear are always of very specific colors for specific occasions. I never ignore the Color Beings. Scarves are a wonderful way to live in color. What one wears also affects one's environment and reminds people that we do have colors to bring joy, courage, and enthusiasm. It is a pity that most people ignore the Color Beings. One will also find that subversive governments and dictators always use colors as a means to control their people. Not being able to wear certain colors or only allowing dark colors for women to wear is an attack on their souls! That is why in the Western world it is really our duty to live consciously with colors and be thankful that we have the freedom to do so.

We have now come to a point where there are no more veils of darkness in front of the light. We do not yet look out into the space that lies behind the light, but we will linger for a while on that spot where there is a perfect balance between what is in front of the light and what is behind the light.

In the yellow-green that we have left behind us the darkness could still withstand the power of the light and gather itself together in small veils of color that for a moment flashed out and then dissolved again. Now we have come so near to the source of the light that the darkness no longer has the possibility of manifesting itself in such a way.

Always bear in mind that the world of color is the world of the *soul*. Light and Darkness are *spiritual* entities, each of them working according to their own laws. Absolute light can never be perceived in the world of the soul, neither can absolute darkness. But there is a moment when the light of the spirit leaves its own realm and enters the world of the soul. At that same moment it is met by darkness in its most rarefied condition. And this particular moment of meeting between strong light and the weakest darkness finds its expression in the color we call viridian green.

In the world of the soul, the light of the spirit cannot maintain its pure self. It enters into another dimension and thereby it changes its character. Because it meets the darkness there it is modified into color. As it falls into the soul substance (darkness) the light of the spirit becomes the light of consciousness. By crossing this threshold the light loses its spiritual quality and thereby loses strength, but at the particularly point where we are standing now it is still all powerful. It lights up the soul-substance of darkness, makes it transparent as the clearest crystal....

Viridian green is the one color that besides soul-qualities has a spiritual quality. It carries the light (the spiritual consciousness) over into the soul. Therefore one may call it the path of incarnation—the path the Ego ["I"] makes for itself and along which it travels from the spiritual world to the Earth. As such this color knows no inner nor outer, it keeps a perfect balance between the two. At the same time it is completely objective, it leaves no room for any subjective emotional movement and that is why people do not like it. Viridian green does not darken itself....

In nature we find the most perfect example of viridian green in the emerald—the gemstone out of which the Holy Grail was carved....

As a carrier of the light the viridian green is a carrier of the destructive forces of death that the Ego needs in order to be able to incarnate. The Ego ["I"] cannot dwell among the forces of life. They have to be cut away to a certain extent so that a path is created along which the Ego may incarnate, a space in which it may reside on Earth. That is done by the power that, in the world of color, manifests itself as viridian green. When I say "path" I do not mean a beaten track but rather a process or a movement. It is important to keep that in mind, because when the person enjoys a good health everything in the fourfold human organism is in perpetual motion, in perpetual flow, engaged in a never-ending process of metamorphosis, forever in a state of becoming, of being created and being destroyed and re-created at one and the same time. All that is included when I use the phrase "path of incarnation."...

The path of incarnation can be damaged, blocked, twisted, broken and then the inner light is intercepted. On the other hand the inner light can get soiled, it can even get stolen or lost. The result of all of this is, of course, illness. But in the case of undisturbed incarnation, in the case of a healthy organism, the human being has for himself a dwelling-place on Earth, a vehicle that enables him to fulfill his destiny.[6]

---

6 Ibid., pp. 154–155, 158–159.

I quote Rudolf Steiner again in a conversation he had with Margarita Woloschin:

> Released from the weight of matter, from what has become, into the realm of the living-becoming, color works to redeem the dead world through the art of painting. In transferring things from their existence in three-dimensional space onto the surface, it grants them a new existence in a new space. In this space, the "inner" of the human being manifests as the "outer." The external world, however, becomes ensouled, becomes inner experience. Time becomes space. The spiritual light of Lucifer and the heavy darkness of Ahriman become color in Christ.

> "Color is the revenge of the gods against Lucifer," Dr. Steiner said to me on one occasion, during a conversation about my work with regard to the healing power of painting. It was only later that the meaning of these words became comprehensible to me. The Lightbearer, who locks up his light in the glow of passion, in the wealth of shades of feeling within the isolated experiences of the human heart, is purged by means of the objective experience of color and offered up to the world. Thus, when, out of the cosmic circumference, the Christ spirit enters the heart that has been brought to rest, the Spirit of Separateness (Lucifer) is freed from his imprisonment in the world and becomes pure Holy Spirit. For this reason, color can have a healing and redeeming Effect. (This is why sentimental, luciferic people often have an antipathy to strong colors.[7]

Some of the beautiful Icons I was privileged to meditate upon in Russia had a beautiful touch of green when the painting was about the Christ. It had the usual carmine red, but the Christ being had a beautiful viridian with a slight touch of yellow in it, a kind of powdery green that is seen in the stone called chrysoprase, a most wonderfully healing stone that I wear every day. The icon painters were aware of the Christ color, and made use of it so that the Christian soul/spirit of the believer would have an easier time reaching, or making their ascent, to their devotion to the Pillar of Light: "Not I but Christ in me."

---

7   Stebbing (ed.), *Conversations about Painting with Rudolf Steiner*, pp. 150–51 (trans. revised).

Turquoise

Now we move far away to distant lands. Picture a beautiful mosque in Persia in the ancient city of Esfahan. It stands in a very large open space, which was used in former times for horse games, and there overlooking an ancient royal residence stands one of the most beautiful mosques I have visited. A large turquoise dome dominates the city and can be seen far and wide from the Persian desert, with minarets calling the faithful to prayers several times a day. The turquoise dome against the clear blue sky is an unforgettable sight. I stood many times in the open-air mosque deep in contemplation, gazing at the powerful, magical, sacred space. The arabesques filled the inside of the onion-shaped dome, as well as the interior space. I loved its clarity, its quiet, peaceful atmosphere, and was overtaken by a deep wonderful mood. It is a place of total repose; nothing comes to create emotional waves in this peaceful setting. One's mind does not wander; it is taken care of. There is no Promethean inclination here. Parceval's realm of asking questions is nonexistent! One is content to enjoy this clarity, this mood of perfection.

This is one of my favorite spaces. The turquoise dome is magnificent and gives an aura of orderliness, peace, and coolness in an otherwise warm desert setting. On a late afternoon one can order a mint tea or a yogurt iced mint drink from the hotel next door in the rose gardens and enjoy a perfect afternoon listening to the warm voice coming from the minaret's loud speakers. There is a bustle of movement in the late afternoon as the Persians wake from their afternoon nap to go to the bazaar to shop. On Friday the entrance to the mosque is filled with believers' shoes on the ground. They are praying. The open space is filled and takes in the fervent prayers, sending them up into the geometrical arabesque space.

Matter is spirit, and as spirit dives into matter it breaks up in thousands of little pieces. The arabesque is formed; it is spirit dying into matter. It is no longer living but in its death it announces its magnificence.

I chose again this turquoise onion dome because one can see similar ones all over the Middle East from Turkey through the former Russian republics—one whole wave of turquoise, calming and cooling the atmosphere of these warm countries. It cools the countries in more ways than one, as we come to understand when we examine the properties of this beautiful color.

We approached the viridian green and then, engulfed in that magic light, we stepped out of the light and now the light is behind us, and we are slowly going toward the darkness. Turquoise is the realm we enter as we slowly leave the magical land of green. It is the first veil away from the light, as yellow-green was the last veil of darkness in front of the light.

To the Greeks the light of the sky was golden and honey-colored, to the people of Byzantium it became a fluctuation between gold and turquoise.... That very first step into a darkness is dangerous when one has lived in nothing but light. The light has passed and is behind one—having to realize that comes as a shock. One feels left to oneself and one has to find one's way toward the darkness.... To be able to go on from here one *has* to have religion.

This was the situation 300 to 800 [years] after Christ. People knew that the Christ had incarnated and all the religious thoughts and feelings centered on this knowledge. The so-called Byzantine Empire encompassed many different nations and ethnic groups. The sphere of thinking and working in Constantinople, where half the town could have taken their vows to the Church, was entirely different from the one in Alexandria with its great Academy and famous libraries. All through the great Councils the various schools of religious thinking fought and excommunicated each other over theological questions and this is an example of turquoise in both its positive and negative aspects: on the one hand deep religious feelings and profound theological thinking, on the other hand the crystallizing into dogmas that caused the splitting up of the Church and intolerance over against schools of esoteric Christianity.

The second dimension was for the people of the turquoise not very far away, they were still rather loosely incarnated. [We are reminded again of the world of the reds, the second dimension.] The pure turquoise is very transparent and clear, like a glacier with the Sun shining through. It has strong qualities of form, of cleanliness and of upright morality. The turquoise people were exposed to all that, their nervous system was very open to it and they had no means of sheltering themselves against it. But they did have the support of their religion....

The consciousness of the people of the Byzantian epoch was as it were fluctuating between dream and objectivity. They did not perceive perspective in space, but they were very much aware of left and right. Theirs still was a two-dimensional perception....

The nervous system had begun to clear and thereby he had come to a different orientation on Earth....

Turquoise is the color that has the greatest coldness. When the soul is only filled with turquoise there is sharp thinking, clearly formed and formulated, that when it goes too far can become an imprisonment for the spirit. In the world of feeling there comes then cruelty for which Byzantium has a reputation. On the one hand the cruelty may be the outcome of cold calculation, on the other hand it may spring from religious fanaticism. There is an entire lack of compromise in this color, an extremity of things than can only lead to a split....

[Turquoise] is very clear, very crystalline, very transparent and its coldness is very objective. It can give form, the formative forces are very strong in this color...

This color belongs to the sunrise and to the sunset and to the coldness of the winter sky. It is an expression of cosmic, objective, creative antipathy. It is without compromise and in its movement it is the most strict, severe and mathematical of all the colors.

Turquoise is entirely dependent on the light and to a certain extent it leans on the light. It can give support inwardly, because in it one can stand with the feeling that one is being carried...there is support behind one.... One can think of a pillar of pure green light that is behind one and when one steps back into it, it gives one a support in one's backbone so that one can stand firmly upright.

Turquoise is the beginning of another kind of inwardness. In carmine one's soul moves more or less from the inside outwardly,... but in turquoise one makes the reverse movement, ... that is from outside to the inside. One has walked *through* the light toward the darkness into a new world. Those are inner steps toward the eventual threshold....

Turquoise can clear things up and make things transparent....

The healing quality of the turquoise is that it can give a certain morality. This color is an expression of the cosmic order that rules the courses of the stars and planets. The creative reality that makes the star has its movement, and in that there is an objective morality. One comes here into a world of laws that is almost mathematical and that is geometrically perfect, that is quite objective and very beautiful. When one wants to partake in that cosmic order, then one can be called moral.[1]

Now we return to turquoise and understand its significance in the world of Islam. As the human being enters the realm of the green light, the Christ being enters the Earth. Then the human being slowly moves away from the light, entering into the realm of turquoise. Humans are now forming thoughts, clear thoughts, and they move away from the spiritual worlds into the world of abstraction with ideas that no longer live but are cold. The dogmas of Rome are raging; the beautiful emerald green has become the awful dark green of the card table, a dark, ugly green. Moving from the green away from the light, as Liane mentioned, is dangerous business.

Muhammad was born in the middle of this turquoise consciousness in A.D. 500, bringing the visionary impulse that will put a stop to cold, intellectual, abstract ways, and thereby bring some balance out of his visionary experiences. We have to be thankful for that since otherwise the cold ahrimanic sciences, which were striven for in the Academy of Gondishapur in the Iraqi–Persian area would have brought a science that was much too advanced for humanity at that stage. Steiner talks about the Gondishapur Academy, which was a marvelous center of knowledge, but would have brought knowledge to the world that was fit for 2,000 years later. People of Byzantium would have had the intellectual knowledge we now have at a time when barbaric souls were still raging. Thanks to Muhammad, who

---

1   Collot d'Herbois, *Light, Darkness and Colour...*, pp. 179–184.

masterfully took all the strength from that early Gondishapur impulse and channeled it into the religious fervor of the Arabs, the religion of the Muslim world was born. The world of that area was still governed by strong instincts that lived in their blood. Their blood was full of life forces, forces coming from the will, with no strong "I" to be a master of those forces, no thinking yet. They did not have the cool, death forces of thinking, but only the youthful forces of the blood. Steiner mentions this in many lecture cycles. They needed the death forces. In that context we can see how the beautiful turquoise brings an element of morality that is otherwise not present in that area of the world. They live much too close to their raging instincts. When one is born in that part of the world, it takes much more discipline to control one's instincts than for the Westerner who is much colder. Therefore the opportunity is there for certain souls who chose to be born in the Islamic world to acquire great moral strength, etheric forces, and willpower in this lifetime.

The Athenian philosophers who were cast out by Justinian [A.D. 529] were welcomed by Khosrau I (531–579) at his Academy of Gondishapur in Persia, which he had modeled on the great Academy of Alexandria. The same curriculum was followed, and a vast body of knowledge was gradually accumulated. Teachers were gathered from the Syriac-speaking schools of the Nestorian Church, Edessa, and Nisiblis, and learning from the Monophysite Church, which was in close touch with Alexandria, was also bestowed.

In the eighth century, the wealth and power of Harun al-Rashid procured Greek manuscripts, many of them medical, from the Roman Empire and these were translated into Syriac and Arabic. An association had been formed with the Academy by the Abbasid court when it was established nearby at Baghdad, and when Harun al-Rashid and his ardently pro-Greek minister, Ja'far ibn Yahya, a Persian from Marw in Khorasan, sought for scholars to aid in their mission of Hellenizing Persian and Arab subjects, they drew many from this rich source. The luster of the court itself was also enhanced by the presence of learned scholars from Gondishapur. So strong was the Abbasid desire for a brilliant culture that the victor at the poetic contests received a hundred pieces of gold, a horse, an embroidered caftan, and a lovely slave. It was in the scientific realm, however, that Gondishapur excelled, and it was mainly from this center that Greek science passed to the Arabs.

The school of medicine was much to the fore at Gondishapur, and had been established before the time of Khosrau. Medical knowledge was derived through many different channels, notably Alexandria and India. Greek medical science passed through Alexandria to India and returned after being developed by Indian students. Gondishapur had an observatory, where Indian material also seems to have been received. Translators of astronomical works came from Marw, where Harun al-Rashid had been educated, and that was a city of Buddhist and Zoroastrian connection.[2]

Again one can see how this entering into the world of turquoise is reflected in the founding of this great Academy of Gondishapur. The mood was there, the mood of turquoise.

This color is an expression of the cosmic order that rules the courses of the stars and planets. The creative reality that makes the star has its movement, and in that there is an objective morality. One comes here into a world of laws that is almost mathematical and that is geometrically perfect, that is quite objective and very beautiful. When one wants to partake in that cosmic order, then one can be called moral.[3]

However, it also has its negative aspects.

In its negative aspects turquoise is the door to coldness, dogma, imprisonment. There can come a mis-forming.... This can start with the thinking, due to a particular attitude that comes from the soul. The soul is rigid and immovable.[4]

When Christian, Roman, dogmatic proselytizers want to take the Christian impulse into certain areas of the world, they should recognize that human beings need different impulses at different times during their lives on Earth. If human souls choose birth in a Muslim country, it is because

---

2   Steiner, *The Redemption of Thinking*, pp. 165–166 (trans. revised).

3   Collot d'Herbois, *Light, Darkness and Colour…*, p. 183.

4   Ibid.

they need to learn something there that they could not receive elsewhere. So we must become larger in our understanding. Leave people to their belief of choice. The world of Islam has its important place on Earth, and we in the West must keep the way clear for it. Only when people overstep their rights and become dogmatic can we interfere. Then it must be done in a clear, objective manner, such as was done in Holland when it forbade Muslim girl children to cover their heads with the chador when they go to school, which is correct. That is when stepping over the limit is lawful since in their homes they have a right to do as they wish.

In Muslim countries the youth are doing their work internally with courage and determination thanks to the internet. Politically we have no right to impose our own dogmatic religion upon anyone, and youth all over the world, especially the women, no longer have the patience to put up with dictators.

Now you see the strong influences that the turquoise dome has: an ordering and cooling effect on the often hysterical soul of the fundamentalist who has been "whipped into action by emotionalism"—an expression Steiner used to describe the Jesuits (Army of Christ).[5]

> Devotion and gratitude, the fundamentals of true religious feeling, are *the* healing forces for the turquoise people, because both are life-giving.[6]

There are wonderful masters of the spiritual life among Muslims. They live a life full of devotion and gratitude, and they will bring what the Middle-Eastern soul needs. It cannot be imposed by the West. In reality, the West could learn something of the wonderful hospitality that still lives in the Middle East. That was my reason for bringing this beautiful image of the Turquoise dome. If we can see what is lacking in one area of the world, then we can see what will bring it balance. Russia is the world of carmine; the soul that is born with a feeling for true religion. South of Russia lays the world of the Middle Eastern Muslim where Russian warmth of soul could

---

5   See Steiner, *Materialism and the Task of Anthoposophy*, Apr. 16, 1921.
6   Collot d'Herbois, *Light, Darkness and Colour...*, p. 186.

help the "cold, formed, lifeless, abstraction of the arabesque": a meeting of the carmine icon with the cool turquoise/green arabesque.

As young people travel from one country to another, the meeting is already taking place. New artistic souls will do the rest and some wonderful new artistic impulse will result that will change that part of the world. This is a far cry from what we hear on the news, and that is the main reason why I travel extensively throughout Mother Earth. Only by walking on this sacred Earth and meeting her sacred people can we have a true understanding. For me Anthroposophy, which I carry in my heart, becomes the new passport for mutual understanding.

Blue

In the period from the ninth to the eleventh centuries, when man became aware of the blueness of the sky, evolution had reached the stage in which the human organism began to enclose the soul and man became a being with an inner world that was all his own. He began to feel himself as separate from both the other world and the Heavens. The man of the cobalt blue was fully incarnated. He had an inner life and was conscious of it. He truly possessed his soul. Visual perception came to be dependent on the focusing of the eyes. This did not come about from one day to the other.... The focus came and went and came again—sharp, diffused, sharp. And slowly man began to be aware of space and of the optical illusion that we call perspective. Space in terms of perspective is not something that comes from the outer world, it is something that comes from the human being. Through the changing of his organism he has thrown the concept of space and of perspective into the world....

The man of the cobalt blue could feel the wish to be alone, to withdraw into his inner world in order to reflect. In the region of his heart he had the feeling "I am here," and also "I am separate from the world." He felt that his religiousness was his own, that it welled up from the depths of his being. And so he could look up to his God with feelings of devotion and humility. He could understand how Percival had to travel through the valley of humility before he could come to the castle of the Grail. Inner warmth is the quality that is carried in the being of the cobalt blue and so the human being of this period could for the first time have a true inner warmth. The Turquoise man did not have it yet and therefore he could be what we call cruel, although it was not cruelty to him.

The step from turquoise to the cobalt blue meant the completion of a process of incarnation and all movements of incarnation bring about warmth. In cobalt blue man could be self-contained and from an inner core establish a relationship with the outer world and with the Divine.

That is a deed of will. In the earliest times, as in the Old Persian epoch, man was surrounded by will. Will and warmth were all around him and carried him as long as he lived in the spheres in front of the light [magenta, carmine]. He could be aware of the Divinity, working Its creative processes in all the realms of the universe. Cobalt blue has brought about a metamorphosis of that Divine will and warmth, incorporating them in the human being as he went through a process of individualization that cut him loose from the Divine and made him wake up to his inner self. From here the road leads toward an ever more conscious experience of will.[1]

When I was twenty-six, I moved to Persia to work. I spent many Friday afternoons looking at ancient carpets, sipping tea, eating caviar and chatting with the merchants. I marveled at all the beautiful styles of tribal carpets, copper ware, and turquoise, and while browsing in the ancient narrow covered alleys of the bazaar, a beautiful lapis lazuli necklace grabbed my attention, so I bought it. It was not expensive but I simply had to wear those stones. It was not fine-grade perfect stone, but mixed stone with traces of silver in it and it had come from the mines in Afghanistan.

I wore that necklace every day for years and I still do. I became accustomed to its deep beautiful cobalt blue and from that stone I learned devotion—devotion to knowledge, devotion to people, countries, family life, children, friends. That necklace has influenced my life. When things got rough I always looked at my necklace and felt its wonderful warmth and strength and was able to go on. Now as a painter, I love to paint large canvases with cobalt blue and I give them away. People need that warmth these days. They need the encompassing, nurturing warmth of the cobalt blue.

The world of cobalt blue concentrates in the overwhelming city of Florence (read *Letters from Florence*). Cobalt blue is that city. Wherever one walks, one encounters the cobalt blue feeling in the murals, paintings, and icons that can be seen by the hundreds, so one lives in that realm. The Italians take it for granted, but they love their cobalt blue mood; it is in their devotion to beauty, to life.

---

1 Collot d'Herbois, *Light, Darkness and Colour...*, pp. 196–197.

[Cobalt blue] in its coming into being is a balance between the darkness behind it and the light in front. And in that balance it has a warmth that is objective, that is caring and knowing, almost all-conscious because of its light. The light gives it the power of reflection that red has not. Red just surges ahead, prompted by its subjective warmth.

Colors are beings, the beings that through all the culture periods were part of us and worked on us. They were as it were our soul outside of us, and they will be our souls in time to come. We must not think of them existing through the ages of ages formed and finished, because they are continually coming into being, creating and recreating themselves as they work on what we know as the realms of nature and on us.

Before we continue our study of the development of the human being it might be appropriate at this point to recapitulate the evolution, or maybe one ought to say the process of incarnation, that we have traced through the colors in front of the light.

When man came out of the consciousness of the magenta and went over to the carmine he left the all-embracing one-ness and woke up to a world of duality. Carmine has to do with man's mission in connection with the Earth. In this color man became for the first time conscious of his feet and of their touching the Earth and every footstep was like a prayer to him. The fact that one can stand upright and can walk is really the foundation of being human—and all that was laid in our consciousness in the carmine of the Old Persian time. In the Egyptian culture period, through the activity of the orange and the yellow the astral body became more closely connected with the nervous system. The transition period of the yellow-green on Crete was the preparation for the consciousness of form. At that time (which was before Troy) the living forms still contained a remnant of the divine: one could still perceive the creative processes. In the play between gravity and the heavens (which found expression in dance and acrobatism) the brain began to play its part as the central organ of the nervous system. In the Greek time it was to a certain extent finished. The unconscious picture-consciousness was transformed into the faculty of logical thinking philosophizing, which was still permeated with the etheric forces of life.

Today man is living in the world far behind the light, in the deep blues. Thinking has for the greater part become lifeless and mechanical and humanity has to revivify it and come to a conscious picture-consciousness. Working with color in accordance with the laws of light and darkness can be a help here.[2]

I am looking now at Raphael's painting, the Garvagh Madonna 1509, depicting the Madonna and Child with the infant Baptist. If we look at it with our knowledge of colors we see that she has a wonderful carmine dress that covers her chest, her heart area, and is wrapped in cobalt blue. The carmine belongs to that area, the warmth that wants to spread out everywhere in emotions, feelings, love, care, the maternal. All of that is enveloped in the other warmth, the objective warmth of the cobalt blue. It is objective warmth—warmth that includes reflection within it. It does not go everywhere unattended, but is collected warmth, thoughtful warmth. In that masterpiece, as well as in all the other Madonnas, we have the symbol and image representing the task that is required of us.

We maintain the warm liveliness of the carmine we saw in the icon in the Russian soul, but surround that with our objectivity—not with the coldness of turquoise that has too much light—and the wonderful encompassing warmth of the cobalt blue, which is devotion and then compassion. When one devotes oneself to something, it is a thoughtful act toward something one loves; our selfishness disappears to encompass something else. Cobalt is that warm space. Then in the middle realm, the green pillar of light, the Christ child is born. Out of the sphere of the unbridled will, passing through the light of consciousness with the birth of the "I," we move toward the darkness, but now with the ability to reflect and act with love. In *Intuitive Thinking as a Spiritual Path,* it is thinking with will, and willing with thinking, the realm of morality.

In the realm of the red carmine mood there is no reflection; we are taken by the wonderful, rich warmth of the darkness moving toward the light in a loving gesture. However, there is no thinking, no reflection. For that we needed to incarnate more and join in the light. Then with the birth of the light within we move toward the darkness once more with the

---

2   Ibid., pp. 177–178.

light, and that is cobalt. This is the realm of reflection, of thinking while still retaining warmth.

When we live in the cobalt blue realm we are living with devotion; we are in a devotion mood. This calms the nervousness of our excited lifestyle and helps us in making important decisions so that what we decide is not dominated by our raging will, but our thinking. Cobalt blue is a great healer nowadays.

In the same manner, for people who are too much in their thinking and reflecting all the time and have lost the ability to act, plunging themselves in the carmine mood of an Russian icon with its lovely red will awaken the will and bring one to activity. Both pictures belong together, and this is the work of the Collot d'Herbois therapist who has lived with the Color Beings for years with total devotion and is able to bring balance in the otherwise unbalanced soul.

When one enters the San Marco's Church and monastery in Firenze one lives in that mood of devotion. Fra Angelico was cobalt blue. The frescos in the cells are all exquisite. If people have lost something within themselves, and if they can just step into one of these cells and take in the colors, it will rejuvenate them and bring great healing to their souls. It is much, much better than taking chemical drugs or spending thousands of dollars on the therapist's couch. Live with the colors for a week and let them move you; then you will recover from your symptoms, whether they are symptoms of a lack of something, emptiness, boredom, apathy, cancer or too much of something—nonessentials, business, drive, heart attack—the atmosphere in these cells brings healing to a sick soul.

I am a great fan of traveling, so I recommend you buy yourself a ticket and spend ten days in the city, especially in the San Marco's cells. Find your favorite and live with it; let the colors be your medicine. Your heart will bring you to the one you need. Your heart does not lie. There might be several paintings, so live with them and feel their strength. At night you will dream in those colors, and the Color Being will come and rescue your soul. If that is not possible, then buy an art book of San Marco and live in those cells through the pictures. Live for a week with the paintings you feel attracted to and watch the result. You will be more than surprised! Changes will occur.

We have been talking about this path for the painter in terms of color, but now one of the greatest of meditation teachers, scientists, and true Christian souls speaks about the process, as a cognitive process.

The human being became the dwelling place of the light....

The path of modern training consists in liberating this movement of the soul from the compulsion of the egocentrically binding experience of the self. It can do so only if it never abandons the principle of cognition. Therefore, training begins with thinking, which is the basis for every judgment: every choice goes through thinking. What is done with thinking becomes the model for the transformation of all the other capabilities of the soul.[3]

Now we come to the heart of the challenge that faces us today.

This brings us to the connection that cobalt blue has with two colors in front of the light: carmine and magenta. With carmine it has in common a certain inner polarity; carmine was the beginning of dualism [ancient Persia, light and darkness, Zarathustra]. Both are an expression of cosmic will: cobalt blue in an objective way, carmine in a subjective way. Looking at it from the point of view of the soul, one may realize that the soul-warmth of the red is more egoistic, especially where it goes toward vermilion. Red can be the expression of all kinds of wishes, desires, passions—hence its intense movement. Magenta is not quite so warm, but like the cobalt blue it is all all-embracing, all carrying. Both colors are nursing, but it is typical of cobalt blue that is all-overlooking, almost all-conscious, because of its light. It has a power of reflection in it, of care and of knowing, but it is always looking to the past. It is like something that sweeps from the past. Red does not have any power of reflection, it just sweeps ahead, seeing nothing but the future.[4]

The challenge is this: How do we live in the *present* and not in the past as in the cobalt blue and not in the future as in the carmine? This is

---

3   Kühlewind, *Stages of Consciousness*, pp. 101, 89.

4   Collot d'Herbois, *Light, Darkness and Colour...*, p. 199.

the realm that Rudolf Steiner mentions as creating a new color that lies somewhere after cobalt and indigo. In this space, as we leave the realm of the light with the birth of the light within, how do we enter the realm of *living in the present*? This was brought to our attention earlier, but from another perspective. We spoke about enlivening the Color Being, while conscious of the fact that the colors are *beings*. In that recognition that we face *beings rather than just colors,* we infuse life into the otherwise dead concepts living in our cold intellect. The Color Beings *become alive within,* and just like in the domain of language, we infuse life into the dead words through our meditation, and that is the creation of stepping out of the past, not forging ahead into the future, but living in the presence of the *beings, joining them and thereby creating new colors.*

That is the task of the painter, a real painter who lives out of what Rudolf Steiner brought to us with such enormous sacrifices. Liane Collot d'Herbois devoted her whole life to this process. Living in the present is a meeting of the spiritual *beings, it is an act of intuition* as Steiner explains it. In *imagination* we see the spiritual beings, in *inspiration* we hear the spiritual beings, and in *intuition* we are the spiritual beings.

> The contrast with the assertion that "active production [will/red] and its objective contemplation (blue/reflection)" are mutually exclusive could not be more decisive. In reality there is no contradiction here at all, since intuitive experience is neither objective contemplation [the blue] ["standing over against"] nor "observations" in the usual sense, but rather is presence, *presentness* in the activity, the unmediated experience from within. This presence, presentness *in* the activity, is practiced in every artistic pursuit. The singer does not wait until the sounds have died away to observe and judge what has been sung. It would be much too late then to notice a false note. One "hears" it in the process, even *before* the sound is produced, from within.... To be present in the moment, *in* the act of cognition, and not merely to wake up to what has been already thought, is to experience intuition, not merely its result. This transparency of the act of cognition itself, this not-forgetting of the cognizing behind the cognized, this not-remaining-hidden of the wellspring of cognition, is at once

the experience of living thinking and of the true "I," which alone is capable of this experience.[5]

Here a great thinker grasps the moment of moving from the cobalt blue realm into the realm of the indigo. There is an enormous step that we need to go through in order to enter the darkness, total darkness, but we cannot survive without *the inner light,* given to us by *an experience of Golgotha.*

Beyond the Madonna picture, another picture comes to mind in the realm of cobalt blue. If we have devotion and add love, then reverence comes into being. I found that aspect very helpful in moving from the cobalt-blue experience/space to the next experience, indigo, the color of the consciousness soul.

> Whereas the mystics of all ages, together with Goethe, have spoken of the unknown, undefined element to which the soul is drawn, as the *eternal feminine,* we may without misunderstanding, speak of the element that must always animate reverence as the *eternal masculine.* For just as the internal feminine is present in both *men and women,* so is the *eternal masculine,* this healthy "I"-feeling, present in all reverence by men and women. And when Goethe's *chorus mysticus* comes before us, we may, having come to know the mission of reverence that leads us toward the unknown, add the element that must permeate all reverence—the eternal masculine.[6]

With the cobalt blue, the final movement of living in an enclosed space, comes a feeling of loving embrace portrayed by the Madonna. Here we have an indication of how we move forward and the beautiful statement of the *eternal masculine* is a great picture that gives us the strength to go on to the next stage of entering further into the darkness. To add to reverence, the *eternal masculine* is something about which people do not think. It is always about the Madonna. To add the *eternal masculine* makes the

---

5 Kühlewind, *Stages of Consciousness,* p. 34 (trans. revised).

6 Steiner, *Metamorphoses of the Soul,* vol. 1, Berlin, Oct. 28, 1909, p. 62 (trans. revised).

transition from cobalt blue to indigo more palpable, more living. Without a strong "I," we cannot face up to the darkness and we get lost.

Perhaps because I am in a female body "this time" I can understand more readily what disturbs me when people these days are focused on Sophia, Madonna, and the eternal feminine (mostly men and not-incarnated females) and they forget, just as Steiner mentioned here, that the eternal masculine has its tasks as well. Without it, our weak egos would not be up to the task. We have dreamy human beings stuck in the Madonna mood and failing to move on to the next consciousness, which is indigo, then on to violet, then darkness, the unknown, and death.

> All things transient are but a parable;
> Earth's insufficiency here finds fulfillment;
> the indescribable here becomes deed;
> the eternal-masculine draws us on high.[7]

---

7   Steiner, *Metamorphoses of the Soul*, vol. 1, quoting Goethe, p. 52.

Indigo

The stormy weather has not subsided and I think winter is arriving in Cornwall. Today it is raining, not as windy as yesterday, but foggy and I can't see anything. I go for the shorter walk to Port Williams just south of this village by the coastal path. I encounter a little rabbit running to his hole, and then I am plunged into the misty atmosphere, sliding on the muddy path, and enjoying the green-grayish veil of colors of the ocean and the waves flattened by the westerly winds.

To my surprise the little hotel is busy with older couples having a drink in the afternoon and enjoying the scenery in the cozy rooms. I am completely wet and enjoy my coffee. Then I bundle up again and climb the cliff back to the path and home. In between the high thorny edges of the inland path, I feel the joyousness of the path and concentrate on that. Who is there? There are a host of elemental beings frolicking in the misty, wonderful airy, muddy, rocky paths.

I am reminded again of Collot d'Herbois's comments when I asked about painting using her method, and she said, "Look out the window!" and I did. "See there in between the space of the branches? Look not at the branches, but concentrate on the space in between the branches of that tall tree. Concentrate on that space!" And she is right. One has to concentrate on the space where there is apparently nothing, and there find something. It is called negative space in projective geometry, for which I have a special love. I have spent hours in deep enjoyment doing projective geometry in very large notebooks. It is good training for the painter.

So today, walking on this path, I concentrate on the space where there is apparently nothing, and the little elemental beings enter and make themselves seen, furtive and quick but nonetheless present in this area where they abound, especially on days like this. This in turn is reflected in people's wide smiles when they walk around here in the rain, the mud, and the stormy winds.

With the experience of one's own true "I" (and humanity is on the verge of becoming conscious of this experience), one experiences an existence that is purely spiritual, without any sort of "matter," an existence as insubstantial as the thought world. By means of this "I"-experience, one avoids picturing the spiritual being spoken of by the spiritual researcher as spatial and substantial. On the other hand, one has a cognitive experience in which one does not stand over against the object [*duality* = object vs. subject]. This "standing over against" was, after all, ingrained through cognition in the sensible world. It follows that this same cognition cannot continue to exist in the cognition of the spirit. Here there is no "standing over against," but only conscious self-surrender, conscious identity—penetration into the object of cognition and mutual interpenetration, as one knows the thoughts of another only when one thinks them through oneself so as to become one with them and make them one's own. One can cognize the spiritual only when one has united with it. Standing over against is appropriate only when dealing with objects, even inner sense objects. We cannot stand over against the spirit; it immediately becomes non-spirit. It is not outside us; if it were, it would be non-spirit (*Ungeist*).

From this it follows immediately that Spiritual Science is no thing, no object, no knowledge toward which one can set a course in order, perhaps, one day to reach it.... Spiritual Science is, or should be, pure activity, and moreover, experience activity. It is no teaching, no doctrine. It is a possibility of modern humanity, which originates in living thinking, in the awakened, experienced core of being. Whoever studies or practices Spiritual Science must move from dialectical thinking—however subtle that may be—to spiritual experience. Otherwise everything remains pseudo-knowledge, dogma, or belief, which nonetheless fails to recognize itself as such and, therefore, is unbelief: superstition....

Once humanity said, I think, therefore I am. People felt their own being sheltered, anchored, and preserved in thinking. However, what of those who are able to experience their "I" outside—independently—of their thinking? What do they say? They no longer need any support to *be.* One's essence, one's own being, answers for itself—it is its own guarantor. Thus one can say the primal word: "I AM."[1]

This stage in our painting work is the movement from cobalt blue to indigo and living in indigo. This is the color in which we live in this twenty-first century, and as you will experience, it is mind shattering. It also has a loving sacrificial mother-of-pearl quality.

> Then humanity took its first step into the darkness. In the turquoise one was still strongly supported by the spiritual light, in cobalt blue one could stand on one's own two feet because of the inner strength one found in one's devotion. People felt themselves cut off from the spiritual world, but they had gained the possibility of reflecting. With the closing of the top of the etheric head the soul had closed, but the physical eyes had found their focus and they could see perspective from one point in space.... Candles, torches, and open fires were the only lights that could brighten their nights, but they did not have the fear of darkness that today can torment man of the indigo. One cannot go through indigo without the deep devotion of the cobalt blue. When one has come to the point where cobalt blue turns into Indigo one realizes that the journey into darkness has really begun. One has to come to the abyss and there is no bridge and only through devotion one can get across.
>
> Indigo is an inner experience, it is a realm without boundaries. When one can go far enough in it, it lightens—even though one has to go through despair and hopelessness before one can see the light.[2]

For the indigo I choose an experience, an imagination, and some paintings. One is a cognitive feeling that I experienced while reading *Intuitive Thinking as a Spiritual Path: A Philosophy of Freedom;* another is Hiram as he jumps into the Sea of Molten Lava,[3] another is El Greco and his "indigo" paintings, and finally is a painting by Raphael, which hangs in the National Gallery of Art, Washington, DC. It is Michael on his horse vanquishing the dragon in a deep indigo armor.

---

1 Kühlewind, *Stages of Consciousness*, pp. 54–56 (trans. revised).
2 Collot d'Herbois, *Light, Darkness and Colour....* p. 216.
3 See Steiner, *The Temple Legend,* part 2.

Several decades ago I lived in Buffalo, New York, for several years and I joined the wonderful Anthroposophical group in Aurora, led by the charming Bruce McKausland. We were reading *The Philosophy of Freedom*, which I had never read. Each one of us had to prepare a chapter and introduce it. I showed up at the meeting without reading or preparing. I could not stand the book and could not see the point of it, although I loved Steiner's lecture cycles and was deeply into them. So I sat and listened. When it was my turn to prepare I had still not read a thing, so I went back home and proceeded to read up to the chapter I was presenting. Then, since I had studied philosophy and rather liked it—especially Bergson, Auguste Comte, Teillard des Jardins, Gabrielle Marcelle, Sartre, Simone de Beauvoir—I really lived into each chapter for the whole week, day and night. At one point I had a feeling that was like nothing I had ever had before. It was the feeling of warmth, utter desolate warmth, and penetrating heat and strength. As I was really studying the sentences, I went more into that feeling. The cognitive feeling was like experiencing my own brain and the intensity was overwhelming, but I stayed with it, and kept on reading. Something was frightfully alive! Then I realized that was the point of the book. It was a door into experiencing the spiritual world. Steiner brought one to that feeling of stepping across the threshold just through reading his well-honed thoughts, clear-cut thinking, like diamonds. One experienced one's thinking! And as Liane Collot d'Herbois says, indigo is a feeling. That is when I recognized the beauty of this book, and it has been my required reading at least once a year, when I plunge again into the exercise of thinking and reaching in a lawful way the crossing of the threshold. It sharpens one's thinking and gets rid of the usual emotional garbage, the nonsense of which people are so fond and in which they spend their lives swimming.

> Through Rudolf Steiner's *Philosophy of Freedom* [*Intuitive Thinking as a Spiritual Path*], in which the strength of Michael holds sway, humanity can rise again to living thoughts and thus reach an experience of the spirit.[4]

---

4   Wegman, *Esoteric Studies*, Sept. 20, 1925, p. 70.

The cognitive feeling that I experienced is the same as the feeling of indigo when one penetrates it very deeply, which is very difficult. One can only go there with total devotion and selflessness.

I chose the jumping of Hiram into the Sea of Molten Lava, because that is the same cognitive feeling that one experiences when reading *The Philosophy of Freedom* if one has the strength to penetrate it with devotion. Lava is indigo color. It is intense heat and molten lava. For me, these two words conjure the world of indigo and what one has to endure to penetrate that world and create the new colors that Rudolf Steiner talks about, the new colors for the future.

> Being so deep in the darkness indigo contains a lot of warmth. It is an inner warmth, like the glow of embers under the ash; a hidden warmth, like the thunderbolt before it bursts from the cloud. In cobalt blue the warmth is more obvious, more on the surface. In indigo it is only perceptible in the sense of warmth.
>
> When in the course of its evolution the soul had penetrated so deep into the world of darkness that it found a foothold in the sphere of indigo the consciousness soul began to awaken. Indigo as it were answers the green and supports it by offering it a form to dwell in: the skeleton. Indigo gives the hardening process its final touch so that it stabilizes into form. The Ego travels a great distance from the origin of the green down to the pure indigo. The incarnation into Indigo is a great movement, the Ego ["I"] reaches a great depth and it touches on a fire that is hidden there. Then the human being finds the possibility of knowing the evil he carries within himself. In indigo the soul has greater heights and greater depths than it ever had before and we have to associate ourselves with this color because we need it for our further evolution.[5]

In the painting of El Greco I have always been fascinated with his use of deep indigo, which other painters of his time did not use. They were seeped in cobalt blue. El Greco had penetrated another world, another dimension. His human figure is totally distorted, perspective is lost, and we swim in an atmosphere of indigo. We see the human beings struggling with all their

---

5   Collot d'Herbois, *Light, Darkness and Colour*..., pp. 220–221.

might trying to control the world of the depths, with increasing fear on their faces. Gone is the smile of Raphael's beautiful Madonna and instead there is enormous fear of entering the darkness. The paintings stand as a foreboding of what humanity is experiencing on a massive scale in our modern world. Its world of dark gray, indigo-colored arms, tanks, gray bombers, gigantic skyscrapers, buildings lost in their world of abstraction and desperate isolation. His is a fear-driven society with massive hysteria, stuck in the quagmire—a marsh of depression, grayish desolate moods. All that is the picture of entering the world of indigo unprepared, with no devotion, no belief in anything except what can be measured, weighed, and counted—a world of selfishness and arrogance.

This can all be witnessed in paintings of El Greco who lived it before we did. In that respect they are most powerful because now we see it ourselves. That world conjured in the paintings exists here in our modern cities, and unless we take up what is spoken of in this book, there will soon be a point of no return.

> Indigo is intensely connected with the problems of our time and the greatest of them all is isolation. In indigo one can feel cut off, not only from the spiritual world but also from one's fellow human beings. . . .
>
> Our time has tremendous drama. The human being now has possibilities of ascending higher in the spiritual world, but also of descending lower in the depths of the netherworld than ever before. Ours is the age in which everyone can be conscious of the evil within himself. The darkness into which the road through indigo leads one is not evil, but what one may meet in it depends on one's morality. A reversal can take place and the evil one carries within oneself may seem to come to one from outside in various shapes and beings. As it gets darker the boundary of the indigo closes ever more in. And because of its deep inwardness it can turn one's whole body into a sense-organ and then one can become aware of beings surrounding one and one does not know whether that is a threat or a foreboding. In so far as one is a carrier of evil the beings come pressing in from all sides, leering, menacing. But when one has the right knowledge of good and evil, and knows oneself to be accompanied by the pure cobalt blue, one can associate oneself with the being

of the indigo without coming to any harm and then one will find that that being is almost motherly. It is the one that sacrifices herself for the beauty of all the other colors as one can see in the mother-of-pearl of a dark shell, where one can see a whole rainbow of iridescent colors against a background of indigo. Then one knows that one can travel on safely because the pure indigo will give one protection.[6]

One can see this beautiful property of indigo in many of El Greco's paintings. One is in the National Gallery of Art in Washington, DC, and it depicts the Madonna surrounded by indigo. She has a cloak of carmine, but her coat is indigo. There are clouds of iridescent light, and a dark indigo play of color that gives a feeling of the mother-of-pearl sacrifice. She is all sacrifice. Her face has a tinge of indigo, and the painting is steeped in an indigo mood, not the mood of Raphael's Madonnas, which are lovely and completely devotional. El Greco has gone beyond that. The Madonna has devotion within and then sacrifices herself so that all can shine. El Greco reached that realm 500 years before it was time. In another painting of the annunciation that hangs in the museum in St. Petersburg the mood is also indigo, and the face of the Madonna is again a light tinge of mother-of-pearl indigo, and the light indigo-white dove over her head swims in this background of indigo, and the angel in some light yellow appears also mixed with indigo. El Greco used both qualities of the indigo to portray his "revelation" paintings.

This is an atmosphere of fear, as well as an atmosphere of sacrifice, of softness, a beautiful world of light indigo in which the other colors can shine.

> One cannot let all patients paint with Indigo, but for those who can, the therapist has to create the imagination of the softness and warmth, of the tender enveloping quality that this color has.... Where there is light there is also a boundary of the light, a circumference. And wherever one goes that circumference is always sheltering and protecting one. In indigo there is as it were a double protection: the blueness of the far circumference has come nearer and nearer to protect one, to give one

6   Ibid., pp. 219–220, 218–219.

a sheltered sphere in which to breathe. There one can be at home. One need not feel walled in, because there is always an opening....

On the whole one can say that the people of our times have lost the inner warmth, the soul-warmth that lies behind the balance of the rhythmic system. That soul warmth one can find when one occupies oneself with indigo. But it is hidden. There is curtain after curtain of indigo between us and the reality that lies behind the world of the senses. One can penetrate that with one's pure thinking, but on the other hand also with the thinking of one's heart. And the latter is the path of color.[7]

Intuitive Thinking as a Spiritual Path: A Philosophy of Freedom can bring the experience of indigo, as I shared a few pages ago, and we can enter that realm if we exert enough tension/power/concentration in the experiencing of this book and it becomes alive within ourselves in a real tangible way, leading to a cognitive feeling, the experience of indigo. The other path is to experience the colors as you have experienced them in this little journey: with your heart.

A friend was telling me that some people do not like Liane Collot d'Herbois's book because it goes all over the place. You can't read it as you would a book looking for information. Everything is everywhere! It is full of life, not intellectual or logical, but written with the Thinking of the Heart. One must experience the book and for it to make any sense one has to meditate on it by painting it. One must paint it, otherwise it leads nowhere. Actually we have to eat the book. That is a much nicer picture. One has to experience it fully, then digest it and make it go through the alchemical process; then we can get somewhere.

It is necessary to realize that living thinking exists. For what is it that people know since the fifteenth century? They know only logical thinking, not living thinking. This, too, I have pointed out repeatedly. What is living thinking? I shall take an example close at hand. In 1892, I wrote *Intuitive Thinking as a Spiritual Path*. This book has a certain content. In 1903, I wrote *Theosophy*; again it has a certain content. In *Theosophy*, mention is made of the etheric body, the astral body, and

---

7   Ibid., pp. 223–224.

so on. In *Intuitive Thinking as a Spiritual Path*, there is no mention of that. Now those who are only familiar with the logical, dead thinking come and say, Yes, I read the *Intuitive Thinking as a Spiritual Path*; from it, I cannot extract any concept of the etheric and astral body; it is impossible; I cannot find these concepts from the concepts contained in the book....

I cannot put a mechanical, lifeless process in place of something living. But picture the *Intuitive Thinking as a Spiritual Path* as something alive—which indeed it is—and then imagine it growing. From it, then develops what only a person who tries to cull or pick out something from concepts will not figure out. All objections concerning contradictions are based on just this, namely, that people cannot understand the nature of living thinking as opposed to the dead thinking that dominates the whole world and all of civilization today. In the world of living things, everything develops from within.... Things that grow and wane develop from within, and so it is also in the case of living thinking. Yet, today, people sit down and merely try to form conclusions, try to sense outward logic. What is logic? Logic is the anatomy of thinking, and one studies anatomy by means of corpses. Logic is acquired through the study of the corpse of thinking. It is certainly justified to study anatomy by means of corpses. It is just as justified to study logic through the corpses of thinking. But one will never comprehend life by means of what has been observed on the corpse![8]

Now that I have emphasized alive thinking yet again, we can go on:

We have almost completed our journey through the realms of color. We began with the magenta—the color that carried us over the threshold into the world of human consciousness and organic life. Now we are about to leave that world again. Violet leads us deeper into the darkness and eventually back into the realms that lay beyond the threshold.

In Indigo we came to an abyss. Indigo spoke to us of death, or in other words, of another knowledge of the Ego. Now the veils of indigo have been torn asunder and we are received by the violet, the color that is like a bridge that we have to cross to come into another world.[9]

---

8   Steiner, *Materialism and the Task of Anthroposophy*, Dornach, Apr. 29, 1921, pp. 186–187.

9   Collot d'Herbois, *Light, Darkness and Colour...*, p. 239.

On our journey from green to turquoise, to cobalt blue and then to indigo we can encounter this Imagination. It is connected with the cognitive feeling experienced while I was studying *The Philosophy of Freedom*. The being that stands behind the strength and life encountered in this book is the archangel Michael:

> The light may come suddenly in indigo. The color will then rush from indigo to ultramarine and cobalt blue and from there into turquoise and then one finds oneself close to the green. And in that moving world of imagination one might meet with what might be called a knight in black armor, with light behind him and shining through him. The blackness may then dissolve and metamorphose into a being of light and one realizes that in our time no other color has such an intense connection with the archangel Michael as just indigo.
>
> …Michael is now guarding a kind of intelligence that is different from for instance the one that Osiris was the keeper of. As humanity developed Michael, too developed and he has a different task now. He who in the times before Christ was the great warrior and the glory of the Heavens now has to wait for human beings to take the initiative. And when in the development of the consciousness soul the human being can find the right connection with the world of indigo, he may become aware of the presence of Michael, may meet him, "see" him in an imagination such as described above. And that will give him courage and inspiration and enthusiasm to pursue his course.[10]

≈

Yesterday I had a most wonderful visit with my "SteinerBooks" neighbors. They are only a few miles down the road and live in a large old renovated church from which one can see the wild coast surrounded by gardens. Henry Golden and his wife Pamela, who is a talented sculptor, offered me a very strong cup of coffee and we proceeded to chat for several hours. The house was full of books and so of course we talked books. Henry at 83 is feeble and facing some health problems, but he is a very sharp thinker and I thoroughly enjoyed his comments. I left their magical site and went for a walk

---

10 Ibid., p. 219.

as the weather had calmed down a bit. I went to pay a visit again to Merlin's cave. It was low tide and I could look down below the cliffs onto the small beaches where birds were diving into the calm ocean for fish. Then I walked to the large cave and collected my favorite things—beautiful rocks polished by the power of the water and wind. They are magical rocks of all colors. I will bring another few pounds of these rocks back home.

Then I sat by the cliffs and let whatever came from the magical setting enter my mind's eye. The same very stern, powerful look from King Arthur came to me, as well as the wild activity of horses and their riders. If he had such a powerful impact on Europe, then he must have left quite an imprint on the area, and I believe it can still be felt without much effort.

> We have seen that each stage in the evolution of the human organism brings with it the perception of a new color. From another point of view one can say that it is the creative power of that color that brings about that step forward in the development.
>
> In the Greek culture-period [green], man had the first glimmer of awareness of an inner world over against an outer world, both on the spiritual and on the material plane. Before everything was inner and outer at the same time, the soul lived in an undivided, all-embracing oneness. The turquoise man, the Byzantinian, lived with the greater part of his soul in the Heavens and the religious feeling…was all around him in the atmosphere, a divine inspiration shining into his soul, which was still very open to influences from outside. The consciousness of the people of the third and fourth century had fluctuated between the world of space in which one was fully awake in the senses and the world of dream where through one's feeling one was able to apprehend what went on beyond the boundary of consciousness. In other words: between the world of three dimensions and the world of two dimensions.[11]

We return to the image of the icon, with its two-dimensional quality in which the viewer still lives in the warmth of the carmine in the spiritual world, and the world of the death of the spirit as seen splattered as it enters the physical world, the Arabesque.

---

11 Ibid., p. 196.

Matter, as it occurs in the universe, is for esotericists no more than form, broken, shattered, and split apart.... *Matter is a heap of ruins of the spirit.* It is extraordinarily important to grasp this definition. *Matter is a heap of ruins of the spirit.* Matter is, therefore, in reality spirit, but shattered spirit.[12]

The Arabesque is a beautifully drawn, lonely line that stands by itself with no life. One has entered the world of the death of the word, the total abstraction that exists in our modern world. Nothing stands behind the word; it is cold. It lives in our cold intellect. Now, however, we have the saving grace of the Renaissance, the world of cobalt blue and finally, the entrance into the world of the third dimension, space as we know it. It is a world that brings magnificence in its wake. As humanity leaves the light, it has entered into the world of darkness, leaving the light behind. As one leaves the cold light of turquoise and moves further into the darkness, one reaches the world of cobalt blue, that immense world seen in the precious stone Lapus Lazuli, a world into itself of which Florence is a fabulous representative. For that world of cobalt blue, I bring Florence, specifically the world of Fra Angelico at San Marco in Florence, and needless to say, the Madonnas painted by Raphael and other painters.

≈

My walk today promises to be the wildest to date. As I start on the path leading through the meadow to the coast, I see a happy brown retriever going for a walk with his master. We both arrive (not to forget the dog) by the cliffs and then a whirlwind catches us both by surprise. I have to yell and say, "Wow, this is at least fifty miles per hour" and he replies, shouting as well, that it is 70 miles an hour and he has never seen it so wild. We wait for the gale to subside, and then he says that I should not walk on the cliff walk, as it is too dangerous, but go through the meadow, which I do. He lives with his wife down the road, and when we parted we agreed that I will

---

12 Steiner, *World of the Senses and the World of the Spirit*, Hanover, Dec. 30, 1911, p. 52.

visit him and his wife for a cup of tea. They are my neighbors and he wants to hear about my project.

I go on walking, bent in two to brave the strong winds and then sit by the cliffs where the waves crash the most, having a wonderful time observing their crashing. They are not as I have observed elsewhere, but it is as if they love crashing on the tall cliffs. They smash with joy and exuberance, sending foam into the air, which lands by me and everywhere else. The waves burst into the air with abandon and disappear into the air in a light shining cloud and then finally into nothing. It is exhilarating to be part of this seascape and the powerful western winds coming across the ocean from Newfoundland as they finally send the waves onto this little piece of land.

I stay for a while then continue for some shopping. Everyone walks around the town in their rain gear with the biggest grins on their faces. This kind of wind brings joy and makes them feel much more alive! A lot of people are enjoying the wild wind today and have come out just because it is so wild. I am just as ecstatic myself, and in the late afternoon head back the same way for an encore performance. This time I climb to Arthur's castle and watch the same waves from another direction. The Sun sets in colors as heavenly as they can be at that time of day. The crests of the waves have a beautiful turquoise tint to them, and the faraway clouds that reflect the last rays of the Sun are tinged with a beautiful vermilion. I walk again through the meadows and the powerful play of sunrays, behind the clouds, peeking a bit here and there, with the quarter moon shining a bit to the east, and a line of dark indigo clouds. I think I have taken at least 100 pictures.

As I sit here I cannot help but think that this place has been used for thousands of years as a sacred place. It must have been a mystery center dedicated to Jupiter, a "Jupiter mystery center" because the land contains tin. The whole of Cornwall was famous for mining tin, and tin is the Jupiter metal, like copper is the Venus, Lead is Saturn and Iron is Mars, and so on. So it would be a matter of course that this place was used for a "mystery school of the past."

A beautiful powdery cobalt blue can be seen along with vermilion and a dark gray mass of clouds advancing toward me, so I hurry back to my cozy home for a cup of tea. It takes me more than an hour and a half to get back, but I enjoy every minute of it, and I will not soon forget this very moving experience. I have been literally moved today, thrown by the wind unto the ground. Let us say I have been moved in my body and my soul. I did want to experience the wild elements here and I got what I wanted.

Here, I think it appropriate to mention the notorious Cornish wreckers. This wild, dangerous coast has claimed thousands of lives and wrecked hundreds of ships, whereby an industry developed of wreckers, which added much-needed goods to a poor community.

Wrecking has gone on ever since ships began to sail the seas. If wreckers of Cornwall obtained more notoriety than those elsewhere, this was partly owing to the high incidence of wrecks on its dangerous coastline, and the inability of the civil authorities to act with sufficient promptitude in preventing plunder, largely as a result of poor communication. Another aggravating factor was the attitude of certain of the local landowners, who pounced like vultures on every ship that stranded on their estates, claiming the justification of ancient privilege for their actions. This example was readily followed by the common people who could at least plead the excuse of poverty for their misdeeds.

Wrecking reached its apogee during the eighteenth century. This was due to a variety of factors, not the least being the rapidly increasing number of merchants, which then began to pass the country's shores bound to and from the Americas, the East, and West Indies, West Europe, and the Mediterranean. These ships were tending to become larger, and to carry richer cargoes; and all too many of them came to grief on rocks and reefs of Cornwall. At the same time, the local population was increasing rapidly mainly owing to the development of mining so that, on the occasion of a wreck, hundreds sometimes thousands, of determined men would quickly assemble, and carry off not only the whole cargo but sometimes every vestige of the ship herself long before anything effective could be done to stop them....

The month of January 1843 was marked by severe gales on the Cornish coast, of which the Jessie Logan, a fine East India trader, became an unfortunate victim. She was owned by Mr. Logan of Liverpool, from which port she traded to and from Calcutta. A vessel of 850 tons burden, she was commanded by Capt. Major. Whilst on her homeward voyage and beating up Channel on the 16th, apparently making either for Tintagel or for Bude Bay, for which the prevailing northwest wind would have been favorable but for its extreme violence, she became unmanageable in the vicinity of Boscastle. Her plight was first observed by the Coastguard at about midday, when she was still 14 miles out at sea, drifting helplessly in toward the coast. The vessel was seen to be in a most deplorable condition—part of her bulwarks were gone, and her sails were blown to ribbons, whilst everything had been swept off the deck. At three o'clock precisely the Jessie Logan struck upon the rocks at the entrance to Boscastle creek, a few miles from the harbor, and continued striking as the tide advanced until 8 o'clock, when her bottom was carried away and the cargo floated out. During the night her masts fell overboard and by morning nothing remained of the vessel but her sides. She had been carrying a valuable cargo, consisting of dyewood, gum, cotton, Indigo, and hides, very little of which was saved. The coast for miles was littered by it; and although the coastguard kept a sharp watch, considerable depredation was carried on by the wreckers, who assembled in enormous numbers. Some hope remained that the Jessie Logan's crew might have saved themselves in the ship's boats, but when both of these were found later that morning, bottom upward, a few miles from the wreck, it became apparent that none had survived. [13]

---

13 Vivian, *Tales of the Cornish Wreckers*, pp. 4, 34.

Violet

With that presence we can go on to the world of violet, the last veil of light before the world of darkness because:

> As this present-day thinking is firmly united with the earthly body, Michael unfortunately cannot approach it. Filled with anxiety, he sees how mankind comes more and more under the influence of Ahriman (cold calculating intellect), and he looks for ways to approach human beings. His task is by his own power to revivify and set free the ethereal bodies of men, which have been fettered by the hardening forces of the physical. Then man will be able to attain to living thoughts again, and will be capable of receiving the divine inspirations.[1]

To enter the world of Divine Inspiration is to enter the realm of violet, the experience of complete selflessness and deep devotion and gratitude. It is the realm in which the Divine can enter, or where human beings can work in cooperation with divine beings.

For this sphere of violet, I am afraid I have no paintings, or painters, or works of art that come even close to representing this realm, just yet. Violet is more of a mood. Indigo is a definite feeling, a strong feeling, and cobalt is a space. Green is a deed, and so forth. But violet is the consciousness of the *future* and we are not there yet.

Having said that, I must honor the fact that I love to paint violet with gold, oranges and yellows, ochre, light violet and black, and vermilion. I love those combinations and have painted large paintings with these colors that bring me tremendous joy—four by five-foot canvases are my favorites these days! To live with those colors is quietly powerful and strengthening, as is working with the other colors too, but these specific combinations bring me real joy and a balancing that is enormously satisfying.

---

1   Wegman, *Esoteric Studies*, Sept. 20, 1925. p. 68.

I have watched sunsets and sunrises with golden light and violet and cobalt violet together, and that is a true religious experience. One definitely is transported into another world. An old Russian woman lighting a candle before a beautiful warm carmine icon—wearing her lovely white headscarf, with the smell of burning honey-wax candles streaming through the space—can evoke the feeling of violet, the feeling I have when I paint violet, and the other beings of gold, yellow, orange. These are deeply religious experiences that I can watch, recognize, but not be part of except when I am painting, and then I am a part of that religious experience.

That one can touch the religious experience but not really be part of that consciousness because it does not exist yet seems to be a contradiction. This can be explained by the fact that we are in the consciousness of the indigo, not the violet, so we can have just a taste, a little "apercu." But there are others who are already living there. With the Color Being Violet, we access that consciousness, as well as with our meditative work, even if it is just momentary.

In this cottage, or rather this large very pleasant house that I have rented in Treknow, I have ensouled the space. I have scattered everywhere on fireplace mantels, bookshelves, and window sills, lots of beautiful rocks I have collected on the beaches. I have set up pictures of icons and prints of sacred paintings. There are bouquets of flower in all corners and I light candles. For me this is living in a mood of violet, a sacred space because what I am doing is sacred work that demands sacred space. It is easily done and not expensive; as a matter of fact it costs nothing. That is the mood of violet. We have it in our home when we set up a sacred space, even a corner, for our meditation. The whole house is a sacred space for that matter. That is the mood of violet. It is the mood that carries one over to the other side where our departed ones go.

In the soft purple-red of magenta where we started our journey we entered the world from the darkness of birth. Magenta, the color of birth and of the Mother giving birth to the child, is the coming into being from the spiritual world. With violet we are about to leave this physical world and step into the darkness again to the world of the Father.

The human being comes in violet to a point where he has to go into the darkness. From then on he has to lighten his surroundings by himself. This is called "Mystical Death," which is the fifth stage of the Christian Initiation. Here one has a meeting with the Guardian on the Threshold. The veil in the Temple is rent and the human being has to leave the Temple. Everything that has carried him until now he has to leave behind and from now on he has to be his own light...

Picture it for yourself: *You* are walking out into the darkness and *you* are casting a light. That is the light of the heart, the light of the second dimension, the light of the dream consciousness, which is entirely unlike the light of the third dimension.

When the heart becomes conscious, becomes an organ of perception, one no longer has a standpoint of "I" over against the rest of the world. Part of the soul is outside of us and it is in that part of the soul that one becomes conscious then. Then you do not perceive from one point inside yourself, but from the periphery outside yourself and from there you can then "see" yourself. In your perception you yourself become an object. But what you really see then is the *space* that your body occupies. It is something similar after death: the space that the body occupies is still there [in cobalt blue], but it is an emptiness.[2]

When one reads these powerful words, one knows deep down that Liane Collot d'Herbois was sent to us to bring us this work. Ita Wegman called her a guest on this Earth. I have often meditated on what that meant coming from such an enlightened individual as Ita Wegman. It has deep significance. The more I work with this impulse the more it becomes obvious that this work was given to us as a great help, a great healing to our overburdened, endangered world. It is an awakening through the Color Beings who are there to help us, and Liane Collot d'Herbois was their messenger, their totally devoted worker. Here are the powerful words of her teacher Rudolf Steiner.

This calling to life of the shadow images of the intellect is not only a human event, it is a cosmic event. Remember what I described in my *Occult Science*—how once upon a time human souls migrated up to

---

2   Collot d'Herbois, *Light, Darkness and Colour...*, p. 257.

the planets and afterward returned to Earth existence. I outlined in my *Occult Science* how the human beings of Mars, Jupiter, and so on came down again to Earth. Now, a most important event took place— it can only be described from the facts that are confirmed as truths in the spiritual world—a very important event occurred at the end of the seventies of the nineteenth century. Whereas in ancient Atlantean times these *human* beings descended to Earth from Saturn, Jupiter, Mars, and the other planets—and it was therefore a matter of *human* soul beings entering the Earth existence then—now a time is beginning when beings who are *not human* are coming down to Earth from cosmic regions beyond. These beings are not human but depend for the further development of their existence on coming to Earth and on entering here into relationships with humans....

Heavenly beings are already here in our Earth existence. And it is thanks to the fact that beings from beyond the Earth are bringing messages down into this earthly existence that it is possible at all to have a comprehensive Spiritual Science today.

Taken as a whole, however, how does the human race behave? If I may say so, the human race behaves in a cosmically rude way toward the beings who are appearing from the cosmos on Earth, albeit, to begin with, only slowly. Humanity takes no notice of them, ignores them. It is this that will lead the Earth into increasingly tragic conditions. For in the course of the next few centuries, more and more spirit beings will move among us whose language we ought to understand. We shall understand it only if we seek to comprehend what comes from them, namely, the contents of Spiritual Science. This is what they wish to bestow on us....

Since the last third of the nineteenth century, we are actually dealing with the influx of spirit beings from the universe. Initially, they were beings dwelling in the sphere between Moon and Mercury, but they are closing in upon Earth, so to say, seeking to gain a foothold in earthly life through human beings imbuing themselves with thoughts of spiritual beings in the cosmos. This is another way of describing what I outlined earlier when I said that we must call our shadowy intellect to life with the pictures of Spiritual Science. That is the abstract way of describing it. The description is concrete when we say: Spirit beings are seeking to come down into Earth existence and must be received. Upheaval upon upheaval will ensue, and Earth existence will at length arrive at social chaos if these beings descended and human existence were to consist only of opposition against them. For these beings wish to be nothing less than the advance guard of what will happen to Earth existence when the Moon reunites once again with Earth....

The fullness of human potential, however, will not be included in this intellect [dry-dead-abstract thinking] and people will have no relationship to the beings who wish graciously to come down to them into earthly life.[3]

Liane Collot d'Herbois never stopped talking about the importance of living with colors and of making colors come alive within ourselves, saying that it has deep consequences for the future—as we can see from the quote above. If that is not done, this lack of making the colors come alive, this lack of infusing life into our dead thoughts will also have consequences.

All the beings presently conceived so incorrectly [such as Newton's theory of color] in people's thoughts—incorrectly because the mere shadowy intellect can only conceive of...the mineral, plant, animal or even human kingdom—these thoughts of human beings that have no reality all of a sudden will become realities when the Moon and the Earth will unite again. From the Earth, there will spring forth a horrible brood of beings. In character they will be in between the mineral and plant kingdoms. They will be beings resembling automatons, with an over-abundant intellect of great intensity. Along with this development, which will spread over the Earth, the latter will be covered as if by a network or web of ghastly spiders possessing tremendous wisdom. Yet their organization will not even reach up to the level of the plants. They will be horrible spiders who will be entangled with one another. In their outward movements they will imitate everything human beings have thought up with their shadowy intellect, which did not allow itself to be stimulated by what is to come through new Imagination and through Spiritual Science in general.[4]

---

3   Steiner, *Materialism and the Task of Anthroposophy*, Dornach, May 13, 1921, pp. 260–263 (trans. revised).

4   Ibid., pp. 263–264.

Liane Collot d'Herbois was more than aware of the tasks ahead, and she worked tirelessly on this mission. Her students have the task of taking up this work seriously, with selfless sacrifice—the mood of violet. The future of humankind is at stake and we must act. Everyone can, and everyone's effort in this work is important.

> The pure light violet is a very valuable color. It can give one an experience of complete selflessness and deep devotion, a state of consciousness in which one can approach the higher Ego [the "I"]. And then one can become aware of one of the fundamental laws of existence: that Creation is based on continual sacrifice. That which is higher was generated by that which is lower, the higher owes its existence to the lower. And when one has really become aware of this truth one is filled with reverence and thankfulness.
>
> The light violet is not an actual support for the Ego, but it helps in overcoming egoism. It does not give form, but it gives the possibility of sacrifice and mercy and its background is gratitude. Gratitude is a faculty that gives air and the possibility to breathe.[5]
>
> For man as he is today violet brings the future. It is connected with a development in consciousness that is still to come....
>
> ...[A]ll the colors, except indigo which belongs to the present, belong to the past. Only violet belongs to the future, it is an experience that still has to come.
>
> To create oneself a picture of that future consciousness is not easy. All the words we have are related to things from the past. Where will one find the words to describe something that is yet to come, that has never been before? Still, we shall try and make an attempt.
>
> The consciousness that the violet will bring will be much larger and much more spiritual than the one we have now. Today violet immediately begins to work in the aura of all people who are interested in the spiritual—either in a positive or in a negative way. In the future it will open the way to greater spiritual heights and deeper spiritual depths than man can possibly imagine today.
>
> In that enlarged consciousness violet will give man what may be called a sense-organ for his karma. Speaking figuratively one could say that violet has a memory and that it will carry the past to us.... Perhaps

---

5   Collot d'Herbois, *Light, Darkness and Colour...*, p. 251.

one could say that violet brings the karma to us and that the other colors carry it out.

Violet will change the human being in body and soul, in such a way that in the far future we shall no longer have the experience of our personality with a name and everything that is attached to it as we have now. The demarcation lines between the individual and his environment, between what is personal and that which individuals have in common, will not be so sharply drawn.... The consciousness of the violet will bring...with it a more intensified, a more conscious "sense of the Ego"—the sense-organ by means of which one can be aware of the Ego of the other person and grow toward a nearer conception of what the Ego is. It is a very important sense-organ and we have not yet woken up to it....

Being only one step away from absolute darkness the all-pervading and all-enveloping violet has great will-power, a will-power that as it were comes from outside us, from the wide circumference. That too will be one of the qualities of the future consciousness: an objective and impersonal will-power.

In this respect violet is the antipole of the magenta which (in ancient India) brought the will-power *into* the human being, into the blood. With the growing consciousness of the carmine the will descended a little deeper as man separated himself a little further.... But in the darkness of the violet the will-power will come to us from the circumference, from outside.

The faculty of religiousness goes through the reverse process. In the consciousness of the turquoise religious feeling was something that came to man from outside, in cobalt blue it became an inner activity, in indigo even more so. In violet religiousness is an innate quality that is deeply rooted in the human soul.[6]

Let thy *will be done.*

≈

My walk yesterday on the way to visit Henry and Pamela took me by the cliffs up and down little valleys carved by streams coming from the uplands. The

6   Ibid., pp. 239–241.

ocean was an unearthly green brought about by the reflection of the indigo-gray skies that was lovely to contemplate as I walked the coastline. The soft and misty rain did not drench me, but kept me inwardly alive. The clouds and the sea were ever changing, moving, and no one was walking. Finally I found my way to their village through fields and meadows to their delightful home in a converted church. We chatted again, had some soup, and they walked me back some distance through the fields, this time as it was getting dark. It was rainy and muddy 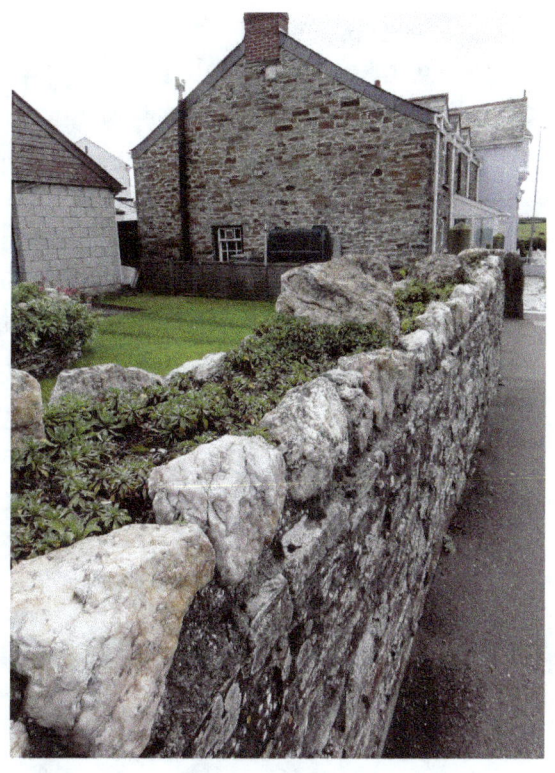 but the sunset was glorious as seen from the heights. The entire horizon was filled with indigo, grays, and tones of vermilion through the clouds, reflecting here and there the rays of the setting Sun. What power lives in these colors that accompanied me all the way to my village! By then it was getting rather dark and I was glad to be back to a warm cozy home.

Again I was thinking about the Druids, or the ancient "Jupiter Mysteries" that were probably celebrated and taught in these special areas. One can feel the power of the marvelous stones sitting on everyone's walls or in their gardens. The enormous stones stand like guardians as I walk the very narrow alleys of these ancient villages, or cross a little bridge in a wooded valley, stepping on some enormous white hard stones here and there. They are everywhere in the fields, and one marvels at their naked beauty. Then one knows that old Druids or other wise men and women walked on these old paths a long, long time ago. And some of the people who live here have not lost that awareness.

Today the Sun is too much to resist, so I end my working day an hour early to take another walk from a little village where I left the car when I walked to the old mill that has a granite-carved labyrinth on the sheer vertical wall. I head north to my favorite town Boscastle. The warm sunshine has brought out many walkers. The sea is calm, and just a few clouds drift in the blue sky. I walk for more than a hour, through the little town and then head back for another splendid time with the elements. Again I feel privileged to be here in these sumptuous surroundings. I think that the Irish monks did not come and settle here; it was the site of other mysteries and for some reason they did not come on this Cornwall coast, preferring the lonely wildness of the Irish coast. This place was the site of totally different mysteries, and one can feel this in the strength of the elements. The Earth has a lot to do with it, with these massive rocks strewn about everywhere pell-mell. In the little stream flowing down by the mill there is a huge white marble-looking rock that just screams for attention. "I am here," it says and one can't ignore him. Every time I walk by him, I have to honor his presence.

Here are Rudolf Steiner's comments on this part of the world from when he spoke at Penmaenmawr, Wales, August 1923, just a half-day drive from here.

> Thus our walks abroad among the rocks or across such mountains as these, if guided by true cognition and not by mere imagery, may reveal to us in the physical light reflected from the rocks, a manifestation of sleeping elemental nature-beings, who will presently reach the dreaming-stage and later arouse to full waking-life; and someday become pure Spiritual beings....
>
> The different parts of the Earth, the different localities, show each in a different way this sleeping of the Spiritual beings; in the mountains and in the solid surface of the Earth. In regions such as this, for instance, we can say that the sleep of the beings awaiting their future, is different from that of those in various other parts of the world.
>
> Here in Penmaenmawr we have a region where, on account of the particular configuration, the particular form assumed by the strong substance, these sleeping beings are able to penetrate through to the forms of the air. Indeed they can even weave themselves into the light,

which is far from being the case in other parts of the Earth. Thus if we do not merely take the material atmosphere into consideration here in Penmaenmawr, but also consider the ruling of the psychic atmosphere, which permeates the air as the human soul, the human body, we find the soul-part of the atmosphere different here from what it is else where.

Suppose you try, by means of imaginative cognition to set up an Imagination and keep it before you. It may be more or less easy, according to the region you may be in, to hold it in your consciousness. In some parts of the world it can be held longer, in others it melts away at once. Here, however, the Imagination remains intact for a remarkably long time; it can therefore grow into an intensely vivid picture.

The Druids and people of like nature, sought out regions such as this for their Temples and Holy Places; regions possessing the quality that there the Imaginations are not immediately dispersed like clouds dissolving one into another, but remain steady for some time. It is therefore quite comprehensible that regions such as Penmaenmawr were sought out as Holy places by the Druids, even in comparatively recent times.

They always realized that it was not so difficult here to hold Imaginations. Of course everything has its light and shadow-side, and for the very reason that the Imaginations stand so firmly, Inspiration is more difficult to attain; but when attained it is the more forceful. Therefore what is to be said out of the Spiritual world pours in here with greater intensity, but it is more difficult to put into words; it is weightier.

Thus, in a Spiritual respect, it is quite possible to note differences in different parts of the world. One might take a map and paint in one color those places in which unimaginative consciousness can more easily hold the Imaginations firmly, and those in which they soon disappear might be painted in a different color. That would make a very interesting map of the Earth. We should have to paint Penmaenmawr a very intense color to represent what governs the psychic atmosphere; a radiant, luminous, ardent color.[7]

There is no need to mention that this Tintagel area is within this atmosphere of strong psychic forces. Otherwise why would people have chosen that little hidden rocky wall to engrave such powerful symbols: the

---

7   Steiner, *The Evolution of the World and of Humanity*, pp. 104–106.

labyrinth, the birth of the intellect. So long, long ago some sages felt the urge to carve it on the rock. Once again, it is pure joy to walk in these paths and breathe in the strength that fills the air.

Here is another picture of violet:

Imagine now that you move toward the sunset-colors and that you come near them. The outer world slowly fades and disappears and then there is only the deepening darkness, with in front of you the glow of the sunset. As the visual world disappears the ear becomes more sensitive and you listen to the ever deepening silence. You reach the sunset-colors and they let you through: between the crimson and the scarlet there is a passage that leads you deeper into the violet, until you come to what can only be called a world-altar, the altar of the Earth. Standing in front of it you are filled with devotion and earnestness and you experience a calling upon your will-power as you have never known before. The violet in its transparency demands something of you. And when you feel that you have become this color, that it has penetrated into the very core of your being, you are full of its carrying stillness and you have, at last, peace. And then you lose all consciousness of your personality, you are still conscious but no longer bound to time and place. Then you turn around and leave. You come away from the altar and your heart and soul are full of the courage that one gets from the very deepest depths of the Earth—of the Earth as a star amongst stars. That courage is a golden color; not yellow, nor orange, but something in between.[8]

Again this calls to mind the feeling I had while inside the Russian Church when I felt that this is what is demanded of us in the future consciousness of humankind. It is this deep devotion and selflessness that is the world of the Russian martyrs and saints depicted in all the Russian icons. They lived in that future consciousness, in the realm of violet. And now they are helping the Russian soul make giant leaps into the future, as Rudolf Steiner has often told us. The future epoch lies within the Slavic/Russian soul.

In that quiet violet atmosphere the voice of the fathers of the church resound. And as I was deeply listening, I heard that ever-soft message that,

---

8 Collot d'Herbois, *Light, Darkness and Colour...*, p. 242.

like everyone else, I have a long road to travel but at least I am fortunate enough to have the warmth and companionship of the Color Beings and the strength of that mighty helper, Michael. These are available to everyone through the path undertaken for us by Rudolf Steiner.

There is a human being who lived in the violet consciousness through and through! His was a very short life, but through his beautiful poems we are plunged into the mood of violet and into the beyond, the realm of the Father, and that is Novalis. His entire life was steeped in deep religious devotion and love, and he lived in the mood of violet, prepared to enter the realm of the Father. Perhaps his task was to let us struggling humans know that death is not the end but the beginning. If we reflect on his prior lives with the consciousness of colors we can add another level of understanding and know this most gifted, extraordinary human being, Novalis.

LONGING FOR DEATH

Down into the earth's womb,
Away from Light's kingdoms,
Pain's raging and wild force
Ensigns the happy departure.
We've come in from a narrow boat
Swiftly to heaven's shore.

Blessed be the endless Night to us,
Blessed the endless sleep.
Truly the day has made us hot,
And long care's withered us.
The wish for strange lands is gone away,
And now we want our Father's home.[9]

Now that we have made this long journey from birth to death, from being born into the physical world through the Mother, the state of Unbornness, through magenta, meeting the light in green, and then going on to the world of violet where we leave the physical world to the world of darkness again,

---

9 Novalis, *Hymns to the Night/Spiritual Songs*.

to the Realm of the Father into death. We were born into the spiritual world of peach-blossom-violet for a stay until we are ready again to come back into the physical world—or die again into the physical world, whichever way one wants to look at it. We have traveled into the development of our consciousness from the all-knowing, unified world of carmine, of clairvoyance, and then we left that consciousness to enter the world of the light, the birth of our thinking, of our "I," the intellect, with Greece, and then finally into the world of space and our consciousness soul in indigo. And now we prepare to leave that consciousness and move toward the religious consciousness of the future in violet. Although seen through a different perspective, this journey was undertaken by Rudolf Steiner in many of his lecture cycles. It is the same journey. Here we took that journey, a very short one at that, through the realm of colors, the unified substance of color created by the meeting of the cosmic beings of Light and Darkness.

You have moved along from being born into magenta and flowed gently into carmine, slowly picking up speed, warmth, and activity into red vermilion, and then slowly into orange, golden yellow, yellow, yellow green into the viridian, then through the light into the turquoise leaving the light behind us and slowly going into the darkness once more into the realm of cobalt blue. Then we were drawn by the warmth of the darkness into indigo and finally slowly sucked by the forces of darkness into violet and then into the all-enveloping darkness of death. As you live in this all-substance of color, you are living in a space; that space is what we *create* when we work therapeutically. We create a space where often there is no space. The human being seeking help has not developed that inner space and has lived in emotions all his or her life without time or space for reflection, most only living in *reaction* or refractions in physical language, which is the realm of the red colors—all will and no thinking. Then we lead them slowly to experience the beauty of space through a scientific knowledge of the colors and their true being. We help them create a space for themselves; we help them incarnate into the world. We help them gain access to the world of the will by introducing the warmth of red colors and of movement when that has disappeared. We help human beings who have become fragmented into so many parts that they no longer feel their true self. We help them in digesting unlived experiences through our scientific approach to the world of colors and their movements. We help them to go on in a world that is increasingly lived without meaning. We help them in their isolation, in breaking that isolation with the beginning of a feeling toward Golgotha. We accomplish that and much more with the help of the Color Beings seen in their true light. That is the work, the immense work that has been only lightly tapped into by the students of Liane Collot d'Herbois and the woman who stood behind her, Francine Davelaar, and Ita Wegman the master of both of them. And the man who stood behind them is Rudolf Steiner who gave indications that these women followed, thanks to their incredible capacities brought into this earthly world from many previous incarnations dedicated to help-ing humankind.

I could not really do justice to this very special and sacred work with colors, but I had to try in a small and modest way. As a painter, I try to create an atmosphere that the viewer will enter, and hopefully allow him or her to experience something that is not from this world—thanks to the Color Beings! In that way, the painter can help the human being realize that this earthly world is not the only one. People can be brought to experience something with the heart and not with the mind. They can be touched. The space that is created with the help of the Color Being is a space that is healing to human beings. It allows them to breathe more freely, to feel new forces in their souls, because through the colors, they can be a bit released from the world of matter.

One can accomplish this with the world of color as painted following the indications of Liane Collot d'Herbois. We are only in the beginning of such work and I am honored to be part of this beginning. I hope that this will also be a beginning for the reader to live ever more consciously into the world of color. Every day it can be done as an actual deed. You can watch a sunset, wear colors in a more conscious way, do color medita-tions, buy more artwork painted in this manner and look at works of art through some of these insights. You can buy Liane Collot d'Herbois's books and begin to paint in watercolors with enthusiasm for the Color Beings, or simply know that the colors are beings and we must remove them from their enslavement to our "fettered to matter" views and release them into large planes of moving colors weaving between light and darkness.

As this book is nearing its end, I must honor the work of Rembrandt. One cannot speak about light and darkness without mentioning his enlightened body of work. Rembrandt would not be Rembrandt without light and darkness. His masterpieces scattered throughout the world in many museums are testimony to the birth of the light within. "Not I, but Christ in me."

After the celebration of the Madonna in Renaissance Italy, we celebrate in Rembrandt the birth of the light within through the golden light, sienna color, and the play of light and darkness in all his masterpieces. It is the birth of the light, in a country that was the first in Europe to emancipate itself from the monarchial yoke and plunge into the first beginning of citizenship. In Holland, the Dutch feel at home and cozy, welcomed to the Earth, and this is reflected in Rembrandt's paintings. This beautiful glow, the inner light reaches the eyes of the viewer and warms the soul as well. In this we see the beginning of the consciousness soul, not manifested as in the great drama of El Greco, but in a different fashion, as a more loving and warm birth, a welcoming to Earth.

Liane reminds us that...

It may be good to realize that we people of the twentieth century have a lot to do with the Egyptians. With them we have in common this love for things that are bathed in gold, in a golden light. We would not love Rembrandt so much if it were not for the golden light that is so characteristic for his paintings. At one time we were bathed in that golden light ourselves, in the Egyptian time. The Old Persia era brought for the first time a duality, a tremendous difference from the Old Indian epoch with its experience of the all-embracing oneness of the universe [carmine]. The Egyptians are aware of what that inner light is and what the outer light is, and they have an awareness of space. To the Egyptians space becomes formed.[10]

---

10 Collot d'Herbois, *Light, Darkness and Colour...*, pp. 115–116.

Standing in front, one of Rembrandt's paintings is to feel loved, welcomed, earthy, as he portrayed in the painting "Return of the Prodigal Son." We have at last come home, home to the Earth. After the cobalt blue of the Renaissance, we enter the love for the Earth, but not in a materialistic way. It is in a warm, loving way. With that warmth, with the birth of that inner light, we can go on to the next stage, which we saw in the experience of the indigo. We must have that warmth to face the tasks ahead, and centuries later his paintings still give us this warmth. How do we manage to receive this warmth, this love for the Earth without the paintings? He was sending us these gifts more than 350 years ago. Steiner's task in Anthroposophy is to warm our souls, to enliven our senses, to feel with such enthusiasm that we can face the future with unwavering Michaelic strength and *act*. Rembrandt as a great helper of humanity showered us with his great masterpieces. Rudolf Steiner showered us with his great lectures full of life, warmth, and love.

We love the Madonna, but how do we give birth to that inner light, or the Son within? The cobalt blue is one world, and now we have moved on to the next world, the world of indigo, the world of the consciousness soul. Many people are still stuck in the cobalt mood, the Madonna world, and have not stepped into the world of indigo. To go forward, one must join the atmosphere of being active. By stepping into activity help comes. And, as was mentioned before, armed with reverence and the eternal masculine leading to a strengthened "I," we can proceed into the unknown.

Here Rudolf Steiner speaks about this process.

In future human beings will be required to allow their personalities to be *inspired from above*, so that they can receive what flows out of the spiritual world. A personality will receive its stamp from what it has been able to absorb of spiritual knowledge; personality will become something quite different.... In future we must become personality through what we are able to receive from the spiritual world.... In future we will be able to become a personality through the character we acquire by our participation in the suprasensory world. The Michael Impulse—which brings an understanding for the spiritual life into the human soul—will achieve this. Those with a pronounced character and personality will, in the future, have this character and personality because of what they bring to expression out of their understanding of the spiritual worlds.... In the future, the strength of human deeds will come from the strength of the spiritual influence working into these human deeds.[11]

That is why Steiner also mentioned that the karma of his devoted students is to take *initiative* regardless of how imperfect they are, since they are only a beginning. It is in this spirit that these words came into being. And in these beginnings, since being born is a real creation, there can be no planning ahead. That would not be real creation. It stems from an independent impulse that comes from the *inner*.

I must explain a bit about my way of creating. I approach writing, the blank paper, as I do the canvas. I know what I want to bring to light, but the format is totally new, unplanned and left to the act of creation. This leaves space for the unplanned to come to birth, for something to come into being that one would not even think about in their wildest dreams. So is destiny. If we had to plan our life, we would have a very poor life indeed, without much room for the unpredictable, the unknown, the unexpected. So it is with writing. The reader goes on a journey that the writer undertakes with no guarantee as to the outcome. Perhaps there will be no outcome, but just an attempt. Or perhaps, one will be surprised by the turn of events!

---

11 Steiner, *The Archangel Michael*, Stuttgart, May 18, 1913, pp. 58–59.

Leaving Tintagel

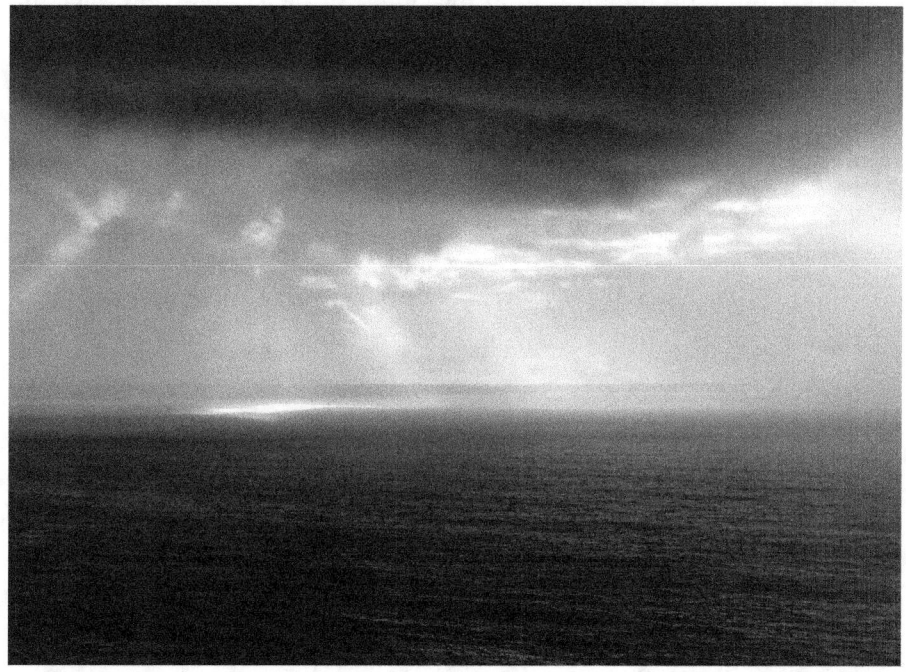

On the last couple of days, I rested from my long walk after entertaining Henri and his wife Pam for lunch when we chatted about everything once again. Henri mentioned that he suffered enormously as a child because at the age of three his mother was taken away from him for a couple of years. He was raised by a "cold-hearted nanny" and then sent to private school as a young child and never receive the warmth of a mother.

It has been typical Cornwall weather with lots and lots of rain. I asked the librarian in the little town, "How long does this rain last?" and she laughed at me and said, "Yes, we have this weather for twelve months." And she was serious!

In the last few days, I have been walking to Tintagel and back in the rain, the mist, and the wind; it is not so much stormy as it is a gentle rain. The clouds are moving across the ocean, and since I walk around at the end of the day, I often witness beautiful light shows. The thicker the atmosphere is with warmth and humidity, the more beautiful the interaction between the clouds and the sunlight behind the clouds. It pierces here and there in beautiful light rays, reflecting on the grayish ocean in marvelous reflection pools. They are brighter than the Sun as they play on the ocean surfaces while the clouds move and as the light rays find space to peek through, gently touching the green-gray sea. It provides wonderful picture-taking and exemplifies how alive this place is. It is mother-of-pearl gray, which later in the day illuminates the skies with touches of yellow or vermilion or carmine. The indigo, the charcoal grays, the tense darkness of the raincloud burst into space and deliver strong, sweet water.

Last week we had massive rain in the area and the train coming from London was unable to come through because of a massive landslide, so there were no incoming or outgoing trains for a couple of days. There was four to five feet of water in some places. Today the Sun is out, and I hear the clop-clop-clop of a morning rider coming through the narrow lane in the tiny village of Treknow.

I really cannot say enough about walking on these paths; it is more than I ever expected. I imagine living here in this beautiful spot one can put up with this never-ending rain. It has not bothered me at all, and I take a walk no matter what the weather. It makes the whole of nature delightfully green. In the Midwest or in New England, nature is now brown, but here it is blissfully green still, and we are almost at the end of November.

> On the path of a soul-connection with the cosmos is bound the
>   ideal, the striving to find and succor that most tragic being; the
>   Isis–Sophia.
> She Who has been robbed of Her living creative imaginations, of Her
>   cloak of stars, of Her "auric colors"—with a brush of illusion
>   swept away from us.
> She the wisdom of the Father God. This we have lost.

> But by the substance of will, by the will of Christ working in our
> hearts, She can be refound.[1]

Let us hope that many more students will embark on this color adventure
and find the strength through the Christ Will to restore our poor "Isis–
Sophia" to her former resplendent power. It was with this aim that this
book was written.

I paid several more visits to Arthur's castle out on the small island, a
large area, and found myself a most beautiful very large white stone on
which to lie. I spent quite a few peaceful hours gazing at the sea and feeling
the power of the elements on my face, the wind, the sea-moist air, the light
of the Sun reflected on the stones, the gentle murmur of the waves. It was a
most wonderful language that spoke of ages past when the land was alive
with knights on horseback, ragged peasants on foot, women with goats
and sheep, outside fires to keep warm in this desolate little place, kettles
full of warm soup in some far corner of a hut, wise old men speaking to
the elements, white dressed men and women performing sacred rites by the
sea, gentle kings, and cruel instincts—all spoken through the winds as I sat
motionless on the enormous white stone.

Then I said my goodbye and thanks to this most wonderful home, drove
to London, and headed across the Atlantic.

---

1   Collot d'Herbois, *Colour*, pp. 151–152.

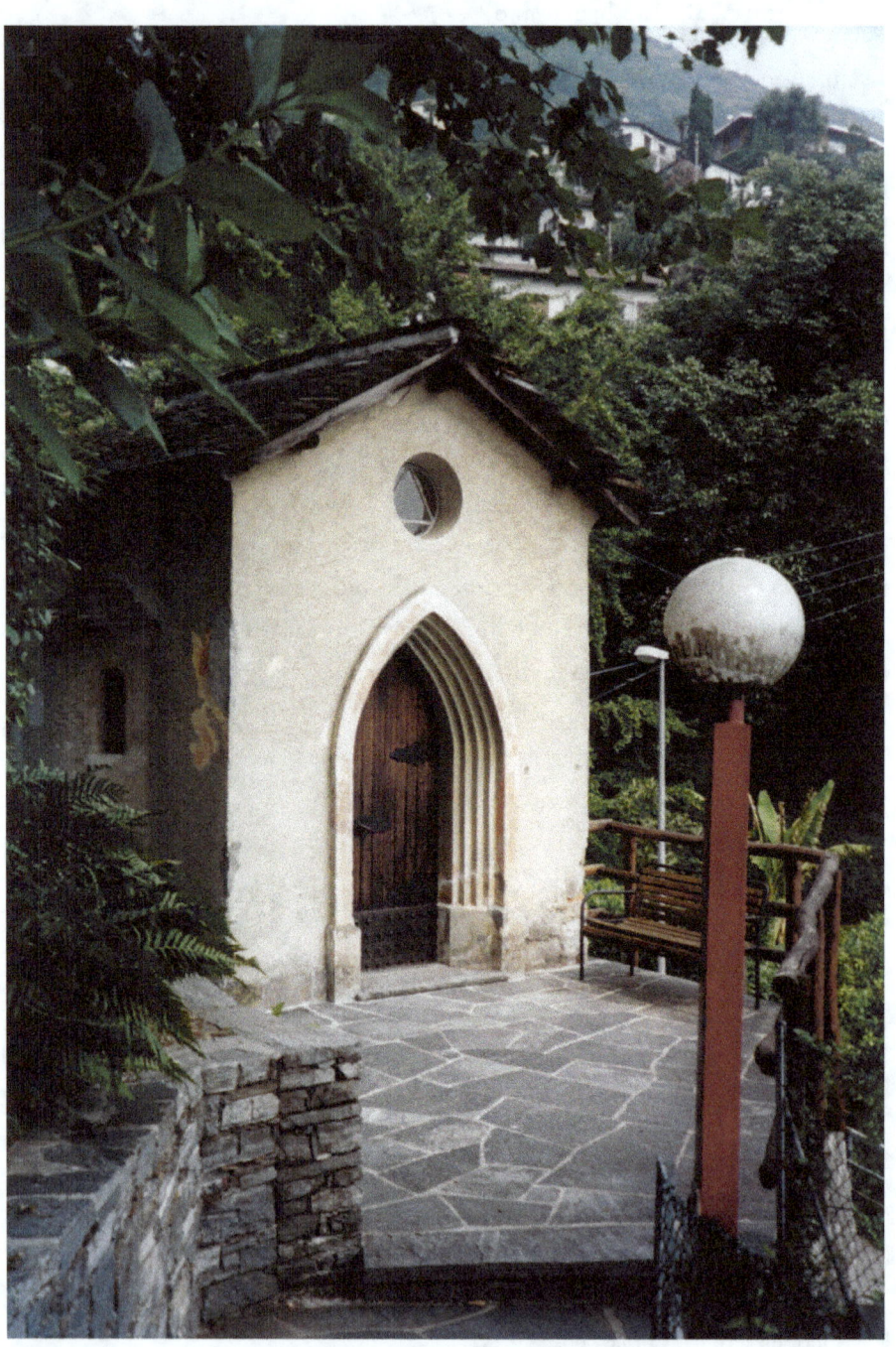

Appendix 1:
The Chapel at La Motta, Brissago

Liane Collot d'Herbois

Ita Wegman loved art. Visiting a museum with her was an exhausting experience; nobody could keep up with her. She had such boundless enthusiasm for everything she saw. Everything had to be looked at with the same intense interest. It all meant something to her. And she was carried by what she saw; she gained energy from it. That was because Ita Wegman had the possibility of using her sense organs purely. She let nothing come between her and the picture she was looking at. She saw *through* the picture; it meant much more to her than what met the eye. And she had a special connection with all those themes in art that are connected with the Christian mysteries and Christian initiation, such as St. John the Baptist, Lazarus, the Stages of the Passion and the Resurrection.

I first met Ita Wegman during an international summer conference in England before the war. There were many people there from different countries, among whom was Elisabeth Vreede. Ita Wegman had various intentions and had made various plans for the future with all these people. She wanted to see me about something, and we went into a room where we could talk. It was a very large and rather darkish room. On the walls were three pictures that I had painted. We went in and talked a bit, and after a while she turned round and then her eye fell on a picture of St. John the Baptist. She walked toward it and looked at it in silence for quite some time. Then she said, *"Ich bin frappiert, ich bin frappiert!"* (I feel touched, I feel touched!). She must have had an inner experience when looking at the picture, because after that she changed all her intentions. All the decisions she had made were swept away, and she did just the reverse of what she had intended beforehand. It took quite a lot of courage to tell all these people that she had changed her mind, not being able to say exactly why; but it turned out to be a very good decision. She was so convinced and so certain that what she had experienced in front of that picture was something, that she changed all her decisions. And she stayed by it, nobody could make her change her mind again. Such was the influence a picture could have on her.

Ita Wegman had asked me to come and live with her in Ascona. When I had settled in, she told me that there was a little chapel in Brissago that she had chosen as the place where her ashes were to be kept after her death. She wanted me to decorate the interior with a mural painting. So I made some sketches of the Way of the Passion. When I brought them and explained them to her she looked at them for a long time. She went out into the garden and paced up and down. Finally, she turned to me and said, *"Ja, das ist richtig, das ist es"* (Yes, this is right; this is it).

The Way of the Passion was a theme that was very near to her. At the time, it seemed curious that she should be thinking about her death, because she was very well then, full of life and laughter. She explained to me that Rudolf Steiner had told her that if her ashes were kept after her death, she would be able to work through them in the earthly sphere, not only in the place where they were kept, but all over. That was her reason for having the chapel rebuilt and getting it in order.

Professor Fiechter had taken that in hand, and later he also helped prepare the ground for the wall painting, giving advice and instructing the Italian artisans who had been hired to do the work. The back wall had the shape of a semi-circle; the ceiling is a dome. All that had to be covered with fresco. The ground for the fresco was put on in two layers. They started with a mixture of sand and chalk, which in about two weeks time dried into a kind of glassy surface. No cement may be used. Even a teaspoon full of cement in the grounding would in time make a large piece of the fresco come off the wall, because cement continues to absorb moisture.

Then a second layer was put on, and on that I painted. I worked from nine in the morning till nine in the evening, almost without a break, because

I could paint on the ground only as long as it was wet. As soon as it began to dry it was no use anymore and it had to be chipped off.

I had to work quickly and as I could make no alterations of any kind I had to be sure of what I did. In the old-fashioned manner, with a nail in the wet chalk I outlined the part of the picture I was going to paint that day. After that, it was just a matter of using the color.

I mixed my colors only with water. In olden days, the painters mixed some chalk in their colors to make them firmer, so that they would still be visible from a greater distance, because the chalk stops the color from sinking into the wet ground. But in this small chapel that was not necessary. I put on one wash of paint, and by two o'clock it was still wet enough to put on another wash. So each color consists of two washes. More than that I could not do, because the ground would have gone too dry. I had to work quick and be certain of what I did. And so the fresco got a rough, unpolished look. All the colors are earth and mineral colors. There are about twelve colors that you can use, that are not eaten away in time by the chalk.

Ita Wegman never saw the finished fresco, because she passed away before I had started painting. Her death was so unexpected. But the mural painting is the same as the sketches she approved.

In the center is the Risen Christ (see next page and page 149). On the extreme left is the second stage of the Passion—the Dweller on the Threshold and the Crowning of Thorns. You see there two little figures, human beings, on the edge of the abyss: man and woman, two different aspects of life, two aspects of reality, two ways of looking at reality. A man has to cultivate in that particular incarnation his "I"; a woman must cultivate and develop her astral body. To the right, I put the fourth and fifth stages together in one picture—the Carrying of the Cross and the Descent into the Darkness of Hell. When you have gone through the stage of the Carrying of the Cross, the cross is no longer heavy and one can carry it easily; it does not mean anything. Between that and the Risen Christ is the angel breaking open the temple, which means the end of the old clairvoyance and the pre-Christian mysteries. That is the fourth stage. When you enter the darkness, you brighten it from yourself. You then see and recognize the other human

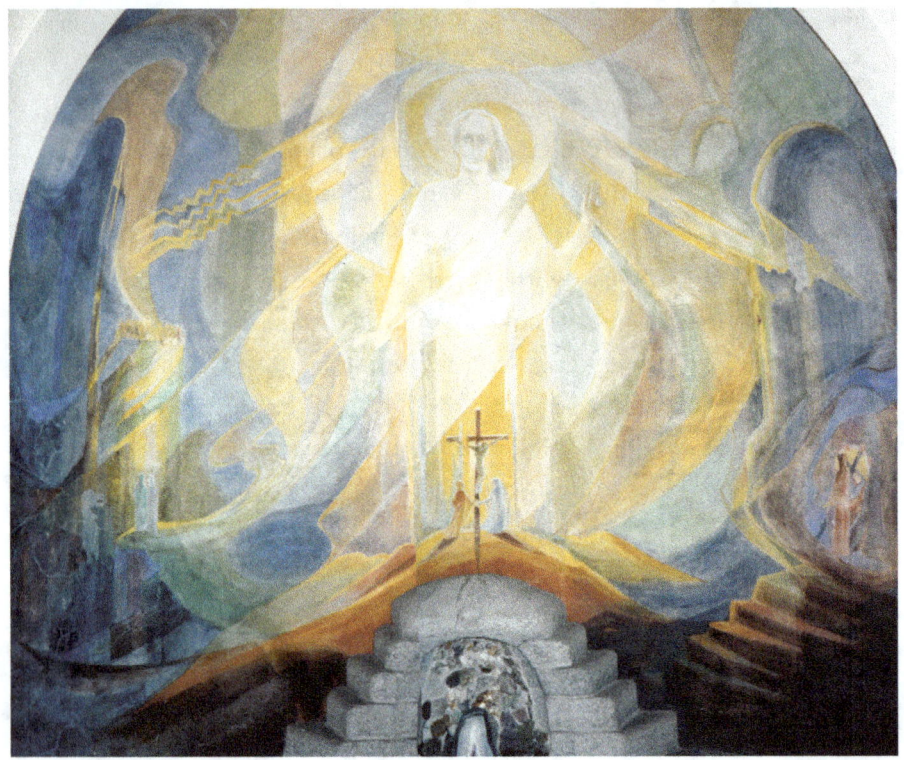

beings who also lighten the darkness, but the rest you do not see other people. That is part of the fifth stage of Christian Initiation.

In her work for Anthroposophy in general and anthroposophic medicine in particular, Ita Wegman had to go through a great deal. How could she come through so much (for instance, to be ostracized by the Society, by thousands of people) and not become bitter, but have so much humor and lightness of soul?

She often laughed, and when she did she laughed with her whole being. She had a sense of humor, and that carried her, because it gives that steadfastness to the Earth. An angel cannot laugh, and an animal cannot laugh; only human beings can laugh.

Remember that Ita Wegman was born Dutch. One thing that is typical of the Dutch is their *gezelligheid* (something like "togetherness")—the condition of cheerful contentment that they mutually create whenever they meet. It is a commitment that consists of an interweaving between soul and soul. They cannot do without it, and they need it, because they live on soil of water and sand. They have to create their connection with the earth for themselves, and they do that in their *gezelligheid*.

I think Ita Wegman derived part of her inner strength from this faculty and that it gave her a connection with the Soul of the World. That is one thing. On the other hand, there was this lightness of soul that she had. At first glance, one might call it superficiality, but the truth is that she could see what was really important. She could see that, after all that had happened, one still had a connection and in the spiritual world would be all together, united through the work with Rudolf Steiner. That she always said. These earthly difficulties were therefore not so important to her. It was karma and she accepted it. And therefore she could laugh. It is all part of that one attitude.

But her deepest source of inner strength she had found in Rudolf Steiner's lectures about the Christian mysteries.[1] She always said, "The only thing that gives life is devotion"—devotion to the Mystery of Golgotha. (Rhythm gives life, too, but not so much as devotion, especially in the case of chronic illness.) She often spoke about that. The Way of the Passion, especially its fifth stage, as described by Rudolf Steiner, meant so much to her. It moved her and she was inspired by it.

The chapel in Brissago is a place from which Ita Wegman can work. While I was painting the fresco, Elisabeth Vreede died. I was then working on the second stage, the meeting with the Dweller on the Threshold. And I was happy, because I felt I was doing it for her, too. Because she and Ita Wegman are united in the Mystery of Christian Initiation.

(From Ita Wegman-Fonds fuer soziale
und therapeutische Hilfstaetigkeiten, Michaeli 1990)

---

1   See Steiner, *The Christian Mystery: Early Lectures.*

Appendix 2:
A Brushtroke on the Portrait of Ita Wegman

Liane Collot d'Herbois

"*Ja, ja, tun Sie das dann!*" (Yes, why don't you *do* it!). These words one could hear from Dr. Ita Wegman after she had listened, half laughing, but radiating a loving interest, to an outspoken idea without hands or feet.

With her, everything was possible. How often one could hear her say, "The gods can take part in what you *do*; the activity can be corrected and taken up by them." Sometimes, filled with self-importance, one came into her presence, and afterward, having spoken with her, one saw oneself ridiculous and one had to laugh with her at oneself outwardly. Because through humor filled with great wisdom, she could place everything at a distance, objectivating all problems. Therefore she could create (one always had the feeling that she was "creating") lightness around her, but knowing on the other hand "evil," thus being able to objectivate that, too; and through her psychological insight with that lightness and humor filled with wisdom, she could help and heal in the true sense of the word, led by compassion. Other people will have experienced, I am sure, this other aspect of her during and through their work and will be able to tell about it much better than I can.

Ita Wegman looked upon it as one of her greatest missions to combat the multitude of phantoms who have the roots of their being in Gondishapur. During the war, she often spoke of it, meanwhile striding up and down the room, saying, "*Die Phantome bekaempfen, das tue ich!*" (Fighting the phantoms; that is what I do!). And for those who knew her well, she added, "*Das wissen Sie, nichtwahr*" (You know that, don't you). In this connection, she spoke at the same time of the negative impulses coming from "The Royal Society" (natural science) in England, in the eighteenth and nineteenth centuries especially.

Air—Ita Wegman created air—air radiated with sunlight. She created movement; one could be carried in her movement. Because of this movement there in her being, one had the feeling that everything was possible. In her speaking, this movement was there, too; in the pictures she called up, in an absolute non-intellectual way—and so her talks and lectures were carried.

Then there was enthusiasm that she carried with her like a flame and she fired others with it.

In her desire to fulfil Dr. Steiner's work, Ita Wegman filled other people with this enthusiasm, to work with sacrifices. At the same time, giving work to people, whoever they were, who could not find their way in life, positively accepting them and at the same time helping them by accepting their impulses. In this regard her immense compassion was working and influencing the people in their work.

Her soul was easily moved through unusual extremities—the depth of earnestness on the one hand, the lightness on the other hand (the latter being a virtue in the Middle Ages), together with the humor that carried her through many difficult periods in her life, which was also one of her most outstanding features.

All these movements, these qualities, these attributes of her soul—the earnestness, the courage, the enthusiasm, the certainty with which to take resolutions—were far greater than one usually met.

Excuse me for talking about pictures now, but in my relation to Ita Wegman in the many years before, and in the last three years during the war, pictures played a part, of course. Pictures meant a lot to her and she could be intensely moved by them. A picture was able to change a resolution absolutely in one direction or another. I am thinking of a picture of St. John the Baptist; she stood in front of it and said, "I am touched, I am touched!" and previous resolutions were entirely changed.

She always judged a picture first by its healing qualities, sometimes looking for "the Michaelic light," and was rarely if ever satisfied with only the subject. A picture was more than just a picture for her—she could be enflamed with enthusiasm.

Once, during the winter before she died, she was depressed by the limitations to the work, and she foresaw the coming dangers closing in on humanity. To describe this mood in her words, she felt herself "cut off from the spiritual world." A newly painted picture was brought in to her and suddenly, full of fire and sureness, she sprang up and said, "The spiritual world *is* here! The connection with the spiritual world is restored!" No wonder that pictures meant so much to her; in her talks and lectures, she used pictures and could call up the most vivid tableaux in front of the audience.

Ita Wegman intended to make journeys after the war, to travel all over the world to meet young people and give Anthroposophy in a new form, because, she said, if that new form was not found, then the war had been for nothing. This new form should be non-intellectual, with even more heart qualities.

About the fresco in the chapel of Brissago, I would like to say only the following: when the content of it was talked over with Ita Wegman and she had said that she was happy with the sketches, I asked her why she wanted a protected place on Earth for her ashes. The answer was because Rudolf Steiner had told her that where the ashes of a person are laid, there on that spot had become a radiating point on Earth, so that the dead could work through that particular place.

I could fill a book with memories of Ita Wegman, memories of what she said, of how she coped with situations, etc. But I would like only, with these inadequate words, to join in the chorus of people who knew her and tell about her many-sided work in manifold ways and who witnessed her radiating Michael-inspired being.

When Ita Wegman was with you, the future was open. She could put her soul qualities on other people; that was really a giving—and thus the future was open.

(Published in the Dutch monthly for
members of the Anthroposophical Society)

The Work of Liane Collot d'Herbois

Liane Collot d'Herbois's books were published as follows:

Colour Part One—her first effort, published in 1979
Colour Part two—published in 1981
Colour Parts One and Two in one volume—published in 1985
Light, Darkness and Colour in Painting Therapy 1993, first appeared
    in 1988, privately for therapists and doctors only, until the 1993
    edition, available to all.

In addition to these books, Liane Collot d'Herbois leaves a legacy of many recorded talks (not yet transcribed), and many notes from her students that are available to all who go through the proper schooling. She leaves as well hundreds of very specific watercolor exercises, which have been developed further by Yanny Mager in Holland. A book on these exercises is in the making. In Germany there are several texts available by Eleonora Hambrecht, a longtime therapist and Collot d'Herbois painter who has one of the largest selections of patients' archives to substantiate the light, darkness, and color therapy work. In the Hague, the Emerald School has a large selection of her paintings. Collot d'Herbois was a prolific painter, and several thousand of her paintings are scattered around the world. She never wanted people to know where her paintings went. In France, her work is being furthered by Chantal at her "Aletier du present" in Chatou. Chantal has been working with patients for many years, and has schooling in light, dark, and color. She also works with French doctors who are very interested in this therapeutic work.

References

Allen, Paul Marshall. *Vladimir Soloviev, Russian Mystic*. Great Barrington, MA: Lindisfarne Books, 2008.

Bird, Sheila. *Tales of Old Cornwall (County Tales)*. Newbury, Berkshire: Countryside Books, 1992.

Collot d'Herbois, Liane. *Colour: A Textbook for Anthroposophical Painting Groups*. Edinburgh: Floris Books, 2008.

Collot d'Herbois, Liane. *Light, Darkness and Colour in Painting Therapy*. Dornach: Goetheanum Press, 1993 (current edition, Edinburgh: Floris Books, 2000).

Kühlewind, Georg. *Stages of Consciousness: Meditation on the Boundaries of the Soul*. Great Barrington, MA: Lindisfarne Books, 1984.

——. *Wilt Thou Be Made Whole? Healing in the Gospels*. Great Barrington, MA: Lindisfarne Books, 2008.

Leloup, Jean-Yves. *Writing on Hesychasme*. Paris: Albin Michel, 1990.

Novalis. *Hymns to the Night/Spiritual Songs*. London: Temple Lodge, 1988 (texts quoted here are from Internet sources).

Stebbing, Peter (ed.). *Conversations about Painting with Rudolf Steiner: Recollections of Five Pioneers of the New Art Impulse*. Great Barrington, MA: SteinerBooks, 2008.

Stein, Walter Johannes. *The Death of Merlin: Arthurian Myth and Alchemy*. Edinburgh: Floris Books, 2008.

Steiner, Rudolf. *Anthroposophy and Science*. Chestnut Ridge, NY: Mercury Press, 1991.

——. *The Archangel Michael: His Mission and Ours*. Great Barrington, MA: Anthroposophic Press, 1994.

——. *Arts and their Mission*. Spring Valley, NY: Anthroposophic Press, 1964.

——. *The Christian Mystery: Early Lectures*. Hudson, NY: Anthroposophic Press, 1998.

——. *Colour*. London: Rudolf Steiner Press, 1992.

——. *The Evolution of the World and of Humanity*. Blauvelt, NY: Garber, 1989.

——. *The Fourth Dimension: Sacred Geometry, Alchemy, and Mathematics*. Great Barrington, MA: SteinerBooks/Anthroposophic Press, 2001.

——. *Genesis: Secrets of Creation*. London: Rudolf Steiner Press, 2002.

———. *Initiation, Eternity and the Passing Moment.* Spring Valley, NY: Anthroposophic Press, 1980.

———. *Materialism and the Task of Anthroposophy.* Hudson: Anthroposophic Press/London: Rudolf Steiner Press, 1987.

———. *Metamorphoses of the Soul: Paths of Experience,* 2 vols. London: Rudolf Steiner Press, 1983 (current edition *Transforming the Soul,* 2 vols., Rudolf Steiner Press, 2006).

———. *Practical Advice to Teachers.* Great Barrington, MA: Anthroposophic Press, 2000.

———. *The Redemption of Thinking: A Study in the Philosophy of Thomas Aquinas.* Spring Valley, NY: Anthroposophic Press, 1983.

———. *The Riddle of Humanity: The Spiritual Background of Human History.* London: Rudolf Steiner Press, 1990.

———. *Rosicrucianism and Modern Initiation: Mystery Centres of the Middle Ages.* London: Rudolf Steiner Press, 1982.

———. *Rosicrucianism Renewed: The Unity of Art, Science and Religion. The Theosophical Congress of Whitsun 1907.* Great Barrington, MA: SteinerBooks, 2007.

———. *Occult Signs and Symbols.* NY: Anthroposophic Press, 1972.

———. *Spiritual Science as a Foundation for Social Forms.* Hudson, NY: Anthroposophic Press, 1986.

———. *World of the Senses and World of the Spirit.* NY: Anthroposophic Press, 1979.

———. *Wonders of the World, Ordeals of the Soul, Revelations of the Spirit.* London: Rudolf Steiner Press, 1983.

Tennyson, Alfred Lord. *Idylls of the King.* New York: Penguin, 1983.

Vivian, John. *Tales of the Cornish Wreckers.* Redruth, UK: Tor Mark, 1969.

von Keyserlingk, Johanna Countess. *The Women around Rudolf Steiner.* (unpublished manuscript).

Wegman, Ita. *Esoteric Studies: The Michael Impulse.* London: Temple Lodge, 1993.